DALES
PONIES

DALES
PONIES

IONA FITZGERALD

Whittet Books

FRONTISPIECE *Miss P.A. FitzGerald and Mrs J.C. Ashby with the mare Stainton Darkie at the water hazard during a combined driving event at Tatton Park.*

First published 200
Reprinted 2005

Text © 2000 by Iona FitzGerald
Whittet Books Ltd, Hill Farm, Stonham Road, Cotton, Stowmarket,
Suffolk IP14 4RQ

British Library Cataloguing in Publication Data. A catalogue record for this book is available from the British Library.

ISBN 1 873580 49 5

The Publishers and Author are grateful to the following for permission to reproduce photographs on the pages indicated: The Dales Pony Society Archives (2, 10, 11, 12, 37, 41, 43, 45, 48, 49, 52, 59, 61, 71, 79, 80, 85, 89, 91, 99, 103, 105, 127, 129, 137, 140, 142, 146, 148, 153, 157, 160, 162, 164, 165, 177, 187); Beamish North of England Museum (60, 61, 62, 74, 76, 83, 88, 100); H.C. Clarke 914, 15); The Farmers Guardian (189); Carol Gilson (193); Wills Keevil (180); Phil Nixon (179); North of England Newspapers (146); Pleasure Prints (183); David Snowdon (172, 181, 196), Sally Anne Thompson (142).

Printed and bound by Cromwell Press

CONTENTS

INTRODUCTION

◆

'Here on my farm of about 40 acres they do all the general work, are used in the mowing machine, the binder, leading corn and hay and ploughing - all the season's work as it comes round. I find them little castles of strength for these jobs, besides being perfect riding hacks. I have in recent years exhibited my Dales ponies at local shows with a fair amount of success. This combined with their usefulness, does create for me a great deal of interest and pleasure from this sturdy breed'

G.H. Hodgson,1955

DALES PONIES ARE NOW APPEARING IN MAJOR SHOW RINGS in increasing numbers. They always attract attention and spectators are curious about them. Until a few years ago many thought them extinct but there was always a pocket of excellent jealously guarded ponies in the dales of North Yorkshire and County Durham.

From the mid-nineteenth century up to the end of the Second World War, thousands of Dales ponies were to be seen in our northern and Midland towns. They were familiar light tradesmen's ponies, particularly favoured by butchers for their speed and style. They worked on pit banks and in lead mines and were to be found on virtually every small farm in the upper dales of the Pennines.

The Dales pony is an 'improved' breed of some antiquity, bred along similar lines to the Welsh Cob but from different foundation stock. Robust all-rounders, the ponies are able to accomplish most of the work of hill farms; are comfortable under saddle, stylish in harness and able to perform well in most disciplines in the show ring. In their heyday Dales ponies carried off a number of Supreme Championships from the National Pony Shows then held in London.

In writing the history of the Dales breed it is essential to include that of the Fell pony, as both are rooted in the indigenous equines which roamed northern England in the past. In relatively recent years they have been closely entwined and it becomes necessary to record this for the benefit of new breeders who no longer have access to old stud books. Both Fell and Dales ponies have always been known as galloways in the North of England, a 'galloway' signifying a strong, hardy pony, good for riding and driving, from 13 to 15 hands.

The Fell Pony Committee of the Polo Pony Society, now known as the National Pony Society, opened a Stud Book in 1898 but failed to differentiate between Dales and Fells, believing them to be two types of the same breed. In 1916 the Dales Pony Improvement Society was established, and their Dales Pony Stud Book was opened with a large entry of ponies.

After the First World War, the Committee of the Fell Pony Society embarked on a publicity campaign to save the Fell breed from threatened extinction. Unhappily, some of the publicity used so successfully to save the Fell pony was at the expense of the more popular Dales, which was dismissed as an over-grown, coarse type of Fell, full of Clydesdale blood. This adverse publicity played no small part in the ensuing decline of the Dales pony.

During the Second World War many Dales ponies were taken by the Army for pack work and Mountain Artillery. Others, including young mares, were in great demand for town work. Few came back for breeding and Dales ponies faded from the scene. In 1955, only four Dales ponies, all mares, were registered.

Fortunately, a few dedicated Dales men and women stood by their ponies throughout the bad years, believing that the day of the heavy pony was not yet over. The breed came under the watchful eye of the Rare Breeds Survival Trust in 1977, which placed it in Category 2 (Rare). Since then the breed has improved steadily in numbers and is now in Category 3 (Vulnerable).

Until 1980 publicity about the breed was sparse and ill-informed, usually as an addendum to that promoting the Fell pony. The Dales Pony Society revised and reissued the breed description in 1963, to little avail. Few post-war equestrian journalists had seen a good Dales pony and the usual description, still to be found in some books and articles, was of a docile type of carthorse, of little use for riding unless required for the nervous and novices in trekking centres. Nothing could have been further from the truth and it is time to expose this undeserved and defamatory myth, which has been perpetuated for well over seventy years.

Although there is an affinity between the Dales and Fell, there is a marked difference between the two breeds, which is unmistakable when comparing good specimens of each. Because so few Dales ponies were to be found following the last war, it became customary for Fells and Dales to be classed together at the few post-war shows which still included classes for heavy ponies. It was not until 1983 that the numbers became healthy enough for the Dales and Fell ridden classes to be separated at the National Pony Show.

In recent years Dales ponies have competed very successfully in-hand, under saddle and in harness, at most of the major shows. There is a now a growing demand for them at home and abroad. Stock is of excellent quality, the ponies are bred to keep all their old-fashioned attributes and cannot be bettered for hardiness, soundness, thrift, good temperament, stamina and courage.

The little known history of the Dales breed is a long tale of service to man in some of the most difficult country in England. Of great renown in the past, the Dales galloway is once again being recognised as a superb all-rounder.

1

THE DALES PONY

◆

DURING QUEEN VICTORIA'S DIAMOND JUBILEE in 1897, the London Horse Show displayed an assembly of horses and ponies from each of the recognised British breeds, consisting of a stallion and mare. No trouble or expense was spared to ensure that the most typical representatives of each breed were selected. A commemorative book, *British Horses Illustrated*, was edited by Vero Shaw. It is interesting to note that photographs of the breeds shown are of Cleveland Bay, Clydesdale, Hackney, Pack Horse (Devonshire), Shire, Suffolk Horse, Thoroughbred and Yorkshire Coach Horse. The pony breeds were Dale (s), Dartmoor, Exmoor, New Forest, Rum, Welsh (Mountain) and Shetland.

This description of the Dales pony was written by Lord Arthur Cecil:

> The Dale or Fell pony is a native of the North of England, his strongholds being Cumberland, Westmorland and Durham, in which localities he is much appreciated on account of his endurance, robustness of constitution, and adaptability for hard work. It is probable that there is an affinity of blood between the Dale and Rum ponies, as the resemblance between them is striking, the good points in one variety being frequently reflected in the other. So far as mere showiness goes it is very questionable whether an ordinary specimen of the Dale pony will compare favourably with certain other varieties, but there is a wear and tear look about the breed which cannot fail to recommend itself to horse lovers, in fact in the case of the Dale it should be accepted as a fact that 'handsome is as handsome does.' In his height the Dale Pony very often attains the maximum permissable in a member of the family, and in some instances he exceeds it, as specimens of the breed of over 14 hands are not uncommon. At the same time the height referred to may be regarded as a fair average, though many of the cross-bred animals are considerably taller.

The accompanying photographs are of two of Lord Arthur Cecil's Dales ponies, the three-year-old colt, Edengrove, and a three-year-old filly, Crackenthorpe, bred by Mr Gibson of Widdy Bank, Middleton-in-Teesdale. Both ponies were sired by **Blooming Heather** and later entered in the Fell Stud Book. Lord Arthur Cecil firmly believed that

The three-year-old filly (2071 Fell) Crackenthorpe, foaled in 1894, bred by John Gibson of Middleton-in-Teesdale.

the blood of one native breed could always improve that of another. Edengrove was used as an improving sire of Exmoor ponies and sired registered Exmoor mares. Crackenthorpe went to Hampshire and produced foals by New Forest pony sires.

The following detailed description of a Dales pony was given in *The Standard Cyclopedia of Modern Agriculture and Rural Economy* published in 1908, eight years before the Dales Pony Society and Stud Book were established.

These ponies are principally found in the upper reaches of the Wear and Tees rivers in north-west Durham, the vales of Westmorland, more especially in the neighbourhood of Kirkby Stephen, and Allendale in Northumberland. The name `Dales' is significant of the nature of the places where they are chiefly bred. In only one or two books of reference concerning horses is particular mention made of them as a distinct breed. This is somewhat surprising, inasmuch as they are a very old breed, and most probably an original English cart-horse breed. Unfortunately they have no stud book. The place to which they are sent for sale by breeders in very great numbers is Brough Hill Fair, near Warcop in

The brown three-year-old colt Edengrove (160 Fell) foaled in 1894, bred by Gibsons, Middleton-in-Teesdale.

Westmorland. The Fair is held in October and was at one time a very important rendezvous for buyers and sellers of Dales ponies. Appleby is also a good market for these ponies. Good individual ponies make from £20 to £30 pounds each.

In conformation and build, the best type closely resembles a good miniature cart-horse. The size especially favoured varies from 13 hands 2 inches to 14 hands 2 inches. The neck is short, thick and well arched, and the natural carriage of the head most graceful. The general bearing of a good Dales pony is very pleasing. Face straight, wide at the eyes and nostrils, the eyes themselves being full and intelligent. Their walking and trotting action, though not so marked, closely resembles that of a Hackney. They are as a rule quiet, docile and easily broken. While not good at cantering, they make excellent trotting harness and riding ponies, and have great powers of endurance. The great stamina of these ponies is one of their strongest points. For their size, their legs have bone of good flat quality and plenty of it. Their feet are sound and hard though somewhat steep. The best of them have nicely sloping shoulders and short, thick, shapely bodies of good depth of girth. They have particularly strong, muscular backs, short, slightly sloping rumps,

A Dales pony - Blooming Heather (as described and depicted in 1908).

thick thighs, and hocks well set down. Their general appearance is altogether indicative of great strength in a small compass. Fine silky hair at the back of their fetlocks and above denotes good breeding. Greys, browns and blacks are favourite colours. In their native homes they are largely used as the general-purpose horse of the pastoral farms. Away they are eagerly sought, for pit-bank work, milk floats, tradesmen's and general hawker's carts.

Originally these ponies were chiefly used to carry in specially constructed wooden saddles the ore from the lead mines to the smelting works. Some of the older farmers remember them being similarly used to carry coal of inferior quality with which to burn lime in the farm lime kilns. Unfortunately a limekiln on farms, where they were in former times of frequent occurence, is now a rarity. On many of the farms in the districts mentioned, carrying hay by sledge is still a common practice. The Dales ponies are particularly intelligent and quick at this work. A good pair, if carefully driven, are sufficiently strong to work consistently an ordinary mowing machine. Most of the land where these ponies are bred is either fell or under permanent pasture. Many of the farmers are small holders, and on the holdings use a single-horse mowing machine with shafts. A good Dales pony is frequently the only horse kept for this and other work.

Speaking generally, these ponies are sound, active, very hardy, and extremely sure-footed. Thoroughbreds and Hackney stallions out of good pony mares usually beget offspring which make excellent roadsters. For farm work on pastoral farms, however, such crosses are not especially liked, as in nearly all cases the progeny are of greater height and lighter in bone than farmers favour. Swiftness and action are secured at the expense of strength, hardiness and durability. On the other hand, the progeny of good pony mares by lighter cart-horse sires of the Clydesdale type are greatly liked for general farm work and the carting of minerals of various kinds from the mines and quarries to the nearest railway station. Pure-bred Dales ponies are of such all-round excellence that it seems regrettable that sufficient interest and enthusiasm amongst breeders have not as yet resulted in the establishment of a stud book devoted to their interests and welfare.

(F.P.W.) Frank P. Walker. Lecturer in Agriculture, Armstrong College, Newcastle-on-Tyne.

The accompaning illustration was of Blooming Heather described as a Dales Pony, although entered retrospectively in the Fell Section of the Polo Pony Society Stud Book (NPS), Volume 13.

The following description of the Fell pony in the same publication gives an indication of the status of the two breeds at the beginning of this century.

This hardy breed of native ponies ranges pretty much at large throughout the Lake District of Cumberland and Westmorland, and even reaches as far as parts of Durham and Yorkshire, being named from the fells or hills of those districts. They are larger and heavier than any of the more southern breeds, and can often be distinguished from any other breed of ponies by the tuft of hair on the fetlock joint. They are fast, active and hardy. It used to be no very uncommon thing for them to be covered up in the deep snows of their native mountains. They are thick-set, possibly with better set up tails than other breeds of English ponies but as a rule have not quite such good flat bones nor such bright-looking heads and eyes.

It is not easy to find really pure specimens of the breed, but there must be many such ranging the hills almost wild. For the most part they belong to farmers owning land which has allotments of hill land attached to it, but they usually put them to selected sires, which it is to be feared are not always the most suited for getting stock able to withstand the rigours of the northern climate. It is a pity that a society could not be formed to keep up the breed in its original hardiness.

It is very difficult to speak of their origin, but it is pretty certain that they are closely connected with the now extinct breed of Galloway ponies (which have become merged into the smaller type of Clydesdale) and with the breed of ponies found all along the west coast and islands of Scotland.

Two good mature Dales mares, H. Barron's Black Silk, aged 12 years, and Burdon Winsome, aged 11 years.

Good specimens of this breed can often be picked up as yearlings or two year olds at Brough Hill Fair on the last days of September and the first of October.

(A.C.) Lord Arthur Cecil

The modern Dales pony compares very well with the 1908 description. It is an old-fashioned pony which has been carefully preserved in its original breeding grounds. The longevity of the breed has helped; many ponies of today go back to mares and stallions that were among the first entries in the Dales pony Stud Book of 1916, within four or five generations. The favoured height remains the same at 14.0-14.2 hands, but ponies and cobs can be found under and over this.

The appearance and bearing of good Dales ponies are much the same. Fronts in general are improved - most ponies now have good shoulders and longer necks. Stallions display a high crest when in good condition, as do some mares. The high head carriage of a Dales pony gives a very impressive bearing. The straight face is unchanged and dished profiles are never seen. A convex curve of the nose from below the eyes is quite common, a clear sign of Spanish blood somewhere in the past. It is said that a Dales galloway should be able to drink out of a tea-cup,

*Black Silk, Burdon Winsome and twenty-three-year-old Heather Mixture III,
showing their powerful quarters and good flat bone.*

meaning that the mobile muzzle should be fine. Large plain heads with
long ears are usually a sign of past Clydesdale influence; however,
these are now becoming rare. The ears should be pony-like and
incurving. The almond-shaped eyes should be full and alert.

The withers of many ponies are not always well defined and can be
flat, ('harness topped') especially in strong ponies with shoulders
buried in muscle but the high head carriage and bold outlook
compensates. Good ponies are short-coupled with long muscular
quarters and well-laid shoulders. They should be very broad across
the chest. This applies to a mature pony of about eight years of age; the
width of a four-year-old is less, as is the furnishing of the quarters, and
this should be understood when comparing ponies of differing ages.
The tail is well set but not high; a few ponies have a high croup which
slopes steeply to the tail which in America is known as the 'trotting
pitch'. Ponies which display this are usually exceptional trotters with
a remarkable ability for jumping.

The ponies have always been renowned for the quality of their feet
and limbs. The muscular forehand should be set square and running
into broad shield-shaped knees. Good ponies have fine, muscular
second thighs above broad, clean, well let-down hocks. This gives them

the ability to reach high and forward with their hind legs. Ponies which are wide above the hocks are unlikely to use their hocks so well. Mature ponies should display eight to nine inches of knife-like, dense cannon bone with well defined fluted tendons. Viewed from the side, the cannons will appear wide but should look surprisingly narrow from the front. Legs can be deceiving; coarse, round bone may look to have the required measurement, but will not have the essential quality. The cannon bones of Dales ponies may appear to lack inches to the untutored eye but a tape measure will tell the truth.

The hooves of a good Dales pony are large, round and open at the heels with a well-developed frog. The pasterns are of a good length and very flexible. The fine silky hair, known as 'feather' falls from behind the cannons and curtains the coronets. This is much valued by Dalesmen; coarse, curly feather is not favoured and is thought to denote some heavy outcross blood. The hooves were habitually described as hard and blue but as the Dales pony carries white markings, it follows that some hooves must also be 'white', which appears as a tawny cream. There is no difference in quality between the blue and tawny, they are both equally elastic and hard-wearing and much praised by farriers. The Dales mare Galphay Supreme, owned by Rosemary Walker, was never shod but competed successfully in the show ring, including qualifying for the Ridden Native Pony Championship Final at Olympia in 1980. She was also successful in Working Hunter Pony classes, Hunter Trials and Dressage. In long distance riding competitions, veterinary surgeons at check points, who questioned the mare's ability to continue unshod, were intrigued to find her hooves in excellent condition at the finish. She was retired in 1987.

The Dales pony is the prototype 'hairy' native, but the hair should be silky and straight. Enthusiasts like the heavy mane to be as much as a yard long with a long foretop (forelock). The tail should also be full and reach the ground. The coat is very fine with a natural satin-like sheen in the summer but changes to a double coat of thick wool with longer 'cat hairs' to direct water away from the undercoat in winter. Snow will lie for some time on the well insulated back of a Dales pony. Until 1948 the ponies were usually docked but with enough hair left to protect the pony in severe weather. This was tied up with ribbons for show days. Following the prohibition of docking, some exhibitors favoured the unsightly 'Scotch dock', (tail hair shortened and tied with ribbons, the dock shaved) but this grotesque fashion is no longer seen among Dales ponies. The fashion for tail ribbons has persisted and become a traditional option. A few exhibitors who wish the breed to be correctly identified in mixed native classes find it useful when showing away from their home ground. There

Mr B. Marshall driving Brymor Mimi on a Yorkshire stage of the 1977 Jubilee drive, 20 miles from Ripley to Masham. This a good example of a Dales trot.

are many tales of owners being amused or otherwise when presented with the Best of Breed rosette for a Welsh Cob, Highland, Fell or, believe it or not, New Forest and Exmoor.

The walk of the Dales pony is distinctive. Flexible fetlocks give a jaunty, stepping movement, each foot is picked up sharply and placed neatly. When viewed from behind the whole of the hoof should be displayed when walking, the best ponies showing the clip on the front of the shoe. The stride is long, ground-covering and deceptively fast.

The natural crisp, elevated knee and hock action when trotting is both distinctive and speedy, akin to the old roadster movement. There is great strength and drive from behind, the best ponies giving a flick of the hocks. An up and down, 'going nowhere' action is frowned upon, and may be the result of heavy shoes. The extravagant extension from the shoulder, as displayed by Welsh cobs is not seen. The good Dales pony trots with a well-balanced, energetic, rhythmical, 'all-fours' action, which gives the appearance of the pony going on wheels. This seems to be economical of energy as the pony can keep going for great distances at a good speed. Many ponies can trot at 20 miles an hour or more. The ponies were carefully bred to produce this way of going and it has held good throughout the years. A newspaper report of the Royal Show, held in Darlington in 1920, contained this extract:

> Closely allied to the Highland pony is the Dales and the Fell pony of the North of England. Both of these breeds were well represented at the R.A.S.E., Darlington. The Dales pony is an extremely stout pony, well ribbed and a particularly good mover. Some of the older class at the Royal, notably the first and second prize winners, had as good an action as the Hackney, but were much more speedy.

The ponies mentioned were the stallions, **Linnel Comet** and **Gentleman John**.

Dales ponies have always been described as quiet and docile. This has never been an accurate description. They are spirited and high-couraged but are sensible and will rarely panic. They can usually be relied on to look after themselves and their rider or driver in tricky situations. If they have been roughly broken or mishandled they can become stubborn; it is of no use to bully a Dales pony as they are far too intelligent to be subservient. They are, however, kind and willing and if they understand what is wanted, will usually oblige very quickly. Following centuries of working with man, they are very domesticated and are therefore extremely easy to break and very forgiving with novices. They can become greatly attached to their owners and when transferred to new homes will take some months to settle properly. The reason why it is difficult to buy older experienced Dales ponies today is because owners of such a pony will very rarely part with it.

Until recently Dales ponies were never allowed to canter as their trotting ability was highly prized, both in harness and under saddle. Driving ponies likely to break into a canter are not popular. The trot of a Dales pony has always been comfortable under saddle, due to their tremendous forward movement and very flexible joints. Their roadster forebears were famous for travelling long distances at this pace under saddle. The ponies can canter and gallop and frequently prove this by winning in Mixed Mountain and Moorland Ridden classes in good company. They are also willing and clever jumpers, as are most horses with high knee action. Mrs Stroma Bedell's Dales mare, Raygill Duchess and Mrs Jan James's Stainton Jewel are among those which were hunted regularly and showed the way over rough moorland and heather, where horses tend to flounder. Rebecca Harrison served as a Whipper-in to the Goathland Hunt on her Dales stallion Moorend William and her mare Sungreen Black Velvet.

The Dales has always been, and still is, a favourite of travellers and most of the black-and-white trotters seen at Appleby Fair are Dales-bred. Travelling to the fair from Durham villages, it is possible to see among the local travelling caravans many that are drawn by Dales ponies. Durham Candy (Hett Randy / Hilton Carousel) standing under 14 hands, drew a caravan from Spennymoor to Appleby and back. This pony also won under saddle many times and has produced a good selection of foals.

The stamina of the Dales pony remains supreme but these days they rarely get enough work to prove it. It has been reported that veterinary surgeons manning check points during long distance rides have been surprised at the low heart rates and speedy recovery of any Dales ponies they meet during the competitions.

The ponies are very thrifty and flourish on short comings. They do best on upland pasture, which is much higher in fibre than lowland grassland. On their home ground most ponies winter out with hay. They

Richard and Freda Longstaff's Dales brood mare, champion Lowhouses Anna with two Lowhouses' foals, Middleton-in-Teesdale.

work best on natural feeds such as meadow grass, hay, oats and carrots.

Colours are black, brown, bay, grey and rarely roan. Black coats are sometimes ticked with white, which older breeders describe as 'the iron in the black.' There is also a very dark brown with lighter dapples, known as 'heckberry or hackberry'.

There is an unusual rule regarding white markings which has been in force since 1966. In the belief that excessive white markings showed Clydesdale influence following the Second World War, the council, when instituting the grading-up scheme, decided to down-grade any pony displaying a blaze or any white on the forefeet. In the confusion at the time when so many ponies had been lost or cross-bred, this odd rule can perhaps be understood. However, it is a fact that Dales ponies have always carried white markings and the thirty-year bar has had no effect on the percentage of ponies with 'wrong' markings, which is the same now as it was in 1916. It was an arbitrary compromise of preferences at the time - between any white and whole black, and a matter of fashion rather than science. The fact is that all stallion lines carry white forefeet, as do most of the female lines, particularly those carrying the oldest blood. However, the Council of the Dales Pony Society is to be congratulated on having had the wisdom to ensure that the blood lines of such down-graded, 'mis-marked' mares are continued by up-grading their correctly marked filly foals. Mis-marked filly foals are kept in the same section as their dams. Correctly bred but mis-marked colts must be castrated, though their correctly marked full-brothers are eligible for stallion status.

The preferred height of a Dales pony is 14-14.2 hands but there has never been a stated minimum height. Until 1963, under the Dales Pony Improvement Society rules, all Dales mares were allowed a height of 15 hands. Under the rules of the reconstituted Dales Pony Society in 1963, height was reduced to a maximum of 14.2 hands to keep in line with the National Pony Society rules. This meant down-grading the Dales cob, whereas in the past, it had merited a sub-section of the Stud Book. This rule has now been amended to 'preferred height' rather than a fixed maximum height. However, the Dales cob is still with us and eagerly sought for performance classes, where it will compete successfully against the larger Welsh Cobs. The Council of the Society is wise enough to realise that if the preferred height of the ponies is to be kept, the large mares hold a very valuable pool of genes to counteract the influence of any Fell blood, which has tended to reduce height.

The Dales Pony Society can be proud of their efforts to ensure that Dales ponies have been kept up to the old standards throughout the vicissitudes of the twentieth century.

2
THE EARLY HISTORY

◆

Bring me out my black Dales pony,
Put a saddle on his back,
There's more value for your money
Than in Clydesdale, Barb or Hack.

Talk of Welsh or Exmoor pony
Shetland, Iceland or what other,
Put me on my doughty crony
For to me he's like a brother.

Not so big as ponderous Shire,
Not so soft as Suffolk horse,
In him what I most admire
Is his mettle, but of course.

Look upon his noble forehead,
Note his flashing, rolling eye,
Mark his flanks so strongly knitted
Scan his flattened shins, forebye.

See the bony feathered fetlock
And his stout and ample chest,
When I laud, it should not shock
If I say he's of the best.

Put him into any harness,
Yoke him into cart or trap,
Mount him, ride to any farness,
You'll be proud of this fine chap.

He has blood and he has wildfire,
Yet as quiet as any lamb.
A Spanish entire was his sire
And mare of Galloway his dam.

What d'ye expect of such a creature
What can but blood avail,
There is every solid feature
In this breed of old Weardale.

J. J. Graham 1865-1941

This poem was written by one who was born and brought up in Weardale. It was based on local folklore and carries a clue to the history of the Dales pony.

The early history of northern British ponies is buried in antiquity and the many hypotheses regarding this are difficult to confirm. Horses were in Britain before it became separated from the Continent and there is archeological evidence of the existence of a small type of pony dated about 100,000 BC and a larger pony around 60,000 BC.

It is generally believed that all horses and ponies developed from three early types:

• One like the modern Przevalskii horse, with an erect mane and a tail like a mule, a long convex head, large ears, a straight shoulder, slender limbs and broad hooves; the type sometimes known as the Steppe horse.

• The second type, frequently known as the Forest horse, differed in having a broad head, prominent eyes, and a convex profile with a long mobile muzzle. It had a longer body than the Steppe type, with short, strong limbs and broad hooves. The mane and tail were long and full. This type is considered the likely ancestor of heavy horses and ponies.

• The third type, which goes by the name of Plateau horse, had fine limbs and small hooves, a narrow head with small ears, large eyes and a small muzzle. All three types were thought to have been dun with black points and zebra stripes.

These early equine types crossed and intermingled, adapting to differing habitats and migrating throughout the world. From Paleolithic times man has had a hand in the evolution of horses, first by hunting them for meat and then by domesticating them for use.

The first people in the British Isles to leave clues of familiarity with domesticated horses were the Iberians of the Bronze Age. They were a dark people which inhabited Britain from around 3,000 BC and are thought to have built Stonehenge about a 1,000 years before the arrival of the Celts. Iberia is the name given to the peninsula which holds Portugal and north-eastern Spain, from whence Iberians migrated to Britain. They knew how to smelt copper and tin together to produce bronze. The remains of a four-wheeled cart with bronze-mounted horse harness from this time was found in Weardale, near Stanhope, and can be seen in the Bowes Museum, Barnard Castle.

Spanish cave paintings, radio-carbon dated at 4,000-5,000 BC show horses being used by Neolithic man. Two types of horse are depicted, one with a 'dished' (concave) profile and a short neck, the second showing a convex profile and long neck. There is a theory that both types were primitive Iberian horses, the like of which can be seen in Portugal and Spain today, in the Sorraia and the Garrano.

The Sorraia is recognised as an ancient breed and one of the the ancestors of Andalusian and Lusitanian horses. It has a convex profile from below the eyes, with a flattened muzzle, high trotting action, a thick arched neck and a close coupled body. It is a very hardy animal which thrives on poor quality grazing. The Sorraia has distinctive, primitive colouring, being dun with a black list down the back and black points which include a luxuriant mane and tail. The legs are nearly always zebra-striped and in the summer coat spots can sometimes be seen on the belly. Rarely over 13.2 hands, it was used by the herdsmen who roamed with the herds of horses and bulls, but now lives in a protected habitat.

The second type of primitive Iberian pony, the Garrano, comes from the mountain valleys of Northern Portugal. The modern specimens are between 11 to 13 hands and they have a distinctive dished profile. The pony seems little changed from those depicted in the cave paintings. It is a strong, hardy little beast used as 'a maid of all work' in the mountainous northern areas and as a Mountain Artillery pack pony by the Portuguese Army. The Garrano has always been favoured by gypsies who use the ponies for the highly popular trotting races. The colours of pure-bred ponies are predominantly bay or brown.

There is also a third type of native Iberian horse, the Asturian and Galecian ponies from the mountains of north-west Portugal and Spain. These were well known by the Romans and were described by Pliny, the Roman naturalist (AD 23-79) as having a special easy gait brought about by moving both legs on the same side alternatively, later known as ambling or pacing. The breed still exists wild in the same region but is said to have degenerated due to neglect. The pure-breds are now about 12 to 13 hands and black is the dominant colour. The Romans did not have stirrups so the pacing Asturian and Galecian ponies were the favoured mounts for long journeys - being comfortable to ride.

Trade in horses is known to have taken place between Iberia and Britain long before the Romans arrived. In her book *The Royal Horse of Europe*, Sylvia Loch writes of Iberian horses being introduced into Britain as early as the Iron Age, around 500 BC.

When the Celts arrived in Britain the Iberians and earlier peoples retreated into the mountains of the north and west. The powerful tribe of Brigantes settled in the region which now covers County Durham, North Yorkshire and the Yorkshire Wolds, which stretched from the the Humber to the Mersey and which was known as Brigantia. The Brigantes also settled a small area on the coast of County Waterford in Ireland and on the coast of north-west Spain around Corunna, which was known to the Romans as Brigantium. Renowned as horse breeders, the Brigantes were known to have imported a small breed of horse from north-west Spain for their chariots.

Among later invading Celts, came the tribe of the Belgii who settled in East Anglia and spread up to the border of the Brigantes' territory. They traded with North Africa and Spain and were known to have imported Barb and Iberian horses. They were renowned for breeding larger horses, which enabled them to ride to battle. The first flagged causeways of stone were laid down along difficult sections of packways and the earliest horseshoes found in England were discovered in Belgii territory from about this time. It is interesting to note that those parts of Britain where the Brigantes and Belgii settled are regarded as the cradles of British horse breeding.

The Roman occupation of Britain, which began with a tentative expedition in 55 BC, was complete by AD 45 and lasted over 400 years. The Romans were not horsemen but they did employ excellent auxiliary cavalry which was the cream of the Roman Army. A Decurion (cavalry troop comander) held a higher rank than a Centurion (infantry troop commander), and cavalrymen were better paid than infantrymen.

The cavalry was the Roman Army's scouting and pursuit force which later became an effective strike force. Fourteen alae (regiments) of 500 cavalrymen served in Britain. Seven were raised in Gaul, three in Spain, two in Hungary and one each in Belgium and Bulgaria. A Cohort Equitana was an infantry battalan of 360 foot with a cavalry wing of 120. A Cuneus was a force of irregular cavalry which was used to strengthen existing garrisons. All draught work was done by oxen, and pack work by mules.

Spain was the main remount depot for the Romans and as they brought horses with them, it is likely that many were Iberian. However, the Romans had a great regard for the high-spirited little chariot ponies of the British and were known to have exported many of them to Rome during their occupation.

The southern tribes and eventually the Welsh were subjugated. The real problem was that of the northern moors, then still covered with forest, where the Brigantes and the Picts were formidable and inaccessible. In an effort to subdue the northern tribes, Hadrian's Wall and later the Antonine Wall was built. Hadrian's Wall took four years to complete, between AD 122 and 126. It was restored in AD 210 and finally abandoned in AD 383. Many military units were required to police the walls and patrol the roads leading to them, over the 261 years. Five alae served on the walls, being stationed where cavalry was of most use - east from Chesters near Hexham, to Benwell and Wallsend. However, the 1,000 strong Ala Petriana, raised in Gaul, was stationed permanently at Stanwix, north-east of Carlisle, as it was the only fort large enough for the double strength force.

Roman horseshoes and blacksmith's tools can be seen at Roman Museums along Hadrian's Wall. The horses were about 14.2 hands but larger ones of 15 hands were found at Newsteads on the Tweed. Little is yet known about stables on the wall, though most forts had enough for a cohort equitana. It is thought that all livestock, including remounts, breeding stock, cattle, mules and up to 200 draught oxen would be in guarded grazing enclosures. The Romans were occupying most of Brigantian territory in the north and trading was considerable with horses, cattle, sheep and timber coming from upper Teesdale.

It is interesting to note that stationed on the eastern sections of Hadrian's Wall were two alae from northern Spain, Ala I Asturum at Benwell and Ala II Asturum at Chesters and I Asturum Cohort Equitana at Great Chesters, all raised in Asturia, Northern Spain. The Austurians were probably originally mounted on the popular Galecian or Austurian ponies. It is inconceivable that cross-breeding with native stock did not take place and is the most likely explanation of the origin of the Scotch Galloway which was also said to be a pacer.

Infantry was stationed at Housesteads, near Haltwhistle, and was augmented at one time by irregular infantry known as Hnaudifridi from Germany with a Cuneus Frisiorum, an irregular cavalry unit, from Frisia (the Low Countries). Another Cuneus Frisiorum was stationed on the west side, at Burgh-by-Sands. These are believed to have been mounted on two types of horse, the first being the ponderous German war-horse, of about 15 hands. The second is thought to have been a cross between the German type and something smaller.

There is a theory that the horses of the Friesian cavalry interbred with natives because the Fell pony looks similar to a modern Friesian. The modern Friesian was derived from the cold-blooded German horse and improved by Spanish blood which is thought responsible for the luxurious hair of the mane, tail and fetlocks and the high stepping action. Later improvement came from Arabian and Thoroughbred blood. In the mid-eighteenth century the height of the Friesian was fixed at 15.2 hands and from this time the only colours allowed for stallions were black or bay with black points, but if an owner had three stallions one of them was allowed to be a roan.

Something very similar to the Friesian was probably evolving from the German war-horse type interbred with Spanish and native stock along the English/Scottish Border, the smaller size resulting from the harsh environment. This is a more likely explanation of the similarity in appearance of the Fell and Dales galloways and the modern Friesian horse.

Besides the various types of horse used on the wall, there are also records that the Crispinian Legion stationed at Catterick (Caturactonium) and Danum (Doncaster) in Yorkshire was mounted on North African stallions, thought to be Barbs. There was plenty of opportunity for cross-breeding with local stock as the Romans used only stallions for riding. Some cross-bred stock would naturally degenerate in the harsh conditions, particularly on the eastern side of the north country which is generally colder than the west. Cross-bred stock that survived and bred successfully would have been extremely valuable.

When the Roman legions departed they left a very peaceful country which easily fell prey to succeeding invasions of Anglo-Saxons, Scots, Jutes and Norsemen. This began in earnest in AD 410 and resulted in the dereliction of almost everything Roman except the roads. The invaders were illiterate and left few records. Little is known of this period, the Dark Ages, until the Christian foundations were established and educated monks in the great abbeys left manuscripts telling of life in Britain. There were, however, records of continued horse trading between Ireland and Spain, when palfreys (horses that paced) from Asturian and Galecian roots were imported. In Ireland their descendants became known as the Irish Hobbys, in northern England they may have become known as the Scotch or Border Galloways.

The first Norsemen, the Vikings, arrived around AD 600 and settled the northern islands of Orkney and Shetland, followed later by the settlement of the west of Scotland and Galloway. In Norway at this time, horses were sacred to the Gods with which they were associated. They were kept in enclosures until required for use in religious rites and processions. The priests, who were usually also chieftains, were in charge of the horses which were selectively bred. Surplus stock was of great value for use in warfare. Known for their sea-faring skills, the Vikings were also considerable horsemen and brought to Britain the first stirrups, made of leather.

During the seventh century Vikings were known to have carried small, hardy horses in their longboats for raiding purposes. Warfare in the north of Scotland at this time seems to have been conducted on horseback. Bones found from this period show a pony of about 14 hands, unusually large where most of the ponies were small. This may confirm that the Vikings brought some of their own horses with them.

The horses of the northern continent of Europe were thought to be similar in colour and type, having a heavy, low form with bushy manes and tails, probably black or dun. The Norwegian Fjording pony of today is a heavy pony of about 14 hands, usually dun with a marked eel stripe (list). Many modern Highland ponies are duns and as late as 1837, William Howitt writing about Dent, in the northern Pennines, described a breed of dun ponies 'remarkably sure-footed and highly prized for drawing lady's carriages'. The great grandfather of the late Mr J. Relph, of Threlkeld, near Keswick, used to tell that there were many more duns and greys among galloways of his day. Some black Dales ponies of today can be found with golden eyes, which are probably dark dun or 'dosk'. There is an even more striking similarity between the Dales pony and the Norwegian Døle. The Døle (Dal) is also an active trotter with a profuse mane and tail, displaying the same colours, black, brown, bay and occasionally grey and dun. Even their name is similar, the English 'Dale' and Norwegian 'Dal' - both mean valley. The Døle comes from the valley of Gudbrand and is known as *Gudbrandsdal*, *Døle* or *Doelhest* (horse of the valley).

The Danes followed the Vikings, overwhelming East Anglia. Here they found the breeding grounds of horses and learned to use them for mobility, almost conquering England. However, the early successes of the Norsemen could not be maintained and Alfred the Great was able to contain them by agreement, in the north-east of England. This great area became known as the Danelaw and was established in AD 878. It extended from the north-east to the borders of modern Derbyshire, taking in Galloway, Cumberland and Westmorland, but leaving the northern part of Northumberland in Anglo-Saxon hands. The inhabitants of the Danelaw were pledged to pay a tax known as Danegelt to their overlords, the Anglo-Saxons.

In the districts where they settled the Danes tended to break up feudalism, consequently there were fewer serfs and more freemen. There was a great mixture of races as people migrated to the area which allowed farming and trading to be practised so independently. Sandwiched as they were between the Anglo-Saxons in the south and the Scots, Picts and Strathclyde Welsh in the north, the people of the Danelaw became adept at keeping their warlike neighbours at bay by playing them off against each other. They would pay the Danegelt just long enough for safety, then let it lapse until threatened with war, when they would hand it over again for a few years. The Anglo-Saxons could never really control them. Eventually the old area of the Danelaw became known as Northumbria and the old Roman city of Eboracum (York) became Jorvik, the flourishing administrative and trading centre. In AD 947 the King of Northumbria was Eric Bloodaxe, and Wulfstan was Archbishop of York.

The last big Norse invasion came under Harald Hardrada, King of Norway, in the north in 1066. Almost simultaneously, William, Duke of Normandy invaded the south of England. Harold, King of England, had one of the best fighting forces in Europe, which consisted of his mobile, well-mounted housecarls, who fought on foot behind a shield wall. He had to leave his southern defences to ride at great speed north to York, where he met and defeated the Norsemen at Stamford Bridge. He then had to ride hot foot back to the south with a depleted army, to face William and lose his Kingdom and his life at the Battle of Hastings.

Normandy had been settled by the Norsemen and the Normans, more Scandinavian than French, were ruled by a family of strong Dukes. The Normans followed the European custom of importing Iberian horses to improve their own breeds. They had also perfected a method of fighting on horseback in chain mail, as armoured cavalry. Their horses seem to have been wiry weight-carriers of about 13 to 15 hands, known as destriers.

The Normans were well organised and attempted a survey of the whole of England in the Domesday Books. This was well accomplished until they attempted to cover Northumbia. The Northumbrians still enjoyed a different society from the feudal system of the Anglo-Saxons. They had an ancient tenancy system, traditional social customs and were always changing their constitution, which completely confused the Normans and resulted in the records of York being somewhat vague. It is not difficult to understand the reason why there are no entries at all for the upper dales of what is now North Yorkshire, Durham and Cumbria. The Northumbrians had been described as a treacherous, stubborn, rebellious people and the Normans found them as difficult to deal with as had the Anglo-Saxons. Over the centuries northerners were drawn into line but their descendents still show the same stubborn, indomitable spirit. Maybe they still regret the passing of their ancient Danelaw independence, for they tend to cast a cynical eye on all southerners! As Welsh ponies seem to reflect the fiery character of the Welshman, so Dales ponies appear to reflect the indomitable independence of the inhabitants of the former Danelaw.

The church was very powerful in this region and over the centuries the great abbeys were enlarged and enriched. In 1131, during the reign of Henry I, Rievaulx Abbey in Teesdale was granted extensive new pastures. Bernard Balliol built Barnard Castle, which included rights of pasture for 60 mares and foals to be grazed from the Feast of St

Martin to the beginning of April. This allowed the lower part of the dale above High Force to be used as winter pasture for nursing mares. It is a bleak and inhospitable part of the country and the mares would have been of a hardy race to have lived and bred successfully, even in the lower part of the dale, but there is no description of the type.

Throughout the Middle Ages horses of many types were in use and continually being improved. The small Norman destrier had been crossed with heavier German blood until it became quite ponderous and slow. Following the Crusades, it became desirable to have a faster, more mobile horse for use without encumbering armour. Once again Iberian horses were imported and brought with them the fire and courage which the heavy destrier lacked. These Spanish and Portuguese horses were such good looking animals that they became the favoured mounts of the Royal Court with every nobleman needing at least one. The Iberian horses were imported in great numbers and became available for use by tenants on the estates of the aristocracy. Thus, throughout the British Isles, another good dose of Iberian blood was used to improve British stock.

The destrier had been ridden into battle at a trot and when on the road was led by a squire mounted on a trotting cob, known as a rouncey or rounsey (a cob used as a saddle pony or pack-trotter). For travelling the knight would ride a horse with an easy gait, usually a palfrey which paced. Palfreys were descended from Asturian and Galecian ponies crossed with Iberian Saddle Horses or suitable native stock. It is interesting to note that palfreys were bred in large numbers around Richmond, in the Norman estates which lay around Nidderdale, Swaledale and Teesdale.

The improvement of horses has gone on throughout history, and although we have a good idea of the types bred from this time forward, the ones which the population of the British Isles could not do without were trotting pack ponies, known in the Middle Ages as rounceys or sumpters. These had to be energetic, large enough for the load to clear obstacles but not too tall for loading; strong enough to cope with heavy mud; hardy enough to stand harsh weather and docile enough to be easily handled. There is little detail of the breeding of these animals but it is possible to get an idea of the type from pictures and descriptions. They were used in increasing numbers and the early successes of British industry were based on their sturdy backs. By 1760 there were said to be more pack ponies in Britain than all other horses, and the last of them worked well into the late nineteenth century.

3
THE LEAD MINING INDUSTRY

$\blacklozenge$

LEAD MINING IN THE PENNINES began in Celtic times and the industry flourished throughout the centuries. Cheap imports of lead in the late nineteenth century saw the beginning of the decline which ended with the Depression in the 1930s. Throughout the ages until good roads and the steam locomotive took over, one of the absolute necessities for the industry was a handy supply of strong, hardy pack ponies.

Lead ore was found in long rakes of limestone which were situated on the eastern ridges of the Pennines, where conditions are hard and the environment bleak. Before smelting, the mixture of ore, stone and other materials had to be sorted and the ore washed. A good supply of water and fuel was required and when adjacent wood or peat was used up, fuel had to be transported from further afield. Smelting boles or hearths were always sited on the tops of hills to catch the prevailing wind. The method of smelting was unchanged throughout the early centuries. The ore hearths held the ore and fuel, the slag which was left was then smelted with charcoal on an iron grid and the lead collected in a pit or mould.

The Romans discovered the lead mines of the Pennines and exploited them with considerable success. It appears that the Hurst Mines in Swaledale and Greenhow, near Pateley Bridge, were Roman penal settlements where captives were sent into slavery. In 1735 two pigs of lead were found near the pack road which descends Greenhow Hill, stamped with the head of Domitian, a Consul of Rome about AD 81. The Roman settlement at Bainbridge in Wensleydale was thought to be a trading centre for lead sent out of Swaledale.

The Anglo-Saxons later carried on the trade as Bede tells of traders visiting Catterick in AD 672 to buy lead from Swaledale. The ensuing invasions of Vikings and Danes resulted in settlements of the dales and many place names in these parts, particularly in Swaledale, are of Scandinavian origin. The settling of such difficult country usually points to rich mineral deposits.

Following the Norman Conquest records were kept, with many

references to lead mining. The Cistercians founded the great abbeys of North Yorkshire, Rievaulx in Teesdale in 1131, Fountains near Ripon in 1132, Byland in Nidderdale in 1138 and Jervaulx in Wensleydale in 1145. They were great agriculturists with a particular interest in sheep. The interests of Rievaulx lay with iron working and lead-mining as well as farming and the abbey owned many mines and large tracts of land. Jervaulx concentrated on breeding horses, based on the local stock. Being a white-robed order, the preferred colour of horses was grey, this colour acting as an easily indentifiable 'trade-mark' when monks travelled between the farm granges, lead mines and abbeys. Most abbeys and castles had a smelting hearth for their own use.

There is a roll of tenants of Jervaulx Abbey who lent their horses for use in the war against the Scots which ended at the Battle of Flodden Field in 1513. Most of the tenants came from Swaledale, Teesdale, Westmorland, Wensleydale and Durham. Of the 253 horses, 163 are described by gait, 129 are noted as 'trottyng' and 34 as 'ambling or racking'. The trotting horses were all for pack work in the supply train or for hauling guns; the amblers were saddle horses. All but one of the 253 mentioned are described by colour, of which 95 were grey and 43 white, 57 were black, 46 bay, eight dun, three 'soreld or red-soreld' (chestnut) and one 'dosk' (dark dun). Many among the blacks, browns and bays are also described as 'bazand' in various spellings, which in those days meant having white on legs and head. The 'trottyng' horses are believed to have been the local breed from Teesdale, the forebears of the Dales galloway, which still carries white markings.

The history of the northern lead mines followed a similar pattern throughout the Pennines down as far as Derbyshire. In 1184, lead from Derbyshire and Yorkshire was shipped from Boston to Rouen and it is said that English lead was used to roof buildings in Jerusalem and the Church of St Peter in Rome.

With improvements in methods of smelting, England was the major lead producing nation by the late sixteenth century. New methods of smelting were introduced by rich landowners in the mid-sixteenth century. These were powered by water and fuelled with 'white coal' (chopped dried wood). In the eighteenth century, the larger cupola furnaces were set up and coal was used which was much more expensive than wood. As the lead mines became deeper, they required a greater workforce and more pony power for the new drift levels, where the way into the workings was by a graded slope from the surface.

Some of the mine owners, such as the Quaker-owned London Lead Mining Company, were aware of the independent life style of the miners and the difficulties of their situation. They pioneered better ventilation of the mines and stipulated the hours of work for the men, and in true Quaker fashion, when they built houses for the miners, they also added a few acres of land and rights to moorland grazing. The London Lead Mining Company ran their mines from 1692 to 1905, and are remembered for their compassionate management.

Until roads were built, the only transport of ore, fuel and lead was by pack galloway to the smelting mills and the nearest waterway to London or Europe. This was known as 'jagging' and many Jaggers Lanes are to be found in Pennine villages. Once roads were built and could be maintained in good order, carts were used for transport. Galloways brought the lead down from the Swaledale and Arkengarthdale smelting mills to Richmond, for transfer to carts for the journey to Stockton and the Tees, or to York for transport down the Ouse. From Teesdale and Weardale it went to Yarm and Stockton, from Greenhow and Pately Bridge to York and Stockton, and from Alston Moor most went down the Teesdale route but some was taken over the lead roads to Tyneside.

Derbyshire lead from the Hope Valley went from smelting mills by wainloads to Boston, on the Lincolnshire coast. From the south Peak it went by wains (wagons) to Nottingham, for transport by boat up the Trent to Hull or to the Midland towns. From the northerly Derbyshire smelting mills, the lead went by carts from near Chesterfield to Bawtry, for transport down the River Idle to the Trent and Humber; and the lead smelted around Sheffield went overland to Doncaster then down the Don and the Humber.

Eventually, the lead was all routed through the new railway system, but lead and ore was still moved by galloways around the mines on the high moors until quite late in the nineteenth century.

The galloways which carried the ore and lead needed great strength and endurance and were specifically bred for the job. A maximum pack load was given as 240 lb by Mr Joseph Willis in a House of Commons Committee in 1758, but was often more. An ingot of lead, known as a 'pig', weighing a hundredweight (112 lb = 8 stones/51 kilos) was slung from each side of wooden pack saddles in 'pokes', which were sacks made of 'harden', a very strong sacking material. Eleven galloways working loose-headed could move a 'fother' of lead, which weighed 1 ton 2 hundredweights. The ore and fuel were bulkier, the ore was usually measured in 'bings' (1 bing = 1 hundredweight).

The galloway carriers or 'galls', worked in gangs of from 12 to 25; each knew its name and none wore a bridle, but they did wear muzzles. This became necessary to prevent them from eating grass which grew along the lead roads, onto which fell fine powder from the sacks of lead ore. If this was eaten it caused the ponies to become 'bellond', an incurable form of lead poisoning. In the years before the laying of roads, these tough little galloways used to traverse up to 200 miles a week, under heavy loads and moving over some of the most difficult country in England at a good speed.

These Pennine galloways were strong, hardy ponies which had evolved over the centuries and were indigenous to the upper moorlands of the eastern slopes of the Pennine chain. They lived in harsh conditions. The bleak uplands fall into deep, long dales where the farmland was not enclosed until about 1820. Before then, the smallholdings followed the old pattern of raising hardy sheep, galloways and cattle which grazed on the fells.

Most of the farmers also worked in the lead industry, usually as carriers, at first independently and later for the landowners. It was customary for the farmers to breed galloways for the lead industry. They were well cared for and well fed to cope with hard work, whereas the wild herds of ponies had to survive on the poor upland grazing in a very unfriendly environment. It follows that the well fed ones grew larger and stronger than their wilder relatives. Weatherwise, wild ponies would have probably migrated to the western slopes of the Pennines during bad winters and it is possible that these became their preferred breeding grounds and could have been the schism which originally parted the breed of black Pennine galloways into Dales and Fell types.

Throughout the years of horse transport, improvements were continually being made to get the best type of animals for specific jobs. The lead industry needed a strong hardy, weight-carrier, speedy, sure-footed and enduring. Breeders found the perfect improver of pack ponies by looking to the Border and Scotland.

The Scotch Galloway

In the sixteenth century, Scotch Galloways were known for their stamina and considered the best ponies for fast travel over rough ground. They were a breed of swift little horses about which very little is known, although they were famous in their time and are well remembered. Descriptions of the Scotch Galloway are few, but they were familiar to Shakespeare who recognised their reputation for endurance and performance and used it in *Henry IV Part 2* in the scene where Pistol, boasting of his sexual prowess, compares himself to a Scotch Galloway, 'shall pack-horses and hollow pamper'd jades of Asia, which cannot go but 30 miles a day compare ... know we not Galloway nags?'

From long before the building of Hadrian's Wall and until the Union of Scotland and England, there were raids across the Border for considerable distances. Throughout the Middle Ages there were continual skirmishes and raids, from both sides. George MacDonald Fraser, in his book on Anglo-Scottish Border reivers, *The Steel Bonnets*, writes:

> The Border robber was a specialist and needed special equipment, the most important part of which was his horse. 'They reckon it a great disgrace for anyone to make a journey on foot,' wrote Leslie, and Froissart had noted two centuries earlier how the Scots at war 'are all a-horseback ... the common people on little hackneys and geldings'. The Border horses, called Hobblers or Hobbys, were small and active, and trained to cross the most difficult and boggy country, and to get over where our footmen scarce dare to follow. The Scots had long been noted horse-breeders, so much so that legislation was occasionally passed to restrain production. By statute of 1214 every Scot of property must own at least one horse, and in 1327 the country could put 20,000 cavalry in the field. Export to England at that time was highly profitable, and was carried on even by men of rank. The Stuart kings imported from Hungary, Poland and Spain to improve the breed and there emerged the small, swift unusually hardy mounts which in James IV's time were reputed to be able to cover as much as 150 miles in a day. However, even allowing for exaggeration, such horses were ideal all-purpose mounts both for peace-time raiders and war-time light cavalry. They enabled the Border raiders to muster and move men at high speed over remarkable distances. A leader like Young Buccleuch could raise 2,000 horse at short notice, able to strike faster and at a far greater range than would have seemed credible to an ordinary cavalry commander; between 60 and 80 miles a day seems to have been within their capability. In addition, the horses were cheap to buy and easy to maintain: there is evidence that they did not even need shoeing.

These became known in England as Scotch Galloways and there is a link with Dales ponies which comes through a name. The most powerful and feared of raiding families were the Armstrongs; one of the most famous was John Armstrong of Gilnockie. Known in legend as Johnnie Armstrong, to the Borderers he was Black Jock. This was the name given to a 'Dales' galloway stallion foaled in the mid-1800s, and who knows how many before and since. Black Jock has always been a popular name among the Border galloways.

Raiding was successfully discouraged following the Union with England in 1603. Scotch Galloways then became the favoured mount of the drovers who brought cattle from Scotland into England for marketing. North-country men always had an eye for a good galloway and would buy if the opportunity occurred.

Daniel Defoe wrote, in *A Tour through Scotland* (1692), referring to the Galloway, 'they have the best breed of strong, low horses in Britain, if not in Europe, which we call pads, and from whence we call all truss-strong, small riding-horses galloways; these horses are remarkable for being good pacers, strong, easy goers, hardy, gentle, well broke, and above all, that they never tire and are much bought up in England on that account.'

The 'pad' was the seventeenth-century name for the palfrey, palfrey being the earlier English name for the smooth-moving, trained pacer, which was also a natural trotter, descended from the Asturian and Galecian ponies. Palfreys were noted for giving a comfortable ride along rough roads. They moved with lifted knee and strong hock action, but flexible joints ensured comfort for riders without stirrups. The Scotch Galloways were apparently pacers and it is highly likely that they were descendants of the Asturian/Iberian/Barb/native crosses, bred by the Romans during their service on the wall.

In the search for improved pack ponies, the Scotch Galloway was a notable find. Tuke in *A General View of Agriculture*(1794), writing of the North Riding of Yorkshire, states:

> Horses constitute a considerable part of the stock of the high parts of the western moorlands, the farmers there generally keep a few Scotch Galloways, which they put to stallions of the country, and produce a hardy and very strong race in proportion to their size, which are chiefly sold into the manufacturing part of the West Riding and Lancashire, to be employed in ordinary purposes.

Scotch Galloways were also bred in Swaledale near Low Row, for the lead industry, where local native mares ran with the breeding herd. Many of the Scotch Galloway mares were also put to the newly imported Eastern sires, Barbs, Turks and Arabs, to produce the finest racehorse in the world, the English Thoroughbred. Thoroughbred or cross-bred horses which were of small stature, 13 to 15 hands, were also known as galloways and richly endowed Galloway races were popular up to the 1930s. In Australia there are still show classes for galloways (ponies of this size).

By 1831, Youatt considered the Scottish Galloway to be virtually extinct. He also writes that there is a tradition that the breed is of Spanish extraction, although he puts this down to the wreck of a ship of the Spanish Armada, containing horses which swam ashore. There is record of a Spanish horse transport being wrecked off the coast of Scotland at the time, and it is quite likely that horses did swim ashore. However, the loading lists of the Spanish horse transports suggest they were all geldings. Spanish influence obviously preceded the date of the Armada, as the Scotch Galloway was already well known in Elizabethan times.

Youatt described them as 'being nearly 14 hands, sometimes more; of a bright bay or brown with black legs, a small head and neck and peculiarly deep and clean legs. Its qualities were speed, stoutness, and sure-footedness over a very rugged and mountainous country.' He also mentions a Dr Anderson who owned a Scotch Galloway in his youth, who wrote:

> There was once a breed of small elegant horses in Scotland, similar to those of Iceland and Sweden, and which were known by the name of galloways; the best of which sometimes reached the height of fourteen hands and a half. One of this description I possessed, it having been bought for my use when a boy. In point of elegance of shape it was a perfect picture; and in disposition was gentle and compliant. It moved almost with a wish, and never tired. I rode this little creature for twenty-five years, and twice in that time I rode a hundred and fifty miles at a stretch, without stopping except to bait, and that not for above an hour at a time. It came to the last stage with as much ease and alacrity as it travelled the first. I could have undertaken to have performed on this beast, when it was in its prime, sixty miles a day for a twelvemonth running, without any extraordinary exertion.

The qualities for which the Scotch Galloway was famed were also instrumental in its demise. It became the foundation or improving stock from which came the English Thoroughbred, the Norfolk Roadster, the Clydesdale and Fell and Dales galloways.

In the Pennines the Scotch Galloways were superseded by the galloways which came from the improving herds of the Pennine lead industry. In a letter on the subject of the best type of pony for mounted infantry, Mr Christopher Wilson of Rigmaden Park, Kirby Lonsdale, wrote, 'The old Galloway was the same as the Fell pony, only it showed a little more breeding. The Fell pony in my part of the country is from 14.1 to 14.2 hands in height and is used for all kinds of farm work - in fact, it is a cart cob in miniature.'

Both Dales and Fell ponies have always been, and are still known as 'galloways' on their home ground. In the 1850s the 'Dales' galloway was considered to be a type of Fell pony. The usual height of 'Fell' galloways was around 13.0 -13.2 hands occasionally up to 14.0 hands at the time; a height limit of 14.0 hands was given in 1895 which was reduced to 13.2 hands in 1926 but rose to 14.0 hands again later. The 'Dales' galloway was usually from 14.0 to 15.0 hands. The little 'cart cobs' described were surely galloways of the Dales type, which Christopher Wilson referred to as 'Yorkshire Fells', as opposed to the

G.H. Hodgson mowing with the Dales mare Hilton Nancy (left) working with a Clydesdale (right) in the late 1940s.

smaller 'Cumberland Fells'.

Lecturing in 1926, the father of the late Roy Charlton told of a Dales pony belonging to Mr Matthew Marshall which, not many years before, had won the class for Galloways at Stranraer. He ended by saying that he considered the Dales pony to be the same type as the old Scotch Galloway.

4

THE CHANGING ROLE OF THE PACK GALLOWAYS

◆

THE WORKING GALLOWAYS OF THE PACKWAYS were eventually superseded by superior vehicles and faster horses on improved roads, and the new railways, although pack galloways continued in isolated regions until the late nineteenth century. To survive they had to fit into the changing pattern of industry and transport.

When the shallow veins of lead became worked out, deeper mine shafts were sunk. The deeper levels were reached by 'drifts', sloping roads from the surface which could be worked by ponies up to the height of 14.2 hands. A new use for the strong Pennine galloways became apparent. The chief fair for the purchase of galloways for the lead mines was held at Tow Law, in County Durham where, after about a fortnight's training, they went into the mines.

Strength and steadiness was necessary for the job, which entailed working underground between rails, standing for the 'tubs' to be hitched and hauling them to the surface. W. R. Mitchell, when writing about Eric Richardson of Nenthead, tells of how the veins of lead lay at an acute angle up or downwards. The miners worked on platforms with the ore falling into hoppers from which the 'tubs' were filled by a 'putter in'. A pony drew the string of loaded tubs along the rails to the unloading point, doing about five journeys a day, the average load of ore being about twenty tons. The underground levels went up to six miles underground. The pony wore a leather back protector, and worked in collar and chains. If the gradients were not too steep, he would be expected to hold the string of tubs back by leaning against the leading tub with his quarters, otherwise his leader would apply the brake. If he was working in wet levels where the water was acidic, he would have to be washed down after the day's work. Unlike pit-ponies, the lead mine ponies were stabled above ground. They were well looked after and often attended local shows in harness and ribbons. Even after locomotives were introduced into the levels for haulage, ponies were still kept for the steeper workings up until about 1936. A Dales pony is still doing this traditional work at the Killhope lead mine, in County Durham, which is now a working museum.

Dales galloways, on the whole, were too large to work as pit ponies in the north but were used underground in a few Midland pits. Many of them also worked on pit banks, moving tubs about on the surface.

Up until the time of land enclosures farming in the upper dales had followed the Norse pattern, of cattle, sheep and horses roaming the fellside. There were also small fields from the early days of lead mining, when every miner had a few acres of small-holding and a run of the fellside. As the lead industry failed, during the depression of 1828-1833, there was a general migration of lead miners and their families from the small villages into the coal mining areas and towns of Lancashire and Durham. Houses were left empty and land fell out of use. Two villages, Dent and Stanhope, benefitted from the quarrying of Dent marble, wanted in London and other large towns for fireplaces and ornamental work. This business was begun about 1780 and provided work for the galloway carriers for some time, as the heavy goods were carried by pack pony and carts over the fells to Newcastle and Stockton for shipment. This continued until the arrival of the railway at Dent.

Limestone had been quarried in Weardale for centuries. Farmers needing lime to improve their pastures collected coal from the small pits of the dales, and limestone from the quarries to burn in the lime kilns found on most farms until the quarries started producing it commercially. All was carried by pack ponies until the arrival of an early railway line from Stanhope to the Tyne. This was partly horse drawn, with sections operated by both steam and gravity. During this time the lead mining industry contracted, and although the remaining mines were improved, it was a time of severe hardship for the dales population. A textile industry based on flax was started in Nidderdale and became very successsful, as were the mills which converted from wool to cotton spinning. The Industrial Revolution had begun and migration to the towns gained momentum.

Seizing the opportunity, farmers began to expand and improve the production of food for the growing towns. The Border raids had long ceased and the cattle and sheep were now coming from Scotland along the drove roads to the northern graziers where they were fattened for the meat market. The Swaledale breed of sheep, with their black mottled faces, were bred from the Scottish Blackface and are still called 'Scotch sheep' in some parts of Yorkshire. Breeds of cattle and sheep were improved. The small farmers of the upper dales found that the intensive grazing improved the pastures, which were also limed, after stripping and burning the thin top layer of turf. This was then walled in and became known as an `intake'.

Landowners looking for better rents and more land, had resulted in the enclosure of much of the common land. Starting on the estates of the Bishop of Durham, 60,000 acres in Weardale were enclosed by 1800. By the mid-nineteenth century, the pattern of small dales fields was well established. The lower dales had good pastures which held large dairy herds and some arable crops. The higher smaller farms ran the beef cattle and sheep, made hay and used dried bracken for bedding. This was, and on some garths still is, cut and then brought in on pony drawn sleds.

The Dales galloway was found to be ideal for working the small farms of the upper dales. It was fully capable of drawing a ton in a cart or sled and was able to take a shepherd in the saddle, with two burdens of hay, one slung each side behind him. A 'burden' was two or three cuts of hay from a rick being roped for carrying over the saddle. They could weigh from 4 to 12 stones; very heavy ones would be taken on a led pony. The hay was, and often still is, carried to sheep some distance up the fell, often accomplished in deep snow and severe weather. There are many tales of farmers losing their way in snowstorms when going up to feed stock on the fell, who were saved by the sagacity of their Dales ponies. The ponies were comfortable to ride and could undertake journeys of considerable distance over rough country at a good speed. Like pack ponies in general, they could trot and proved good trappers, taking the farmer and his wife to market in grand style. They became the traction units of the farms and accomplished all tasks as the seasons came round on the poor quality fodder available and frequently in very harsh conditions.

Throughout the nineteenth century, there was a continual improvement in the breeding of agricultural horses. The heavy horses were coming into their own and by 1850 Britain had three magnificent breeds of draught horse to cope with the new machinery being invented for agriculture which became progressively larger and more efficient. In Scotland and the North of England, the Clydesdale was supreme. These well built, active horses were very popular but were not hardy enough to thrive on the small farms of the upper dales, and, being rather expensive to keep, were not economical enough to tempt such a farmer.

The winter of 1947 will be long remembered by folk who lived

William Iceton with his Dales gelding and Swaledale ewes in Baldersdale in 1974.

through it. Lasting 10 weeks, it almost destroyed the dales farmers, some of whom suffered tremendous losses of stock. In Barry Cockcroft's book *The Dale that Died*, there is a vivid description of conditions. Mr R. Pratt owned 65 acres of land in Griesdale with two good Dales ponies, 35 cattle and 250 Swaledale sheep. The storm began on January 24th, 1947, and it was still snowing in the middle of February. The snow covered walls and gates and cattle were driven over the top of them. All water was frozen except for very deep springs and sheep died, either lost under drifts or huddled in barns, where they started sweating and died of pneumonia. Hay was dropped by plane to stranded farms as the snow continued falling into April and more ewes died, being too weak to lamb. Mr Pratt lost 150 of his flock and got only about 40 lambs instead of 200. However, his losses were nothing to those of his neighbour who was new to the dale and had brought with him two Clydesdale horses, a herd of cattle, 150 ewes and 50 gimmer hogs (yearling ewes). At the end of the winter he was left with 38 ewes and 12 gimmers; he had also lost some of his cattle, and both his horses which lay down and died in the intense cold.

Mr J. R. Longstaff of Lummas House, Marske, above Swaledale, has a photograph of his Dales stallion, Lummas Comet, carrying hay to sheep. The pony is stepping over telephone wires near the top of a telegraph pole, working on top of deep snow and it is telling that Mr Longstaff's mares were wintering out at the time. Dales ponies worked very hard during that winter and were largely responsible for the survival of many farms.

The late Mr Joe Hall, who bred the Stainton ponies, used to tell how he owed his life to his mare, Wharton Beauty, when he was lost on the fell in a snow-storm and only got home safely by holding onto her tail as she found her way through the drifts. Mr Laurie Raine, a noted breeder of Swaledale sheep and Dales ponies, lives in one of the bleakest spots between Bowes and Kirkby Stephen and still relies on his ponies to keep his sheep fed during any heavy snow storms. When motorised transport cannot cope, the ponies are still the safest and most economical means of getting hay to the stranded flocks.

In 1979, the Dales ponies Stainton Darkie, a daughter of Mr Hall's Wharton Beauty, and Brymor Mimi, were the sole means of getting fodder to 300 in-lamb ewes stranded about a mile and three-quarters from a farm belonging to Mr F. Hammond, near Stanage Pole in Derbyshire. Winters always tend to be fierce in the High Peak and this was one of the memorable ones. From January 1st, deep snow lay until March 25th.

The Land Rover and tractor made very heavy weather of the mile

A Dales pony hauling a load of hay on a sledge, Swaledale, 1940.

drive along the road and could not get up the hill track to the flock of hardy ewes which had gathered in a high belt of conifers. Stainton Darkie was hitched to a metal farm gate on which were loaded seven bales of hay and a sack of mineral blocks. She set off, adjusting to her low load and working impressively, hauling the makeshift sled along the snowy road and up the stiff, uphill track. She did this job for a week when a slow, temporary thaw set in, and the ewes drifted back onto the open moor. There was a further very deep snowfall on January 17th. The ponies were ridden up to the moor to see how many sheep had gathered and found about 300 among the trees.

Having already made a rough path through the deep snow, it was decided the ponies should take the hay. Each day their riders, sisters Penelope FitzGerald and Joanna Ashby, took a bale in front of them on the saddle. The ponies stood as the bales were hauled onto the saddle and set off through the snow onto the moor, returning for two more loads each morning. Both ponies carried about 14 stones in weight and the journey was uphill and awkward, with rutted snow and drifts. When the riders arrived, they were surrounded by milling hungry sheep, pushing and jostling for food around the ponies which stood like rocks as the hay was spread.

Eventually the tractor was able to take a load of bales to the bottom of the hill but it was an awkward job hauling the bales off the wall onto the ponies, as they tried to snatch mouthfuls. With the reins often getting caught over their ears or under the bale, the mares were usually working with no means of steering other than word of mouth. Conditions became a little easier as the path became more marked and they became used to the job. Mimi was very clever at it but one morning she fell into a deep drift, emerging through a flurry of snow with the bale hanging off one side of her shoulder and her rider off the other, to balance the load until it could be dropped with the sheep. It was also their habit to set off for the next load at speed, galloping and trotting over the very slippy surface, before their riders were settled in the saddle. Many horses would have fallen under these conditions but their natural sure-footedness saved them many times on the icy surface. The job continued until February 28th, when one of the worst blizzards in living memory hit the Peak.

It raged for three days on a rising wind and it was not possible to get to the sheep. The farmyard was full of snow up to the cowshed roof and the ponies had to stay in their boxes as field gates disappeared under the snow. A 10-foot drift lay in the drive; feeding and watering had to be done by climbing over loose-box doors; any paths dug out were instantly filled in again. When the snow stopped, the road was filled with enormous drifts. Some brave Venture Scouts managed to get up to the farm by walking along the tops of the stone walls. They volunteered to carry bales along the walls to the bottom of the hill if the ponies could break through to reach them. Darkie, being the biggest pony, was chosen to have a try. She was saddled without stirrups and ridden into the drift, which lay across the gateway. She plunged into the drift and got her head under the snow which alarmed her, but she rolled onto her side and kicked her way through. She emerged slightly put-out so her rider walked into the next drift and trampled down the edges. Darkie followed in a series of plunges when she was asked.

The mare soon worked the method out and worked loose-headed, plunging into the drift after her rider, then standing awkwardly while sinking into the snow, until asked to go on. At one point she went right under and looked like a floundering black whale, but got herself out and cleverly avoided stepping on her leader who had fallen under her feet. She soon got used to the job and went on in front. When she reached the bottom of the hill it became obvious that the snow had blown off the hill into the road, so carrying uphill was possible. Darkie was ridden back through the track she had made and Mimi came out to do the carrying. After 11 more days three JCBs turned up to help the snowplough clear a road and eventually the snow disappeared and the sheep returned to the moor.

The ponies had successfully accomplished a job for which their forebears were bred. They never protested about being dragged out in the freezing dark, and thrived on the hard work. The speed with which they bounced downhill on return journeys was not that of tired animals. They were not only working ponies. Brymor Mimi won the Dales Championship at the National Pony Show four times, and was twice

Joanna Ashby and Brymor Mimi carrying hay to stranded sheep in 1979.

Reserve for the Lord Arthur Cecil Cup for the Supreme Native Brood mare. Among her many successes she has won in Brood Mare, Ridden and Driven classes and been Reserve Best Female and Reserve Champion at Breed Shows. She has also been a film star and can be seen flashing past at her customary trot, driven to a wagonette, in the film *Agatha*. Stainton Darkie also had a very respectable career in Combined Driving and Performance classes and did a great deal under saddle during her long life. They have both been good representatives of their breed and there are many like them.

Before the coming of Land Rovers, tractors and Snowcats, it was only the strength and hardiness of the Dales ponies that kept the farms of the upper dales going and they are held in jealous esteem by older dalesmen, who know their true worth.

5
THE NORFOLK ROADSTERS

◆

IN THE SEVENTEENTH CENTURY goods were moved about by ponderous, barrel-wheeled, covered waggons horsed by eight strong, slow horses. Coaches were heavy and unsprung and the rutted roads were dusty when dry and deep mud when wet. The favoured coach horses were the Friesland trotters from the Low Countries which, though very powerful, were also slow. The pack pony trains were still supreme as fast carriers of goods, their bells being a familiar sound as they travelled the moorland tracks. The fastest road travel was still accomplished on horseback.

By the middle of the eighteenth century farmers began to frequent the new weekly markets, travelling on horseback sometimes with a pillion for a female passenger. At about the same time there was a concentrated effort in road improvement, which resulted in roads being surfaced more effectively.

The comfortable palfreys, pads, amblers and galloways, which had eased travel over difficult, unsurfaced roads for centuries, were on their way out. They were superseded by improved roadsters and lighter, sprung vehicles. Horse breeders now searched for stallions with speed. In the past tenant farmers had the use of the Spanish stallions favoured by their noble overlords. These had passed on dense bone, short wide backs, muscular withers, powerful hocks, rounded action and high head carriage to their progeny. The Spanish horses, however, lacked in one particular: they were not very speedy. Arabs and Barbs were proving much faster.

Charles I became a patron of horse-racing and owned a Royal Stud, which contained a collection of imported eastern mares known as the Royal mares. These were preserved by Oliver Cromwell although racing was banned during the Commonwealth. Once Charles II was restored in 1660, horse-racing became very popular. There was a rush to import eastern stallions and mares and the foundation of the English Thoroughbred was laid down.

The three most influential eastern stallions were:

A Trotting Carthorse.

- the Byerley Turk, ridden by Captain Byerley at the Battle of the Boyne in 1690
- the Darley Arabian, imported by John Darley of Buttercrambe, near York in 1705
- the Godolphin Arabian, which was said to have been a Barb.

The latter was imported by Edward Coke in 1730, from France, supposedly stolen from a royal stud in Barbary. From these three, out of English galloway mares, came the early racehorses such as Flying Childers, an unbeaten son of the Darley Arabian and considered to be the fastest racehorse of his day. From the next generations came the Thoroughbreds, improved hunters and the faster roadsters, which had such a strong influence on breeds of horses throughout the world.

In Norfolk, at about the same time, there was in existence a renowned breed known as the Norfolk Trotting Carthorse which was highly thought of as an improving sire. The stock were distinguished by wide chests and round buttocks. They were not speedy but had great endurance and were very comfortable to ride. A description given in *The Sporting Magazine*, in 1820, was: 'having plenty of hair, short legs, a good lengthy barrel and only wanting a little blood'.

Improving blood eventually came through a horse named Blaze, foaled in 1733 and sired by Flying Childers. In 1755 a local mare, produced a colt to Blaze, this was **Shales the Original**, one of the acknowledged foundation sires of the Norfolk Roadsters.

The history of the early years of the Norfolk Roadsters is retrospective, researched by Henry Euren for the Introduction of Volume 1 of the Hackney Horse Stud Book. The absence of the pedigrees of mares leaves tantalising gaps but as the breed became dominant and the fame of the stallions spread, records became more informative.

Racing Thoroughbred sires, of which there were many in Norfolk, were used to improve the speed of subsequent generations, which became known as Norfolk Roadsters or Norfolk Cobs. Eventually, these became the most renowned improving horses of the eighteenth century and were exported in large numbers to Europe, Russia, North and South America, Asia and the British colonies. As with the Scotch Galloway, this practice sadly resulted in the inevitable disappearance of the Norfolk Roadster into many new trotting breeds.

Shales the Original sired two sons, Scot's Shales and Driver. Scot's Shales was reputed to have got the best stock of his day, one being

A Norfolk Trotter.

Thistleton's Shales, the sire of the celebrated **Marshland Shales**, foaled in 1802. As an eight-year-old, Marshland Shales trotted 17 miles in 56 minutes carrying 12 stone. He was described when over the age of 30 years, by George Borrow, in his autobiographical novel, *Lavengro*, when he heard the old horse called the 'best in Mother England' and saw spectators doff their hats to him.

In a Sporting Magazine of 1824, Marshland Shales, at the age of 22 years, was described thus:

> His crest, yet very large, was, when he was young and in high condition, immense, but gradually fell over to the off side, with a remarkable indent. When excited by any passing object, he raises it so as greatly to diminish the indent. In his numerous trials he was never beaten; and was universally acknowledged both the speediest and stoutest trotter of the time. He was fully master of 20 stone and most truely, as they used to style in Norfolk,`a thundering trotter',extremely apt to throw dirt and pebbles into the eyes of those who, of necessity, come behind him. He was not, however, a remarkably high goer though he bent his knees well.

The second influential family of Norfolk Roadsters were the Fireaways, the first of which was Jenkinson's Fireaway which sired West's Fireaway, foaled in 1800, out of a renowned trotting mare by the Thoroughbred, Pagan. West's Fireaway sired Burgess's Fireaway, a chestnut roan foaled in 1815, out of a mare by the Derby winner, Skyscraper. Burgess's Fireaway sired some notable stock, the most famous being **The Norfolk Cob** (Wright & Goold's) foaled in 1819.

In his book *The High Stepper* Mr Tom Ryder quotes from the *Sunday Times* in 1839, a description of The Norfolk Cob, when aged 20 years:

> He was got by Fireaway out of a Shields (Shales) mare, and is reputed to be the fastest trotter that ever stepped. He is known to have performed two miles in 5 min.4 sec., and is also said to have trotted 24 miles in an hour. This surpasses the celebrated Phenomenon mare, or any performances of the fastest American horses. He has a great crest resembling the Godolphin Arabian; is short-legged but standing over a great length of ground. He is strong as a buffalo; indeed his great muscular delineation and the immensity of his bone give him the resemblance of an animal of that class. He shows, however, a vast deal of blood. His colour is bay; he has lost both eyes, but is in other respects, totally free from blemish, very quiet, of excellent constitution and a remarkably safe goer, notwithstanding his almost incredible speed.

In the hands of his owner, Mr Theobald, his name was changed to the Norfolk Phenomenon, and at the great age of 26 years he was exported to the West Indies estate of Sir William Codrington, in 1845.

This was the type of horse Yorkshire breeders were looking for.

The breeders of Yorkshire roadsters and coach horses were improving their own roadster stock with Thoroughbreds, by using them on galloway and chapman mares. The chapman was a pack horse much used in the north-east, particularly on the north Yorkshire moors, from which stemmed the Cleveland Bays.

Jalap was the most influential Thoroughbred used to improve the Yorkshire roadsters. He sired Trotting Jalap, out of a mare by the racehorse Cade foaled in 1734. Cade was a son of the Godolphin Arabian. Trotting Jalap appears in many Hackney and coach horse pedigrees. Ruler (Bethell's) winner of the 1780 St.Leger, stood at Middleham (County Durham) in 1790 and had travelled many parts of Yorkshire as a county stallion. The racehorse Brutandorf also served in Yorkshire as did the grey, Delpini. At this time, the Yorkshire roadsters were generally of high quality and fast but they were light and lacked stamina. In an effort to rectify this state of affairs, the Norfolk stallions, Wroot's Pretender and his son, Performer were brought into Yorkshire by Robert Ramsdale of Market Weighton, in 1806.

Wroot's Pretender, foaled in 1788, was a black, blood-like horse with fine legs and short fetlocks, which became a very popular sire of trotters. His breeding has never been confirmed owing to a plethora of Pretenders, but it was acknowledged that he came from the Fireaway line.

In 1821, the *Sporting Magazine* gave an account of Pretender, then aged 33 years.

> Mr Lawrence must be mistaken respecting his age, as the horse in question is now serving mares in Westmorland and Cumberland. He was bought last year out of the East Riding of Yorkshire by a `break-neck dealer', being `turned adrift,' no one suspecting it possible for him to propagate his species any longer; but I have seen 10 or 12 of his produce (yearlings) as well as foals this season which are very promising. He is dark brown, 15.2 hands, and it appears was bred by Christopher Rook (Wroot), Long Sutton, Lincolnshire. His first performance was in that county, when he trotted two miles in 5 min. 54 sec. with a high weight, upon a green sward. I well remember his first appearance in a market town in the north. The Johnny Raws smiled at his worn out emaciated form, but the moment room was given for him to get upon his pins, every other stallion that was exhibited retired into the shade in an instant.

The same Mr Lawrence also observed that trotters, unlike gallopers, do not lose their speed from old age many having been known to trot as fast at 20, and even 30 years of age, as they did in their prime.

Trotting matches were as popular as racing, the sport having taken

Field Marshall (2986 HHSB) foaled 1889. A Norfolk Roadster owned by King Edward VII when Prince of Wales.

a hold which reached the height of popularity in this country in the mid-nineteenth century and lasted until the turn of the century. In the dales and Wales, the homes of modern native trotting cobs, the sport has had an enduring popularity and to this day can be seen at many local agricultural shows.

Pretender's son, Performer (Ramsdales) was the sire of the Yorkshire roadster, Merrylegs (Lund's). The following quotation is from part of a conversation with William Lund, which Henry H. Dixon, alias 'The Druid', recorded in his book *Saddle and Sirloin*:

> Our auld bay mare was dam of her as bred Merrylegs, and all of them good 'uns... she was tremendous fast; some days beat owt in the world - some days we could mak' nowt of her... I once ploughed a yacre of ground with her, and then trotted 16 miles to Beverley races and back. T'auld bay meer come of a black meer by Harrison's Sportsman, gitten with syke a horse as come of Jerry Broughton - a little bit of fash down the legs, but go for yae summer day after another. They lived like racehorses - there were never no mair syke.

Lund's Merrylegs won the Premium at the East Riding Agricultural Show, Beverley and was Best Roadster Stallion at the Royal Show, York, winning at many smaller shows from 1835 to 1837. He travelled for 12 years in the same district and many of his sons travelled in Yorkshire and Lincolnshire. When he died in 1846, his obituary was published in *The Yorkshire Gazette.*

Another of Old Pretender's (Wroot's) sons was Steven's Bellfounder, foaled in 1797, who became the sire of Jary's Bellfounder, the foundation sire of the American trotters. However, his most renowned son was Read's Fireaway, out of a mare by Scot Shales. He became a famous trotter who, in 1801, went to Yorkshire to compete at Howden Show for Best Trotter; after winning he went on to trot 16 miles carrying 16 stone in 58 minutes. He stayed in Yorkshire for two seasons before returning to Norfolk.

The best known of the travelling Thoroughbreds was Bay President. His son, another Bay President, won the award for the 'Best Stallion for Hunters' at the The Yorkshire Agricultural Show in 1840, and in 1855, at the age of 22 years, won a class for the best Roadster stallion.

The world-wide success of the Norfolk Roadster was not lost upon Yorkshiremen. It had become obvious that the Norfolk breed could improve the Yorkshire one and every opportunity was taken to accomplish this.

INFLUENTIAL YORKSHIRE ROADSTERS

In 1825 Thomas Kirby of York went to Norfolk to buy Burgess's Fireaway to take to Yorkshire. The horse's name was changed to Wildfire and he left some valuable stock. In 1838, Robert Ramsden of Market Weighton brought into Yorkshire, the 15.2 hand, red roan, Bond's Norfolk Phenomenon, a son of the Norfolk Cob. A blue roan son of Bond's horse, Norfolk Phenomenon, (Taylors's) was described by a breeder of Norfolk Trotters in a letter to Henry Euren thus:-

'To Taylor's horse I must assign the palm of pre-eminence over all trotters I have ever seen; from 12 to 15 miles an hour he lifted himself in the air, and seemed propelled by wings rather than feet, whilst his wonderfully rounded action reminded one rather of the rotation of so many wheels than the legs of an ordinary horse.'

This description is of interest as it is the way a good Dales pony should travel.

From the Fireaway line on both sides came Lord Derby II, foaled in 1871, a brown 15.2 hand Hackney which was to have a profound effect on pony stock. A good winner in the show ring, he was held in high regard as a sire in his home country of Holderness. Lord Derby II was also influential in founding Hackney ponies through his use on Wilson pony mares.

During the early reign of Queen Victoria, the railways had been laid down and these eventually put paid to the Stage and Mail coaches which now enjoyed the use of swift coach horses of the highest quality. Breeders changed tack once more and the day of the elegant Hackney to horse smart town carriages was arriving. However, the need for equally smart, small roadsters did not abate and the pack galloways, now becoming redundant, were at hand.

THE WILSON PONIES

It should be recognised that during the evolution of the Norfolk Roadster into the Hackney, the size had increased considerably, up to 16.2 hands in some cases. The most popular size was about 15.2 hands but the pony roadsters still reigned supreme.

The most popular sire of small roadsters in the 1840-1850s was Houseman's **Merry Driver** (1045 HHSB), foaled in 1836 by Pretender (601HHSB) by Ramsdale's Performer, out of a mare by West's Driver (188 HHSB). West's Driver, foaled in 1805, was by Read's Fireaway who had spent one or two seasons in Yorkshire. Read's Fireaway was by Driver 187 HHSB out of a mare by Scot Shales, sire and grandsire by Shales the Original. Many Fell and nearly all Dales ponies carry Merry Driver lines.

In 1872, Mr C.W. Wilson, of Rigmaden Park, Kirkby Lonsdale, Westmorland, was experimenting with cross-breeding galloways to get more speed combined with small size and hardiness. Speedy, weight-carrying galloways had been used as Turf ponies on race-courses in the days when Thoroughbreds competed in two-horse match races. The racing horses were followed closely by spectators mounted on Turf ponies.

The stallion used by Christopher Wilson in his breeding experiment was the 14-hand, brown Sir George (779 HHSB), foaled in 1866. By Hart's Sportsman, out of a trotting mare named Polly, this Yorkshire-bred pony became one of the foundation sires of the modern Hackney pony. His pedigree can be traced back through the Fireaway and Shales lines to early Thoroughbreds, including the Derby winners, Highflyer and Waxy, and imported eastern stock including some of the Royal mares of Charles II. His sire, Sportsman, was by the Yorkshire Prickwillow, by Taylor's Performer, the latter being a son of Ramsdale's Phenomenon out of the dam of Lund's Merrylegs. His grandsire was Ramsdale's Wildfire, formerly Burgess's Fireaway.

Sir George was put to a small Thoroughbred mare, The Pet, a 13.2

hh bay, bred by Daniel Miller of Worcester and foaled in 1869. The result was the filly, Snorer, foaled in 1879, who won at the Royal Show five years in succession. She and two more of her daughters by Sir George, Snorer II and Lady Polo, were in turn put back to their sire, the same procedure was followed with the resulting grand-daughters. This policy of inbreeding to the fourth generation proved a notable success and resulted in the foundation of the brilliant little trotters which became known as Wilson ponies, on which the modern Hackney pony is based.

At the same time Sir George was also put to Yorkshire galloway and Welsh mares and all youngstock was turned out on the fell, to prove their hardiness. Most of the Sir George/galloway stock were not entered in the Hackney Horse Stud book, but their blood lines went by various routes into the Welsh and the Dales and Fell galloways. This gave an extra brilliance to the speed and action of the galloways without greatly altering their appearance. Early Wilson ponies were Sir Douglas (1875), Sir John (1879), Sir William (1879) out of Maggie by Derby 953 HHSB (alias Norfolk Cob) and Little John out of a mare by Comet (1881).

In 1882 Snorer was put to a pony who had been entered in the Hackney Stud Book twice, once as Young Confidence (1237 HHSB), by his breeder, D. T. Armes, and later by his owner C. W. Wilson as Little Wonder (1237 HHSB). He was a 13.2 hh, dark brown son of the Norfolk-bred Confidence (158 HHSB) out of a Welsh mare. The resulting foal was registered in the Hackney Stud Book as Little Wonder II (1610 HHSB), he died in 1906 at the age of 23 years. In 1882 Christopher Wilson bought Dorothy Derby, a 13.3 hands mare by Lord Derby II (417 HHSB) out of Burton Agnes(608 HHSB) by Danegelt (174 HHSB). In 1881, Dorothy Derby foaled Sir Horace (5402 HHSB) by Little Wonder II. Together with his full sister, Dorothy Derby II, Sir Horace had a strong influence on Hackney pony breeding. He was was Champion Hackney Stallion seven times and Dorothy Derby II was Champion Hackney Mare in 1896 and 1897.

Little Wonder II was bought by the Marquis of Londonderry, and stood at the Seaham Harbour Stud, County Durham; he was registered in Volume II of the Polo Pony Society Stud Book (later the National Pony Society Stud Book), as Little Wonder II (25). He sired many trotting galloways before the Dales and Fell Stud books were opened, but some of his and Sir Horace's stock were entered in early Fell and Dales Stud Books. This gave the galloways another boost of trotting blood. The early roadsters were usually under 14.2 hands, as were the early Thoroughbreds, and they 'nicked' very successfully with galloway stock.

It is well to remember that these good stallions were easily available

Sir Horace (5402 HHSB) foaled 1891 - a Wilson pony bred by Mr Christopher Wilson.

to farmers; they travelled districts weekly with time-tables and destinations well advertised. Transport by rail was cheap and easy for mares and grooms to any distance. Farmers were breeding for the market and followed the fashion for small, strong, stylish trappers. It was a dangerous time for all native breeds and not one escaped the influence of some outside blood at this time.

Farmers of the upland farms of the dales and fells had an enduring passion for match races between trotters, in harness or under saddle. They watched the new breed evolving with interest and used the acquired knowledge to add speed and style to the progeny of their own galloways. Dales farmers would have found it impossible to keep one horse for farm work, another for the trap and a third for sport. They were not fools, they used their heads, looked to their galloway mares and bred exactly what was required.

6
THE IMPROVERS

━━━━━━━━━━━━◆━━━━━━━━━━━━

FROM THE 1850s the call for improvement grew stronger, but fortunately there were still many true ponies working on the farms of the upper dales. One early experiment was carried out in the 1860s at Streatlam, County Durham, by Mr John Bowes, who trained and owned many successful racehorses. He used The Spy and other Thoroughbreds on Dales galloway mares in the search for a good breed of hunter. The Spy was by the famous Underhand, three times winner of the Northumberland Plate (The Pitman's Derby), in 1856,1857 and 1858. Mr Bowes found, as in the Dales/roadster cross, that although the added blood improved their size and quality, the appearance of the cross-bred did not alter greatly following a single crossing and he found them to be 'thicker and stronger than ever'. It has always been understood that the best cross is out of a Thoroughbred mare by a Dales stallion, the larger mare producing a taller riding horse. Army Remount officers were always keen to get half-bred Dales galloways for troopers and gun teams, and they were eagerly sought by Masters of the Hunt looking for something handy, with five legs, for Hunt staff.

The next cross to a Thoroughbred produced a good-sized horse, with a record of endurance and strength, which was also popular with the Army for officers' chargers. This method of breeding strong, active and enduring horses was endorsed in 1982, by the late Mrs I. M. Yeomans, a long-established breeder of Welsh ponies and a consultant in Thoroughbred breeding. Giving a commentary for a Mountain & Moorland pony display at Stoneleigh, she stated that one of the best ways to breed a good performance horse was from a Dales stallion out of a Thoroughbred mare, the progeny being subsequently returned to a Thoroughbred. Marjorie Quarton, in her book on her experiences in Ireland, *Breakfast the Night Before*, tells how clever Irish horse dealers made good use of this knowledge between the wars, thus :

> Irish horse-dealers knew that the Army and the Police believed that Yorkshire horses were solid, dependable creatures for which it was worth paying a substantial premium, and found that they could always

sell their Irish bred Hunters to Yorkshire dealers. And so, once in England, an Irish Draught would be transformed into a Cleveland Bay and a Tipperary hunter would find itself sired by a Dales stallion.

Towards the the end of Merry Driver's era in the 1860s, a big brown stallion travelled from Manchester to Shap to compete in trotting races. He was brought from Wales by Daffyd Evans and was almost certainly the 16-hand, dark bay Trotting Comet (1411 HHSB), foaled in 1851. He was by Trotting Comet (834 HHSB), out of a mare named Black Bess by Cauliflower out of a mare by Glory Farmer. He was bred by Ellis Thomas of the Talbot Hotel, Tregaron, and known in Wales as one of the many Young Comets. He was the sire of Briton Comet, foaled 1859, who sired Caron Comet and the dam of Young King Jack, well known in Welsh Cob lore. In the north, he was known as Comet Talbot and, as is customary in the dales, though bay, he was described as brown.

The sire of Comet Talbot was one of the founding fathers of Welsh Cobs. Foaled in 1840, Trotting Comet 834 was registered in the Hackney Horse Stud Book and died in 1861. Welshmen had been improving their own breed of trotting ponies and cobs as the dalesmen had, by using Norfolk sires. Welsh Cobs were at the same stage of development as the Dales trotting galloways, being required for the same reasons. In the north, Comet was responsible for producing 'the Comets', a type of large, active roadster out of galloway mares, which used to sell like hot cakes at Brough Hill Fair.

There was a continual crossing of blood throughout all the native pony breeds in the search for faster and more stylish roadsters. There are records of northern sires going into Wales, around the same time. One such was Highland Laddie, the celebrated pony by Mountain Ranger by Highland Rob by Lingcropper, who won the Cup for the best pony sire at the Royal Show, Chester, in 1858. This pony had been used as a gig pony and was originally sold for £21.14s, at a rate of 6d a lb. but following his win at Chester he was sold to a Mr Starkey for £100. He was a well-known teaser, having accompanied the racehorse, The British Yeoman, when he travelled in Cumberland. Another northern horse who had an influence in Wales was Ruler II, the sire of True Briton, foaled in 1830 and considered to be the fountain head of Welsh Cobs. Ruler II was a Yorkshire Coach Horse, a son of the racehorse, Bethel's Ruler.

In the north, Comet Talbot sired **Comet II**, sometimes known in the north as **Young Comet** and said to have been out of a galloway mare. Comet II was bred by William Hully of Orton, who was a noted breeder of registered Hackneys and trotting galloways. The Hully family bred a line of Comets, and it is difficult to be sure which of the Old and Young Comets was which. However, two important Dales stallions

Comet II owned by William Hully of Orton.

sprang from the line, both by Comet II. These were **Daddy's Lad** and **Teasdale Comet**. Daddy's Lad was a very fast trotter, exported to the Argentine just before the First World War. Fortunately he left behind some good mares and one important stallion, **Linnel Comet,** to continue his line. The grey Teasdale Comet, foaled in 1898, was very influential in both Fell and Dales breeds. He was never entered in the Fell Stud Book, being 14.2 hands, but was eventually registered at the age of 24 years after the Dales Stud book opened.

Following Merry Driver and Comet, the Norfolk and Wilson lines were continued through the brilliant little pony sires Sir George, Sir Richard, Little Wonder II and Sir Horace. The Wilson pony lines were also being extended through the stallions out of galloway bred mares, such as a later Little Wonder II. The following description is given on his Stud Card.

LITTLE WONDER II
Foaled in 1886 the property of William Coltman, Hardberry Hill, Middleton-in-Teesdale.
Will serve mares this Season at £1 and 2s 6d the groom; Grooms fee to be paid at first time of serving, the remainder to be paid when the

mare proves in Foal.

LITTLE WONDER II, stands 14.2 hands high, is a bright bay with black legs, possessing great strength and superior action, has already figured prominently in show rings, and promises to make a good DALE SIRE, as you will observe in the following pedigree:-

LITTLE WONDER II, is by that noted horse, LITTLE WONDER, the property of Mr Pearson, Harbour Flatt, which was sold (to go abroad) for a very large sum. LITTLE WONDER was by SIR RICHARD, the property of Christopher Wilson, Esq. Kendal; SIR RICHARD by SIR GEORGE, winner of the Royal Show eight years in succession.

LITTLE WONDER II, dam, that noted pony which has won twelve first and two second prizes, out of sixteen times exhibited, and was also successful in winning the Silver Cup, given at St. John's Chapel, Weardale, in 1883, out of an entry of 17 excellent ponies: Dam's sire, Glengarry, the property of A.C.Dent Esq., Eden Place, Kirkby Stephen. A whole host of notable ancestors might be given, including that renowned pony HEATHER BELL, which won so many prizes in Liverpool and other principal towns in England - in fact was open to

ABOVE *Teasdale Comet foaled 1898.*

LEFT *Fair Day, 1912. The grey pony is Teasdale Comet.*

the world as a trotting pony. But your inspection will suffice. All mares tried by this horse, and served by another, sold, exchanged or given away, will be charged full price unless by consent of the groom. Will travel part of the Tees and Wear valleys.

Another well advertised pre-Stud Book stallion was Daybreak by Young Comet out of a 13-year-old brown mare by Comet II. Owned by William Coatsworth of Middleton-in-Teesdale, and bred by James Hutchinson of Bowes, he was foaled in 1896 and stood 14 hands. A photograph of him as a two-year-old shows a short-backed, compact pony with a good head and a little feather on excellent feet and legs.

The breeders of the Dales galloways were getting what they were looking for, a speedy, stylish trapper with strength and endurance, economical, hardy and long-lived. These were very popular animals and were produced in large numbers, whereas the numbers of the Fell type were fading. Improvement had become a national habit, bringing with it a looming danger for pure breeds.

ABOVE Daddy's Lad, sire of Linnel Comet.

BELOW The Clydesdale - Silver Cup.

THE DANGER FROM TRAVELLING STALLIONS OF DIFFERING BREEDS

From the beginning of the nineteenth century horse-drawn farm implements were being continually improved. By the 1840s heavier ploughs and cutting machines were being used and at the Great Exhibition of 1851, the reaper was demonstrated. These, particularly the American machines, could still be drawn by a pair of light horses, but by 1877 the reaper-binder came into use. Heavier, more sophisticated machines, with subsequent heavier loads of hay and corn, needed larger wagons and larger fields. Horse breeding corresponded to demand and this resulted in the improved breeds of British draught horses, which became the best in the world by the end of the century. They were not only able to move large weights but were active and speedy. They were also very expensive to keep and the farmers of the upper dales found them of no advantage. The big, powerful horses and heavy machines were not suited to the small, steep fields of the dales where larger horses did not thrive in the harsh conditions.

The Shire was predominant in much of England and in Wales, where the Welsh Cob still worked the hill farms. In Scotland, Cumberland, Westmorland, Northumberland, Durham and the Border, the Clydesdale was supreme. The industrial towns, railways and docks used heavy horses in enormous numbers, which, after a few years on the roads, were sold to farmers for work on softer going. The towns also required good active, heavy vanners and any dales farmer who put his galloway mare to one of the travelling Clydesdale stallions could be sure of a good return for his money. The Clydesdale/Dales cross produced just such a vanner which was in great demand by the army and the railway companies, where they worked in the smart express parcel delivery vans. These were a familiar sight speeding around the streets of large towns and cities well into the 1950s.

The popularity of the Clydesdale also affected fashion in the north. It was generally believed that the Yorkshireman and the Irishman liked of a bit of blood; the Scotsman was fond of hair and the Norfolkman liked a little horse with a lot of action. However, the coming of the Clydesdale, with full feathered feet, changed the north-countrymen into fanciers of feather, although this was usually clipped off working ponies in the army and for town work. Some modern Dales ponies sport more feather than their forebears of 100 years ago.

The Clydesdale is a particularly free-moving animal with good shoulders, wonderfully clean, flat bone and the best of feet. They have always been admired in the north-east. The Dales galloway is of similar make but smaller and more compact. This should not be surprising since both breeds spring from similar galloway roots. Older dalesmen still describe the best type of Dales pony as 'like a nice, tight, little Clydesdale'. They certainly have a similar jaunty way of walking with a long swinging stride and a distinctive flick of the hocks. A certain amount of Clydesdale blood was considered no bad thing if an animal of size and strength was required, but these were on the whole larger, and without the spark of the Dales galloway. They also displayed certain horse features, such as long ears and Roman noses, often with a ratch (blaze), and they tended to display a great deal of white. The next cross, back to a Dales, could produce a high quality pony with beautiful limbs. However, breeding from such a pony was chancy. The quality of the half-bred (Clydesdale/Dales) X Dales cross was sometimes reproduced but could throw-back at any stage in a line.

Clydesdales were also used to impart strength and quality to a group of horses known collectively as general purpose horses. Stallions of this type were also used on Dales galloways to get useful foals and these were the types which sold so well at horse fairs such as Brough. Stallions with a mixture of trotting and galloway blood sired many of the famous Chronicle horses. These were fast roadsters, which were used by both *The Manchester Evening News* and *The Chronicle*, in a race between the rival firms to get the newspapers out to the newsagents first. These nippy ponies were unbelievably fast through the traffic and are considered to have produced times which have never been bettered by motor van.

The real danger of losing the pure breed of Dales galloways at this time was due to the lack of travelling Dales stallions. The Clydesdales had a stud book and were able to get travelling premiums to help with expenses. Upland breeders and farmers found it costly and time consuming to travel a Dales stallion over great distances. A glance at one of the Show catalogues of the time will show another source of pressure on the pure breed. It was customary for the owners of Clydesdale, Hackney and general purpose stallions to give prizes at shows, for good foals out of a Dales mare by their own stallion.

It was touch and go for the breed during these years as to whether the Dales would go the way of the Scotch Galloways or not. Fortunately there was still a good number of the old breed in the upper dales.

7
THE NATIVE BREED SOCIETIES

━━━━━━━━━━━━━━━━◆━━━━━━━━━━━━━━━━

IT IS A REMARKABLE FACT that a game which was popular in 600 BC was a prime factor in the survival of the nine breeds of British native pony. A Polo match between Persians and Turkomans was described by the Persian poet, Firdausi, at this time. The game spread throughout Asia but by the nineteenth century had died out in all but the remote valleys on the northern frontiers of India, where it is still played on small native ponies.

The game was discovered by British Army officers in India who adopted it with enthusiasm. In 1850, Captain Sherer organised the game in Assam, laying the foundation of the Polo Clubs which became so popular in India, where the Indian Princes took up the game. Polo was originally played on 13 hh ponies which had been improved with Arab, Barb or Australian Waler blood, the latter often being bred in New Zealand. The game spread to England, Australia, New Zealand and the Americas.

Polo became popular in England and army officers returning from India found a pressing need for quality, weight-carrying ponies, to replace the ones left behind. Some brought their ponies home with them and there was the possibility that a cross with British native ponies would produce the good nippy, weight-carrying ponies required.

In 1893, a meeting was held at the Royal Show, Chester, where a number of interested pony men gathered to establish the Polo Pony Society. Among them were the Earl of Harrington, W. Scarth Dixon, Sir Humphrey de Trafford, Lord Middleton, the Marquess of Londonderry, Lord Arthur Cecil and W. W. Wingate-Saul, all breeders of harness ponies. The object of the Society was to improve and encourage the breeding of high class riding and Polo ponies.

The first Polo Pony Stud Book was opened in 1894 with the entry of 54 stallions and 316 mares. In the Preface, the Earl of Harrington recorded a wish to see all really good stallions and brood mares likely to produce riding ponies, registered, stating that although youngstock may grow to 15.2 or 15.3 hands, and it might be thought absurd to register them in a pony stud book, the object was to encourage the breeding of valuable animals, and it was impossible to imagine a more valuable animal than a pony bred to that size.

An article was written by Mr John Hill, in the same volume, on the use of native ponies as foundation stock. He pointed out that their freedom of action and dash were ideal for crossing with small Thoroughbred or Eastern sires to produce a Polo pony. He added that he liked to see a pony bend his knee in the trot and that the beautiful ponies brought to well nigh perfection by Christopher Wilson were exactly suited to being crossed with a Thoroughbred or Eastern sire. He appealed to all breeders of native ponies to stop the neglect and use only the best stallions to keep the blood pure. All ponies entered in the Stud Book were inspected for type by District Committees. Believing that all British native ponies stemmed from the same stock, Lord Arthur Cecil felt that there should be a free interchange of stallions but hoped that this would not be to such a degree that eventually there would be only one consolidated section, 'The British Pony'. Only the New Forest, Welsh and Shetland had their own Stud Books at this time.

Most ponies entered in the early Polo Pony Stud Books were harness ponies. Among them, the Wilson pony **Little Wonder II** numbered 25 in Volume 2. He sired a number of registered Fell and Dales galloways. The 13.2, black mare, Queen of Tyne (Midnight/Lady Derwent by Derwent Water) foaled in 1891, was also entered. Both were owned by the Marquess of Londonderry who owned the Seaham Stud in County Durham. Midnight was a 14.2 hh black Hackney. Queen of Tyne was the dam of May Queen II (later registered in the Fell Pony Stud Book) and Brown Lucy (later registered in the Dales Pony Stud Book), both were brown 14.0 hh mares sired by Sir Gilbert by Sir Horace (Wilson ponies).

Two other Dales mares entered in Volume 2 were Quickstep (Blooming Heather/ Teesdale Lass) a bay mare foaled in 1889, bred by W. Raine, Park End, Teesdale, and the 14.0 hand, grey mare Sunrise by Black Jock (14.3 hands) foaled in 1887, bred by T. Coulthard, New Close, Teesdale.

By 1895 the Polo Pony Society was well established but, though well supported by those interested in Polo, interest from farmers in a good position to breed ponies was not forthcoming. To improve publicity a show was organised which was successful but not well attended

In 1896, a second show at Hurlingham had a worse attendance although the schedule had been changed to include classes and prizes for Exmoor, Dartmoor, New Forest, Welsh and Border Country ponies.

These classes were not well filled and the quality of pony was not what was hoped for. However, the organisers still believed that with encouragement Mountain and Moorland ponies would improve and become good foundation stock for Polo ponies.

The 1897 Show was moved to Manchester, at the request of the Manchester Local Committee for a complete pony show. There, the judging of the well filled classes was watched by a large and critical crowd.

Volume 5 of the Polo Pony Stud Book for 1898 contains 24 stallions and 75 mares in the Polo Section and 51 stallions and 279 mares in the new Mountain and Moorland Section. These included, for the first time, sections for Dartmoor, Exmoor, Fell (Brough Hill), New Forest, North Wales, South Wales and Scotland.

Local Committees were appointed to oversee the registration of the various breeds. The Fell Committee consisted of W. W. Wingate-Saul, Dr R.W. Gibson, W. Graham and R.M. Malloch, of which the first three were noted breeders of registered Hackney ponies.

An introduction by Lord Arthur Cecil explained that the title 'The Polo Pony Society' was a mistake as Polo was only one of the many uses to which a riding pony could be put. Although they were expected to carry at top speed weights that were considered ample for hunters of 15.2 hands upwards, it was obvious that a pony suitable for Polo must be of the highest type of riding pony. However, a pony must be of pony size; height was one of the greatest difficulties of the society, as there was no certainty of breeding ponies of 14 to 14.2 hands. At the time, and with pony sizes as they were, it was practically impossible. There was always the danger that the best looking and best nourished stock would exceed the limit. The remedy was to use the stocks of hardy little ponies which were indigenous to the large tracts of mountain and moorland land to be found in North and South Wales, the New Forest, Exmoor, Dartmoor, the hills of the North of England and the West Coast of Scotland. However, Lord Arthur Cecil feared that these stocks were already driven to the barest and bleakest parts of districts with a consequent danger of deterioration. He implored farmers to consider running native ponies on hill land promising them a good return for good ponies, for which there would be a great demand.

It was important to register the ponies and keep the breed pure so that it might be possible to regulate the size of the higher class riding ponies to the desired limit, while at the same time infusing into their blood the hardiness of constitution and endurance combined with a fiery yet even temper, so pre-eminently characteristic of the British native breeds.

He advised that the shape and qualities of a high class riding pony should be fixed in the mind and there was no better description than that given by Captain Moray-Brown in his treatise on Polo, who wrote:

He or she should have a clean, well-bred head, a broad forehead and intelligent eye, a well set on neck, strong, flat legs and good sound feet. The pony's back should be short and muscular, the ribs well arched and the loins strong, the quarters should be long, strong and muscular with length from hip to hock and second thighs well developed. Let your pony shew as much substance as a weight-carrying hunter, the quality of a racehorse, and measure from 14 or 14 hands 2 inches.

This was a good start for the Council of the Polo Pony Society which was aiming to save from extinction and endeavouring to improve the British native ponies and also to establish a stock of approved mares easily accessible to Polo pony breeders through the Stud Book.

At about the same time the War Office had noted that most army remounts had not had the stamina for the long treks during the recent South African campaign. It now supported a move to get more native pony blood into troop horses, as natives and native crosses had acquitted themselves well.

Surprisingly, although the native breeds have had narrow escapes over the years, they are now very popular and more than holding their own. The riding pony, up to weight and speed for Polo evolved into the elegant little 'British Riding Pony' of various heights for children and teenagers. Strength and endurance gave way to a more delicate beauty primarily for show, though the more robust Working Hunter ponies are nearer the original aim of the Polo Pony Society.

In 1912 the President of the Board of Agriculture & Fisheries appointed a committee to advise him of measures which could be adopted for the improvement of Mountain & Moorland Breeds of Ponies. Committee members, under the Chairmanship of Lord Arthur Cecil, were all members of the retitled Polo & Riding Pony Society and the Secretary was Mr A. B. Charlton of the Hunter Improvement Society. The report was comprehensive and many measures were recommended.

Observing that the Mountain & Moorland breeds were of common origin with the same characteristics modified by the environment, it was the opinion of the committee that these characteristics should be recorded with all available history of each breed. Believing that all native ponies were descended from the ancient British pony, they attributed the various types firstly, to their surroundings; secondly, to their treatment by man; thirdly, to selection for the work they had to do; and lastly, to the attempt made at different times to improve the herds by the introduction of crosses of more or less alien blood.

They found that the most invaluable qualities were the sturdy constitutions, keen intelligence and concentrated vitality common to all the native breeds, which constituted their real value to horse breeding generally. However, it was also noted that though their virtues were common to all, so were their faults. Coarse heads, badly set on necks, low withers, drooping quarters, badly laid shoulders and absence of bone (though the quality was close and well knit) were to be found in almost every one of the Mountain & Moorland Breeds. These bad points were invariably the result of three causes:

- Immature, unsound or aged breeding stock.
- Too close inbreeding.
- The curtailment and deterioration of the range and pasture available for the ponies.

It appeared to the committee that the history of any breed of pony was the story of man's neglect and interference with their freedom. It was surprising that they had on the whole survived so well. The committee went on to evaluate all the crosses which, from time to time, all native breeds had suffered. Some breeders had used crosses to increase size and thereby the value of the ponies; others had introduced Thoroughbred, Hackney and Arab blood to improve the stock. However, cross-bred stock found it hard to survive in the rough conditions of the native herds and only the very hardiest stock lived long enough to perpetuate the lines carrying alien blood.

The work for which the ponies were required naturally influenced the type of breed. The committee recognised that in the districts which may be described as the fountain heads of Hunter and Polo Pony breeding, the pony had been used for carrying packs. These passed by natural transition to carrying a saddle; it was also a small step from the pack pony to the roadster.

The committee considered that native blood had filtered into the general stocks of light horses through the Borderland ponies, which were:-

- The Deer-stalking pony, misnamed Garron, springing from the Hebridean pony,
- The Devonshire Cob from Exmoor and Dartmoor,
- The larger Goonhilly out of the smaller Goonhilly
- The larger truck pony of the New Forest, which is itself described as 'a little better nor Forest', an ideal transport animal which, when crossed with Thoroughbred or Polo Pony sires, produced excellent ride and drive cobs as clever as cats,
- The larger Dales pony, springing from the Fell pony, which, with

its great bone and surefootedness, is a foundation for producing ponies of the riding type, and if mated with Thoroughbred or Polo pony sires gets riding horses or artillery lead horses up to 15.2 hands. These larger Dales ponies are found to be essential to the small owner for his farm and gig work.

The above classes of Borderland ponies were proved by experience to be most valuable to the small farmers whose holdings had been situated in the neighbourhood of the mountain and moorland districts. The committee was of the opinion that the value of these ponies depended on the open-air life and the wild conditions under which they were kept.

One of the recommendations made to the President of the Board of Agriculture and Fisheries was that Pony Associations should be encouraged in each district, which would administer grants through a local committee, under the guidance of the Board of Agriculture and Fisheries. The grants were made through the Polo & Riding Pony Society in 1912. For Fell ponies, £30 premiums were awarded at the Kirkby Stephen, Keswick, Shap and Brough Agricultural Shows, and a representative committee was formed, nominated by those shows and approved by the Polo and Riding Pony Society and recognised by the Board, as a separate committee for Fell pony breeding. Lord Lonsdale became President of this committee with Mr F. W. Garnett as Secretary and representatives from Kirkby Stephen, Shap, Brough, Appleby, Sedbergh, Keswick, Middleton-in-Teesdale, and Hesket Newmarket.

Hilton Nancy leading hay, 1948.

8
THE FELL PONY STUD BOOK

◆

THE RESPECTIVE LOCAL INSPECTING COMMITTEES were asked to register only ponies of riding type which, on the dam's side, were of pure pony blood. The general rule, passed in 1901, was that 'the Society (Polo & Riding Pony) considers that the foundation stock of these breeds (Mountain & Moorland) should not be registered unless they contain three-quarters pony blood.'

It was an accepted fact that ponies would always outlast horses when it came to endurance under saddle or in harness. Therefore, this highly valued, improved type of northern galloway was chosen for entry in the first Fell Stud Books. The habit of improvement was deeply ingrained and there was still a tendency to consider pure natives as pretty useless except as pit ponies.

The two colts entered in the first Fell Stud Book (Fell Section of the Polo Pony Stud Book,1898) were Brough Hill and Edengrove. Both were bred by A. F. Gibson of Widdy Bank, Middleton-in-Teesdale, and owned by Lords A. & L. Cecil. Blooming Heather sired both out of Fell mares. Edengrove went into the New Forest.

The heights of the six mares entered were from 12.0 to 14.1½ hands. All were of unstated breeding, one of Dr R. W. Gibson's entries was (fs1425 HHSB) Brown Fanny also registered as (861 Fell), foaled in 1882. The preferred height of Fell ponies was 13.0 to 13.2 hands until 1907. From 1908-1922 a height limit of 14.0 hands was allowed for stallions, after which the 13.2 hands limit was re-established. The modern limit is 14.0 hands but 13.2 hands remains the preferred height for Fell ponies.

In 1899 only one stallion was entered in the Fell Section. This was **The Mikado** foaled in 1889, a black/brown with tan and white heels, owned by Lancelot Pickering. Although only 13.2, he was known for his ability to trot a mile under 3 minutes, carrying his 12-stone owner.

His sire was the 14.0 black **Young Perfect** by the 14.3 **Black Jock** out of a mare by 'Young Merry Driver by Old Merry Driver by Old Gay (Gray) Shales foaled in 1755'. This implies that the mare carried the best Norfolk blood but is confused and brief, probably from word of mouth. Old Gray Shales usually referred to West's Grey Shales, foaled in 1819, four generations from Shales the Original, foaled in 1755. The dam of Young Merry Driver was said to be by Young Fireaway (West's Driver) by Old Fireaway (Read's Fireaway) with lines back to Shales the Original. **Black Jock** was by the 14.0 black **Bewcastle Jock** out of a mare by an unknown Sam out of a mare by 'Old Hero', also unknown but possibly Yorkshire Hero (Lord Derby's) which was an approved sire of Hackneys bred in Yorkshire or Cowlings Yorkshire Hero (878 HHSB) also Yorkshire bred and travelling in 1838, both with lines through Wroot's Pretender to the Fireaways and Shales. Bewcastle Jock was by 'Ayrshire Champion' out of a mare by Richardson's Gilsland, now unknown. **Ayrshire Champion** (Broatch's) was probably the early unregistered sire of early Clydesdales of unknown breeding foaled in 1842, and travelling in the Borders in 1853.

The dam of The Mikado was a 13.3 dark brown trotting mare **Dolly Varden,** winner of many trotting and show-ring victories in Cumberland. She was by a **Highland Laddie** who was by **Merry John** (Merry Driver/Atkinson's Doll) out of Wearmouth's mare (unknown). Doll was by a famous trotter, the grey Little Johnny Lingcropper out of 'Dent's brown mare' (dam of another famous trtotting pony, Heather Bell). **Little Johnny Lingcropper** was by the 14.0 brown **Young Lingcropper** out of the unknown 'Thompson's mare'. Young Lingcropper was by **Lingcropper,** said to be by Shales Merrylegs by 'Old Gay Shales by Marshland Shales by Flying Childers' out of a mare by Old Performer out of a mare by Sportsman out of a mare by Old Fireaway (Jenkinson's). Again, this was pointing in the right direction but sadly confused. Shales Merrylegs (P. Ramsdales') was by Shales (Bonnett's) out of a mare by Merrylegs (Lund's). Little Johnny Lingcropper sired the dam of **Barnum** (3434 HHSB) by Merry John, foaled in 1886. Lingcropper was the sire of the roadster pony, Jack's Delight, and four inspected Hackney foundation mares. Lingcropper would have been from Shales and Fireaway lines which encompass the racehorse Marske by the Darley Arabian. The dam of Lingcropper is untraceable.

The dam of Dolly Varden was **Lády Beaconsfield,** said to have trotted 4 miles in 11.29 minutes at the age of 17, dying when 36 years old. She was by **Glengarry,** full brother to the Highland Laddie who won the Chester cup 1858, said to be by Mountain Ranger by Sandy (unknown) out of a mare by Moorcock (unknown) out of a mare by Lingcropper. Glengarry is said to have been foaled in 1855, yet he was either 1st or 2nd at the Royal Show, Newcastle, 'about 1852'. He was owned by Hodgson Brothers or Rotherhope, Alston, who bred the dam of Lady

Beaconsfield, **Rotherhope Lass**, and owned her sire **Falcon Clint**; he was named after a group of rocks above High Force, the waterfall in Teesdale, bred by Thomas Gibson of Friar's House near High Force. Highland Laddie, bred by J. Wearmouth of Swindale Head, was owned by Thomas Gibson and sired progeny until 26 years old. Black Jock and Bewcastle Jock both served for 20 years, owned by Parkin Raines, Middlton-in-Teesdale.

Whether the pedigree of The Mikado is true but inaccurately reproduced from heresay or a rough guess and wishful thinking to comply with fashionable demand is unclear today. Undoubtedly he was a northern bred trotting roadster of some quality. He sired a few Fell registered ponies before going to Lord Arthur Cecil and later sired registered progeny from registered Highland, Exmoor, Fell and New Forest mares. Lord Arthur Cecil firmly believed that blood of one native breed could improve that of another and always admired the Wilson type of pony.

Among the Fell mares entered in Volume 6, two were by The Mikado, (1082 Fell)Doll out of a mare by Merry John, and (1083 Fell)Lady Alice out of the 12.2 bay mare Fanny, by the 13.3, grey Telegraph, described

Mountain Ranger (598 Fell) foaled 1906. Bred by J.W. Dent of Middleton-in-Teesdale.

as a half-bred Arab. The third mare was the prize-winning brown mare Trip standing 14.1 hands. She was foaled in 1887 by General Gordon (by Little John by Merry John by Merry Driver) out of a mare by the 14.2 Blacklock, unknown. Her brown grand-dam was by Merry John, her great, great grand-dam, the 14.0 dun, Trip II was by Ramsdale's Grey Performer (336 HHSB). Her 4th dam was also dun, Trip I by a grey, Old Highland Laddie.

Trip foaled Lord Briton by The Mikado in 1898 and Majestic by the Hackney Greetland (4292 HHSB) in 1900. She was bred by John Wearmouth of Brough, and it is notable that most of her immediate forebears were over 14 hands, and her 2nd and 3rd dams were dun.

Two stallions were entered in the Fell Section of Volume 7 of the Polo and Riding Pony Stud Book. One was Lord Briton, foaled 1898, the other was Mountain Hero II (Young Mountain Hero/Black Bess), a bay, 13.2 pony foaled in 1897. The 13.3 brown Young Mountain Hero was by the brown 13.2 Rob Roy (by Highland Laddie). Black Bess was by FitzGeorge (386 Highland Pony Stud Book), out of a grey mare by Jack's Delight, a renowned trotter. The grey **FitzGeorge**, by Sir George, was bred by J. J. Spedding of Keswick, who entered him in the Hackney Horse Stud Book as Fitz George II (4265 HHSB). His dam Fanny (fs878 HHSB) was a 12.3 white mare also entered in the Hackney Horse Stud Book, as a foundation mare. She was foaled in 1865 out of Metal, a daughter of Highland Laddie of Chester Cup fame. FitzGeorge was owned by Lord Middleton of Applecross, Rosshire and Birdsall near York, who entered him in the Highland Pony Stud Book as FitzGeorge (386). He is described as 14 hands, of great power and substance with very good action.

One of the nine mares registered was Warcop (Blooming Heather/ Fell mare) owned by Lord Arthur Cecil and bred by John Gibson of Widdy Bank. She had two foals by the Thoroughbred, Lord of the Lea but no registered Fell progeny.

Of the three stallions entered in Volume 8 (1904) the most important and the most famous, entered retrospectively, is

Blooming Heather 325 black, white star, aged (Said to have been foaled in 1880). Height 13.2.
Sire: Little John, brown, 13.2.
Dam: Polly, dark brown, 13.1, by Mountain Hero, black, 13.2.
G.Dam: Spittal Doll,black, 13.1 by Black Prince, 13.01/2
G.G.D: Fanny, black, 13.11/2, by Merry Driver,brown, 13.2.
Owned: John Gibson. Widdy Bank, Middleton-in-Teesdale.
Breeder: The late R.Tunstall. Stainmore, Westmorland.

Blooming Heather II (566 Fell) by Blooming Heather (325 Fell) out of Queen of the Dales by Black Jock, foaled 1902. His great grand-dam was by Merry Driver.

There is contention regarding the true identity of Blooming Heather. Dalesmen always considered him to be a Dales and he was bred and used in Dales country. It used to be said that Teesdale was known for three things, steel ship building, High Force and Blooming Heather. He may have been registered in the Fell Stud Book but his sire and his sire's full sister, Weardale Polly, were considered to be Dales, and he was described as a Dales in *The Cyclopedia of Agriculture* (1912). He was of Fell height but there have always been Dales ponies of 13.2 hands. His sire, Little John, was the son of Merry John (Merry Driver/Atkinson's Doll by Johnny Lingcropper). Little John was reputed to be a very fast trotter and said to have been sold for export at the high price of £180.

Blooming Heather's dam was by the Revd. J. M. Lowther's Mountain Hero, used as an improver on the Caldbeck Fells. He was described as 'a little animal with splendid bone, as hardy as the wildest of his kin' which implies that he was also an improved pony.

The five mares entered in Volume 8, were all roadster bred: (1513 Fell)Attractive, was a 13.0 black mare also entered as a Hackney pony foundation mare (fs1397 HHSB), being by the 14.3, black Hackney Norfolk Swell (alias Perfection), out of Curley by Stainmore Hero and bred by Dr. G.W.Dalston-Ewbanke, who also owned the Hackney,

Stainmore Swell (2281 HHSB). Attractive won 8 first prizes and was Reserve Champion at the London Show in 1895. This was the type of pony the Committee thought right for entry in the Mountain & Moorland Section of the Polo Pony Society Stud Book at that time.

Of the five stallions entered in Volume 9, only Mighty Atom appears to be near the true Fell. The grand-dam of Caudale Swell and the dam of Gay Lad were by the 14.0 hh dark bay, roadster Yorkshire Champion. The grand-dam of Westmorland Model was by the 14.2 black Dales, Norfolk Cob. The 13.2 black Heather's Model, foaled in 1902, was by Blooming Heather (235 Fell) out of a bay mare by the Wilson pony, Little Wonder II (by Sir Richard by Sir George) out of a mare by Black Jock, bred by William Dalton of Snowhope Close, Stanhope, Co. Durham. Of the 9 mares entered, 4 had grand-dams by Telegraph, possibly Yorkshire Telegraph by Yorkshire Champion, all roadsters.

Tenison Pendragon, the sole stallion entered in Volume 10, (1907-1908) was another by The Mikado out of Lady Alice. Five mares, all roadster-bred, were entered in this Volume.

Stallions were absent from Volume 11 (1909-1910). There were possibly two or three true Fell mares among the seven entered. Crackenthorpe by Blooming Heather out of an unknown dam, foaled in 1896, was a 13.2 black mare bred by John Gibson and bought by Lord Arthur Cecil. She had two foals in 1909 and 1910 by a New Forest sire; no further progeny were registered.

Although Dales galloways were entered in the Fell Pony Stud Book, as Fells, they were nevertheless recognised as something quite different by the new Convener of the Fell Pony Committee, Frank W. Garnett, MRCVS, who wrote of the Kirkby Stephen Show, 1909:

> Kirkby Stephen was an excellent show of quite typical Fell ponies, and the question arises to my mind, is the Polo and Riding Pony Society obtaining the registration of mares in this district which it might reasonably expect to get? My impression is that it is not.
>
> There were five classes for 'Dales Horses', i.e. not exceeding 14.2, and there were 32 entries from nearly as many owners. For ponies not exceeding 13.2, there were five classes with 28 entries from 18 owners.

In 1912, it was recognised that few true Fell ponies were being registered and a new Fell Pony Committee was set up, consisting of northern breeders. The President was the Earl of Lonsdale; F. W. Garnett, MRCVS, remained as secretary. The new ccommittee worked hard to encourage the registration of Fell ponies but continued to include Dales.

The winner of the Premium awarded at Keswick Show was Lothian

Prince, a popular brown pony stallion standing 14.1 hh. He was pronounced not eligible for the award, as he was by Royal Lothian 6991 (Clydesdale Horse Stud Book). The Premium passed to the 14.0, black Highland Fashion by the black Dales cob, Yorkshire Fashion out of a mare by Swaledale Comet by Norfolk Cob. Highland Fashion was Dales bred and therefore acceptable. Lothian Prince was never entered in the Fell or Dales Stud Book but had sired the registered Fell stallion General Pride in 1906, and two mares.

Fourteen stallions were entered in Volume 12 (1911-1912). Of these, **British Boy**, foaled in 1901, **Dalesman**, foaled in 1902 and Highland Fashion, foaled in 1908, were all by the 15.0 Dales cob **Yorkshire Fashion** (by Norfolk Cob) out of roadster-bred mares. **Real Fashion**, foaled 1897 by Young Perfect, Prickwillow, foaled in 1896 by the roadster, Little John and Little John (599 Fell), foaled in 1894, were also out of roadster-bred mares; all stood 14.0 hands and all except Highland Fashion, had white markings; Real Fashion had three white fetlocks and Little John 599 had a white face. Little John 599 was by the 14.2 black North Star, by Young Prince by Young Ploughboy, probably by Ploughboy, an early Clydesdale sire or Ploughboy an even earlier Cleveland Bay sire, both were in the area. In 1912 at the Middleton-in-Teesdale Show, Little John (599 Fell) won the Premium but was not accepted for registration by the Board of Agriculture,which certainly pointed to an outcross of some kind. However, his progeny continued to be registered. Another entry was that of **Weardale Hero** (607 Fell), foaled in 1902 by the 14.2 grey Dales, **Teasdale Comet** by Young Comet, out of Nina by Blooming Heather (325 Fell). He was also bought by Lord Arthur Cecil for the New Forest.

One of the Fell stallions was Heather Boy (600 Fell) bred by J.W. Dalton of Snowhope Close, a founder member of the Dales Pony Improvement Society who later became President of the Dales Pony Society. Heather Boy was by Heather's Model (381 Fell) out of Fanny, black, 13.2 ,by Young Merry John out of Blossom, dark brown, 13.2 by Stainmore Hero, unknown.

Thirty mares were entered in the same Volume. The Dales-bred mares were Busy Bee II, foaled in 1903, by Yorkshire Fashion; Darling II, by the 14.2 Inglewood Fashion (out of a mare by Yorkshire Fashion) and Sweet Heather, foaled in 1908, by Stainmore Fashion (by Yorkshire Fashion); Tailbert Peg, foaled in 1906, by the Dales/Wilson pony, Daybreak; the 14.0 Teasdale Jess by the 14.2 black General Gordon out of a mare by Little Wonder II (PPSB 25 /HHSB 1610); Topsy II (Blooming Heather/Jessy by Little Wonder); May Queen II by Sir Gilbert (by Sir Horace 5402 HHSB) out of (fs1088 HHSB) Queen of Tyne and Maid of Honour, foaled in 1900, by Real Fashion out of the Dales mare Poll.

J.W. Dalton with his home-bred Heather Boy (600 Fell) foaled in 1905.

It was a good entry but still dominated by Hackney and Dales-bred stock. Dalesman (572 Fell) and (2359 Fell) Maid of Honour were later transferred into the Dales Stud Book when it opened.

Of the 11 stallions entered in Volume 13 (1913-1914), the 13.3 **Black Blooming Heather** (674 Fell) by Blooming Heather (325 Fell) out of a Fell mare by Young Comet; 13.1, black **Glengarry** (640 Fell) by British Boy by Yorkshire Fashion out of a mare by Blooming Heather (325 Fell) and the 13.3 black, **Highland Laddie III**(642 Fell) by Mountain Hero II (250 Fell) out of Bonny by Sir Richard (Wilson pony), were also later transferred into the Dales Stud Book. (2491 Fell)**White Heather II**, later transferred to the Dales Stud Book, was one of the 41 entered mares, eight of which were by Dalesman and one by Rutherford's 14.0 brown, Dales stallion, North Star II (900 Dales).

Volume 14 (1915-1916) had 8 stallions and 21 mares entered. More Fell stallions were available, but three of the colts were by Dales-bred stallions and one was by Cross Fell Hero by Lothian Prince. The most intriguing entry is that of the 14.0 hand **Lingcropper II** (768 Fell) by **Daddy's Lad** out of Blossom by Norfolk Cob, foaled in 1916, He sported a star and snip and two white hind fetlocks. Daddy's Lad was a son of Young Comet and Blossom's dam was a bay mare by the 14.0 brown

Dales, Lingcropper. On his transfer to the Dales section of the National Pony Society Stud Book, the name of Lingcropper II was changed to **Linnel Comet** by his new owner, Mr Roy B. Charlton, and he became a very well known Dales stallion.

The declaration of war in 1914 had brought changes and wartime necessity was about to bring the Dales breed recognition and their own Stud Book and the Polo and Riding Pony Society title was changed to 'The National Pony Society'.

Mr J. Townson's prize-winning mare (2491 Fell) White Heather II, by Teasdale Comet, foaled 1903.

9

THE DALES PONY
IMPROVEMENT SOCIETY

✦

JOHN DALTON OF SNOWHOPE CLOSE and other Dales breeders were discussing the opening of a Dales Pony Stud Book in 1914 but shelved the project when war was declared. Two years later, Mr Roy Charlton related how he was travelling in the company of Mr William Patterson when he saw in a newspaper that Lord Lonsdale had purchased the Percheron stallion Nonius which he intended to cross with Fell pony mares, to produce light draught horses for the army. He remarked, 'We have the very animal the army wants and they don't know it.' An advertisement was placed in the local paper for a meeting to be held at the Coach and Horses Hotel, Hexham, with a view to forming a Dales Pony Society.

On the day fixed, December 12th, 1916, William Patterson went to the Low Market and Roy Charlton to the High Market to whip up a few likely people, being afraid that nobody would attend. On the way they met Foster Armstrong and got a surprise when he said, 'Why man! the room's full.'

Marsden Drury took the chair and among others present were T. V. Emerson and J. W. Dalton. The following letter from J. E. Rogerson, MFH, North Durham Foxhounds was read.

'The Committee of Durham County has frequently urged upon the Board of Agriculture the desirability of doing something for the breed, such as subsidising stallions, but had always been met with the answer that nothing could be done in the absence of a stud book. Any movement to start a stud book will have the entire sympathy of myself and all my colleagues. The pure bred pony excels in courage and endurance and what is a great point in horse breeding nowadays, it is practically free from hereditary unsoundness. I have had many good hunters which were the first cross between the Dales pony and the Thoroughbred. They stay well and are good tempered, no day being too long for them. As a basis for army remounts they are invaluable and have proved their merits both in South Africa and during the present war. Remount officers are always keen to pick up anything with Dales blood in it. Every effort should therefore be made to encourage the breeding of this type, and I wish your movement every success.'

The object of the meeting was to get local breeders together to arrange for a registration of mares as foundation stock, and to enter into negotiations with the Board of Agriculture for premiums for pony stallions to travel the dales. Rules were drawn up for the regulation of the society and it was agreed that it should be designated 'The Dales Pony Improvement Society'; that headquarters be at Hexham; that its object be to promote and encourage the breeding of high class ponies and that the area of the society embrace the following districts: Tynedale, North Tyne, South Tyne, Hexhamshire, East Allen, West Allen, Weardale and Alston. The important Dales pony breeding areas around Teesdale and Swaledale were not included, probably because 25 of the 38 councilmen were from around Hexham, Allendale and Tynedale and the remainder from Weardale.

J. E. Rogerson was elected President, J. J. Kirsopp as Vice-President and W. Patterson was appointed Hon. Secretary. A council was appointed and councilmen were expected to act as pony inspectors, to get stallions and mares of the proper type registered with the society.

The first council meeting was held in Hexham on January 3rd, 1917, when the Memorandum of Association and Bye-Laws were approved and fees fixed: the annual subscription and registration fee for foundation stock stallions was five shillings; the Registration fee for each foundation stock mare and every foal produced by a registered Dales stallion, two shillings. Non-members to pay treble the fees. At this meeting the maximum height of the pony was fixed at 15 hands for mares and 14.2 hands for stallions. It was also agreed that a breed show should be held at St John's Chapel in Weardale on the 7th April.

Roy Charlton, Foster Armstrong and J. E. Rogerson offered to guarantee a Super Premium and J. J. Kirsopp, A. M. Allgood and J. Sparke, guaranteed the under Premium for two Dales stallions to travel for the season of 1917. Other members donated prizes for mares.

The Board of Agriculture would only give premiums to stallions which would travel in districts where there was a sufficient number of registered mares of the same breed. A further condition was that all Dales pony mares that received assisted nominations to the Premium Dales pony stallions must first be passed for breeding purposes by a Veterinary Surgeon, expenses paid by the Board of Agriculture. It was, therefore, important to get the mares inspected for entry into the Stud Book. A total of 101 ponies was registered up to the end of 1917. On the

The Dales stallion Mettle's Lad by Meteor.

advice of the Board of Agriculture, a Dales Section had been opened in Volume 15 (1917-1918) of the National Pony Society Stud Book. Ponies were not to exceed 14.2 hands, with a sub-section for mares exceeding 14.2 hands and up to 15 hands. Geldings were not registered.

Heavy snow fell before the show and very few roads were passable. The Chairman of the National Pony Society Show Committee, G. Norris Midwood, and F. W. Garnett, MRCVS, President of the Royal College of Veterinary Surgeons and Secretary of the Fell Pony Committee of Westmorland and Cumberland, had promised to judge the mare classes. After covering 50 of the 60 miles of their journey by car, they then found the roads to St John's Chapel completely blocked and had to give up. The judges of the stallion class, Mr John Dargue from Dufton near Appleby, who had braved a difficult walk over the fell, and Mr Thomas Wilson of Wolsingham, agreed to judge the class for Dales pony mares, deemed most suitable for registration as foundation stock.

The 23 little mares were said to be a delight to look upon and no light task to judge. The first prize winner was Westgate Jessy by Blooming Heather, foaled in 1909, a dark brown pony standing 14.1 hh and an exceptionally good sort, bred in Weardale. Standing second was three-year-old Jenny Lind II (by Highland Laddie III out of Polly by North Star) a 14.0 hh black and as sharp a pony as one could wish to see, bred in Tow Law. Third was the black Stonedress Polly by Highland Laddie II by Little John out of a mare by Blooming Heather. Bred in Wearhead, she was foaled in 1910, she stood 13.3 hands and was said to be the model of a true Dales pony.

Six stallions competed for the two Premiums. The winner of the Super Premium was **Silver Top** (by King's Pilot out of Snip III). The Clydesdale King's Pilot (14726 CHSB) was by Silver Cup (11,184 CHSB), a very popular sire of powerful small horses for use in the coal mining industry. Snip III was by Tip Top by Minstrel Boy, a 13.2 black pony by Highland Laddie (by Merry John by Merry Driver) from a tail male line to Shales the Original. The dam of Tip Top was the 14.1 dark brown, prize-winning trotting pony, Jess by Sir Richard (by Sir George) described as 'a true Dales pony'.

Bred and owned by John L. Forster, one of the oldest and most famous of Dales breeders, Silver Top was described as

> a beautiful black, standing 14.1 hands, a powerful Dales stallion built on miniature Clydesdale lines. He has a most wonderful fore-end, showing true pony ears, eyes and nostrils. His shoulders are laid right back into his short back. His middle piece is perfect, and he stands on the very best of feet and legs, with immense bone below the joints. The Society is fortunate to have such a good Dales pony to travel the west end of the Dales pony district

The Premium for the second district went to **Black Blooming Heather.** In 1914 he had held the Board of Agriculture Fell Premium for the Kirkby Stephen district. By Blooming Heather, out of a 14.1 Fell mare by Young Comet. The Show report stated

> he is built on true pony lines, and goes with speed and good style. He is a grand topped one, but in the writer's opinion he could do with a bit more substance below the knee. It is understood that he is leaving some wonderful stock, which was not to be wondered at when one remembers the strain of pony from which he is descended.

Reserve was taken by T. V. Emerson's **Highland Laddie III** by Mountain Hero II (FitzGeorge/Black Bess) out of Heather Belle III (Blooming Heather/Bonny by Sir Richard), also transferred from the Fell Stud Book. Black with a star and white hind fetlocks, he was foaled in 1910 and stood 13.3 hands. He was shown in the rough as he had been running out in deep snow on the Fell until the day before the show, which told against him as he was poor in condition. However, he was considered a real model and a grand mover. Mr Emerson was unable to travel the stallion but Mr Foster Armstrong bought him and

Mr John Emerson, the father of Thomas V. Emerson, outside Hag Gate.

later placed him at the disposal of the society.

All three stallions had a very successful season and there were reports of a promising crop of foals expected. It was also reported that all the ponies shown were black or very dark brown and of a much more even conformation than one would expect to see in a breed which had been left to fend for itself for generations. One of the objects of the new society was to get Dales pony stallions on the road. Until a few years previously there had been quite a few to choose from and the society had been formed none too soon. The Board of Agriculture had given Premiums to Clydesdale stallions to travel in the Dales pony districts for some years. It paid horsemen better to travel a stallion with a premium than one without.

In May, Captain Alexander Campbell of the Board of Agriculture visited Dales pony country to take a general look at the breed. Silver Top and Highland Laddie III were paraded, being stallions of different types and he remarked favourably, describing them as heavy and light, but both good and necessary for the welfare of the breed.

The following day Captain Campbell was taken on a journey through Allendale and St John's Chapel to Langdon Beck in Teesdale, returning through Alston and Whitfield. Many ponies were inspected and seen

Mr T.V. Emerson's Highland Laddie III.

both at work and running on the fells. Here he saw Black Blooming Heather and his half-brother (Valence Heather), another black Dales stallion, which were greatly admired. These Blooming Heather ponies were described by him as being marvellous in bone and substance and quite the most wonderful of all the native ponies he had seen; Black Blooming Heather had 8 $\frac{1}{2}$ inches of bone below the knee.

The following is an extract from a letter subsequently recieved from Captain Campbell.

> I have always recognised ponies of any breed, more or less so, as the foundation stone of any description of horse one may wish to breed. I cannot conceive why your ponies have not come into prominence, which they are bound to do. An 'outcross' is the business of people quite away from your country. It is your business, which I know you recognise fully and more so than I do, to keep the breed pure at home. Your breed has one superb asset, possessed by every specimen I saw i.e. the most perfect foot in the British Isles. Even when broken and made small by bad shoeing there was a perfect substance, perfect horn, and a frog always well developed and of the hardest guttapercha

substance. Keep that a sine qua non, but don't let it be forgotten that there is still a good foot, in fact a perfect one, that has been broken and spoilt by the handiwork of man.

Following Captain Campbell's visit, the Board of Agriculture agreed to award three Premiums for Stallions for the 1918 season. These were to be awarded at Hexham, when it was hoped to offer prizes for mares deemed suitable for breeding Dales ponies, which would be open to registered and unregistered mares with a free entry. The National Pony Society had also offered three Silver Medals for registered mares. The average value of a Board of Agriculture Premium was £50. Premium Stallions were to serve 25 registered mares to which assisted nominations had been awarded by the society on behalf of the Board, and any other registered mare nominated by the society at a service fee of £5 and a foal fee of 5 shillings. The only payment to be made by the owner of a nominated mare was the groom's fee of 2s.6d. but a fee of 5 shillings was paid by the Dales Pony Improvement Society in respect of every nomination issued.

The first Dales pony section of the National Pony Society Stud Book was opened in Volume 15 (1917-1918). Twelve stallions and colts were entered. **Black Blooming Heather** (674), **Linnel Comet** (841) and **Highland Laddie III** (642)were all transferred from the Fell Stud Book.

Black Blooming Heather had collected Board of Agriculture Premiums in 1914 for Kirkby Stephen District; in 1917 for St John's Chapel, and 1918 for Hexham District.

Highland Laddie III had won First prizes at Wolsingham, Stanhope, Bents, Egglestone and Middleton-in-Teesdale in 1911 and was also awarded the Board of Agriculture Premium for Hexham District in 1918.

Silver Top (833) was entered, as was the dun, Kitchener 901, by Borrodale (384 Highland Pony Stud Book) by FitzGeorge which was entered in both the Highland Pony Stud Book as (386) and in the Hackney Horse Stud Book as (4265). His dam was a brown mare by the black Highland, Lord Reay. The line of Kitchener (901 Dales) does not seem to have survived the Second World War, though it may have re-emerged in the post-war grading-up register which catered for ponies which had lost papers or had not been registered.

Linnel Comet was bought by Mr Roy Charlton for the 1917 season and entered in the Stud Book as a Dales with further breeding details. Originally registered in the Fell Stud Book as Lingcropper II (768 Fell), he was described as a most beautiful black pony of the heavy sort. His new pedigree was entered thus:

The Dales stallion Merry Jock, foaled 1907.

Linnel Comet 841 Black, small white star on forehead and small mark on upper lip, white near coronet and off fetlock. Foaled in 1913. Height 14.1.
Breeder, Thomas Stainton, Tebay, Westmorland.
Sire: Daddy's Lad by Comet II by Old Comet
Dam: Stainton's brown mare by Norfolk cob, black, 14.3 (Dales) by
      Black Samson.
G.dam: by Lingcropper, 14.2 (Dales).
G.g.dam: by Bay Performer, 14.0.

Stainton's brown mare was the 14.0 mare Blossom by Norfolk Cob. Norfolk Cob has capital initials in the Fell Stud Book but cob is written with a lower case initial in the Dales Stud Book. It appears that Norfolk Cob is the name of a Dales sire, not just any Norfolk roadster or cob. However, the name would signify a good fast trotter of some substance. Black Samson is given capital letters in the pedigree, so was probably well known but of another breed. He could have been the Clydesdale, Black Samson (62 CHSB) which travelled in the area around 1877. The grand-dam was the13.2 bay Fanny by the 14.0 brown Dales

Linnel Comet, foaled 1913.

Lingcropper out of a mare by the 14.0 Hackney, Bay Performer (Ramsdales) by Brown Shales (Hewson's) by Chadd's Black Shales by Marshland Shales. The dam of Bay Performer was by Performer (Ramsdale's). The dam of Brown Shales was a roan mare by Primo (Taylor's) by a son of Jenkinson's Fireaway. There is a good infusion of the best Norfolk blood in this line which comes into modern Dales ponies through **Prince Comet 1153**. In 1918 Linnel Comet was awarded the Board of Agriculture's Premium for the Western District at Hexham Dales Pony Show.

The entered Dales colts were:-

Beacon Light 842 by Mountain Ranger (598 Fell) out of 3205 Jenny Lind II by Highland Laddie III 642. No registered progeny recorded.

Linnel Heather 888 (Black Blooming Heather/Stonedress Polly) dark brown, foaled in 1918.

Linnel Mars (Heather's Model (381 Fell)/3494 Orton Sally), dark brown with small star and white off hind fetlock. Foaled in 1917. Orton Sally, dark brown with a star and white hind fetlocks, was foaled in 1898 by Young Comet by Comet.

Merry Boy II 873 (Black Blooming Heather 674/Westgate Jessie). Dark brown, foaled 1918.

Merry Jock 849 (Dalesman 572/ Merry by Black Jock) a smart grey colt foaled in 1918 and standing 14.2 hands. Black Jock described as a Dales cob.

Western Star 834 (North Star 900/3202 Linnel Dale by Black Robin) was a 13.3 dark brown colt foaled in 1915, bred by William Carr of East Petrel Field, Hexham. Linnel Dale was bred in West Allendale and was second in the Dales Pony class at Tyneside in 1914.

North Star II 900 was a brown, 14.2 hands entire foaled in 1906 and owned by John Rutherford, butcher of Wearhead, who always had a good stallion. North Star II was by Fashion of Teeswater, a popular stallion out of a mare named Howgill Heather, bred by the Tees Valley Water Board. The dam of North Star II was a daughter of Weardale Polly, the full sister of the sire of Blooming Heather.

The astonishing number of 189 mares were entered in this first Dales pony section of the Stud Book. Twenty-six of these were entered in the Sub-section for Dales Cob mares from 14.2 to 15 hands. Many of the mares were of unknown or unregistered breeding. The only coloured entry, the skewbald Eastwood Daisy, by a sire named Union Jack, produced no registered stock. The dark dun mare, 3241 Prospect Jean, was by a pre-registration Dales sire, the black King of the Mountains: her daughter by Silver Top, the mare (3339)Prospect Damsel, a brown with white fetlocks, was also entered.

Another interesting entry was the 13.3 bay mare 3201 Linnel Lady by Sir Horace, foaled in 1908 out of an un-identified dam. A photograph of this pony can be seen in *A Lifetime with Ponies* by Roy B.Charlton, pictured being driven by his 13-year-old son, Roy.

The famous mare (3331) **Stanhope Beauty** is entered in this Stud Book for the first time, by Messrs. P. E. & Arthur Sanderson of Stanhope. She was described as black with a small star and white hind coronets, foaled in 1915, height 14.1; but without any further pedigree. Her breeder was D. Hutchinson, Newbiggin, Carlisle. She foaled a black filly in 1920, Stanhope Belle to Black Blooming Heather (674 Dales), when in the ownership of Mrs A. Sanderson. In 1928, when the property of Joseph H. Johnson of White Lea Farm, Crook, Co. Durham, Stanhope Beauty went to the National Pony Show in London, still in her winter coat; she returned with first and The Lord Arthur Cecil Cup for the Best Native Brood Mare; and with a second with Ouston Model and (5735 Dales) Heather Gipsy in Mr Johnson's Dales group. She had won 15 first prizes for Dales pony brood mares and three Silver Challenge Cups in 1919. In 1920 she won eight firsts for Best Dales pony brood

(3331 Dales) Stanhope Beauty, foaled 1915.

mare and rounded off with a first and Silver Challenge Cup at the Royal Show, Darlington and NPS Silver Medals in 1920 & 1921. Her full pedigree was entered in the Dales section of the NPS Stud Book, Volume 20, when she was purchased by Roy B. Charlton, then of The Linnels, Hexham. This was:

(3331) Stanhope Beauty
Sire: Young Sir Harry
Dam: (3828 Fell) Emma, black, 13.2 by Crossfell Hero, black, 14.0 by Lothian Prince, brown, 14.2.
G.dam: Black Bess, black, 13.2 by Little John (599 Fell), black, 14.0.
Breeder: T.Dixon Hutchinson.Wythwaite, Penrith.

Her progeny were listed as :
1927 - filly (5633 Dales) May Beauty by Ouston Model (1215 Dales)
1918 - colt Linnel Surprise (1626 Dales) by Bonnie Blooming Heather (1324 Dales)
1929 - colt Linnel Success (1710 Dales) by Linnel Brown Boy (1523 Fell)

Her 1931 filly, (6477 Fell)Linnel Belle II was entered in the Fell Stud Book as by Linnel Darkie (1524 Fell) out of (3331 *Fell*) Stanhope Beauty, which was probably a genuine mistake. She foaled her last foal,the bay filly Generous Gift (7032 Dales) in 1933. Her line is still viable through the Stainton ponies.

The entries in the first Stud Book show a variance of colour which might surprise modern Dales pony enthusiasts. Dalesmen habitually describe dark bay and bay as brown whilst others use the term bay; it is therefore hard to differentiate so bay and brown are separated. The 189 ponies consist of black 60, brown 55 and bay 51 (116), grey 27, dun 2, roan 2, chestnut 2 and 1 skewbald.

In April 1918, the second Dales Pony Show was held at Hexham with 61 ponies forward. The number in the mare class proved that there were many breeding mares left in Tynedale, Allendale and Weardale, after the huge numbers taken by the army four years earlier. The show drew a large number of interested spectators and a high standard of real Dales pony type was seen. Three Board of Agriculture Premiums were awarded, to Roy Charlton's Linnel Comet for the Western District, Foster Armstrong's Highland Laddie III for the Hexham District and H. S. Robson's Black Blooming Heather for the North-West Durham District. The Reserve was John Forster's Silver Top.

The winner of the mare class was the 14.0 Dean Polly, a splendid dark brown mare who won the National Pony Society Silver Medal for the Best Registered Mare in foal to a Dales pony sire. Bred by Mr T. V. Emerson, she was by Mountain Hero II (250 Fell), the sire of Highland Laddie III, and was foaled in 1910. Second was Roy Charlton's 14.1 bay mare, Linnel Martha (breeding unknown) foaled in 1912, who also won the NPS Silver Medal for the Best Dales Mare not exceeding 14.2 hands. Winner of the Silver Medal for the Best Dales Cob was the 14.2½, bay mare Jennie of Blackhall (breeding unknown), foaled in 1906. Standing Reserve was Comet's Dolly (breeding unknown) a black mare foaled in 1913 and standing 14.3 hands.

The owners of Premium stallions had their difficulties in 1918. Mr H. S. Robson, who so successfully travelled his stallion, Black Blooming Heather in 1917, joined the army during the year and was later killed. His father gamely undertook his son's duties and the pony served over 100 mares in the North Durham District. The other three stallions had highly satisfactory seasons under difficult war conditions.

The society was still very short of Dales stallions and the council appealed to the owners of brood mares to keep good colts by Premium stallions entire. The secretary reported that the demand for pure-bred

Dales ponies was likely to be very great for some years to come.

During 1919, the secretary had been driven by an excellent Dales pony whilst helping during the election in Richmond. Upon getting into conversation with local people he learned that there were some good Dales mares in Swaledale. As a result he and Mr Charlton visited Swaledale and were successful in registering 15 mares, all of very good type.

The third Annual Show, held at Bishop Auckland in April 1919, was also very successful in the registration of mares. Ten stallions and 64 mares came before the judges. Eight judges voted on an independent card system for the four most suitable stallions to hold the Board of Agriculture Premiums for the season. The following were chosen:

STALLION	AREA
Black Blooming Heather	West Durham
Linnel Comet	Hexham East & Derwent Valley
Gentleman John	Swaledale
Merry Jock	Western District

Reserves: Highland Laddie III, Western Star and Silver Top.

Unfortunately, owing to the extra expense of travelling, Merry Jock could not accept his Premium, which was taken up by Western Star.

The powerful brown, Westgarth's Sprightly Spark, took the 1919 NPS Silver Medal for the Best Mare in foal to a Dales stallion. Bred by Thomas Blackett of Low Westgarth, Butterknowle, Sprightly Spark was foaled in 1915 and stood 14.1 hands. She was by the Clydesdale, Royal Ratho (12338 CHSB) out of Westgarth's Maid of Honour (3586) foaled in 1900 and originally registered as (2359 Fell) Maid of Honour by Real Fashion (605 Fell) out of Poll (Dales): she was later transferred to the Dales Stud Book. The Reserve was taken by (3399) Jennie III in foal to Teasdale Comet. The NPS Silver Medal for the Best Female Dales pony went to the Misses Sanderson's 14.1 black mare (3331)**Stanhope Beauty**. Reserve in this class was J. B. Metcalf's grey 3601 Marwood Daisy (Teasdale Comet/Cockfield Daisy by Fashion of Teeswater). Foaled in 1912, she stood 14.1 hands. The Silver Medal for the Best Dales Cob was won by (3577)Torrent (breeding unknown) a 15.0 hh bay mare foaled in 1914.

The third year of the society was very satisfactory. The young grey stallion, Gentleman John (907) had been awarded 24 assisted nominations in Swaledale, which was new ground for the society. Some good specimens of Dales ponies had been shown at Muker and Reeth, where J. Fawcett's Dales mare (3517)Fussy , by Daddy's Lad out of a mare by Yorkshire Fashion, won the NPS Silver Medal. Fussy was half an inch off 15 hands, a brown cob with three white feet, foaled in 1910.

All Dales pony owners were asked to encourage their local shows to put on classes for registered Dales ponies and to preclude any Dales mares in-foal to any breed of carthorse.

The season started with the Breed Show at Hexham on April 13th, which produced keen competition for the four £80 Premiums offered by the Ministry of Agriculture. It is reported that nine of the best Dales pony stallions seen up to that date were paraded before the judges in beautiful condition. The following awards were made:

STALLION	AREA
Linnel Comet	Western District
Highland Laddie III	Hexham and East Derwent Valley
Black Blooming Heather	West Durham & Weardale
Gentleman John	Swaledale

The report continued 'the class open to all comers produced a rare stamp of mare, the property of Mr D. Hutchinson of Middleton-in-Teesdale. A half sister to the famous Stanhope Beauty, which although showing a strong cross, is an ideal mare to mate with a Dales stallion'. This was Harvest, a black mare with a blaze and three white feet, foaled in 1914 and standing 14.1 hands. She was by Black Boy (by Sir Harry) out of Emma by Cross Fell Hero. (3828 Fell) Emma was out of Black Bess by Little John (599 Fell). Sir Harry was said to be by Norfolk Cob and Cross Fell Hero was a grandson of the Clydesdale, Royal Lothian (9661 CHSB).

The society contributed £20 towards the prize money and Lewis Priestman gave a Cup for the Best Dales Mare or Filly, to encourage a good entry at the 1920 Royal Show, held in Darlington. There was an entry of 27 in the four Dales classes, judged by the veteran Dales breeder, John L. Forster. The best of the 1,2 and 3-year old colts was the grey Thunderbolt 955 by Teasdale Comet out of a mare by the Hackney, Young Chancellor (II), foaled in 1917. Second was the grey Hilton Jock (965), foaled in 1918 (Mountain Ranger/(2491 Fell) White Heather II, now (3627 Dales) White Heather V.

Third was Fairy King - a pony who was never actually entered in the Stud Book though he was registered and did get one registered filly, Jolly III, out of a mare by Daybreak, in 1926. Linnel Comet won the Stallion class standing above Gentleman John and Highland Laddie III. The class for 1, 2, and 3-year old fillies was won by Captain Christie's 3 year old, Miss Dale (Silver Top/Lady Dale). She also took first prize at Gilsland in 1919 and 1920 when she also won a NPS Silver Medal. Second was Captain Norman Field's 3-year old Dales cob (3696) Cockfield Topsy (Black Blooming Heather/Marwood Topsy), a bay cob with four white feet, standing 14.0 hands. Third was Mr John Dalton's 3-year old Dales cob, (3743)Dewdrop , by Bendle Squire by Royal Ratho (12,338 CHSB) (Clydesdale) out of a mare by Teasdale Comet. She was a 14.1 dark bay with a star and three white heels. Dewdrop was one of the group of Dales ponies which were Reserve to the Welsh group in the 1921 National Pony Show, London. At the same Show in 1927 she won the Lord Arthur Cecil Cup for the Best Mountain & Moorland Brood mare and was also one of the winning group of three.

The class for mares with foal at foot had a number of very good mares forward. The winner was Stanhope Beauty, second Linnel Martha and third, Westgarth Sprightly Spark.

For the first time, a Dales Group had been entered at the National Pony Show, consisting of the Stallion Linnel Comet and the mares, Stanhope Beauty and the Dales cob Dewdrop; the group came second to the Welsh and were Reserve for the Challenge Cup. It was a promising end to a good season.

An innovation was the decision of the council to hold the Annual General Meeting at Barnard Castle, with a view to bringing the society into greater prominence in the southern area of the Dales pony country. At last the Dales pony breeding areas of Durham and the North Riding were becoming recognised.

10
1916-24

◆

THE RESPONSE OF THE FELL PONY SOCIETY to the newly formed Dales Pony Society was not one of whole-hearted approval as shown by this extract from their Annual Report for 1917 written by Frank Garnett, MRCVS:

The present spring brought with it the entry of a new Pony Society to encourage the breeding of pure Dales ponies. If it continues with the energy of its initiation, its success and that of the breed are assured.

That the Dales pony has ever been a distinct breed from the Fell pony is more than doubtful. Their only real difference is one of size. The Dales pony running up (some of its adherents would wish) to 15 hands, is in itself a source of weakness of proper pony character. Their usefulness is however unquestioned, especially for army purposes and on all Dales farms that require a larger and more powerful animal than the Fell pony.

The foundation stock of both Fell and Dales ponies is to be found in the old galloway, common to the Border country and Scotland. The larger size of Dales is got by crossing with a heavier and bigger breed, the Clydesdale, and (though to a much lesser extent) the Hackney.

The Dales Society offered two premiums this spring at St John's Chapel, in Weardale, for stallions to travel their district. Of the three stallions shown two were registered Fell ponies, and the third was a horse of the Clydesdale type. Since that date I have received requests for other registered Fell stallions to be transferred to the Dales Section of the Stud Book. The difficulties of re-establishing an old breed, or creating a new one, under such circumstances are very great, and to make a distinction between the two breeds would be a very great achievement.

The size of the Fell pony is governed by the land upon which it is produced, and it is a foundation stock from which any sized horse may be bred. The Dales are, with very few exceptions, two-thirds Clydesdales, and have gone on the heavy side as far as the Polo Pony has gone on the blood side. The consequence is that in each instance they have lost their native Pony character. The Dales are fourteen to fourteen two hands, strong built, and rather long drawn. But where they excel is in their great clean bone, legs and feet of the very soundest;

for Army purposes they are second to none in the country.

From the National point of view it is a question worth consideration if the bringing back of these animals to the true pony type is altogether in the country's best interest. Unquestionably from the pony breeder's point of view it would be a great achievement, and one deserving the encouragement of all pony lovers.

The Dales Pony Society have been given a section in the National Pony Stud Book, but as has already been shown, there are strong reasons for not dividing the Fell and Dales Sections. At our meeting I will ask the Committee to carefully consider this question.

Although many breeders kept both Fell and Dales, the enthusiasts of either breed did not see eye to eye. If the breeds continued as they were it is quite possible that either the endangered true Fell would have disappeared or there would have been a dichotomy within the mixed breed into a pony and a cob, as with the Welsh. In fact the Dales pony was never 'from 14.0 to 14.2 hands'. A minimum height was never laid down and there have always been good Dales ponies around 13.2 hands. The stallions that were transferred to the Dales Stud Book were all Dales bred and there were more Dales and roadster-bred ponies in the early Fell Stud Books than pure Fell ponies. Fell men believed they were all the same but Dalesmen believed there was a distinct difference. Clydesdales, to a small degree, and Hackney roadsters to a greater, went into both breeds. The situation resulted in keen rivalry and much public debate which was often carried on through the pages of the The Live Stock Journal.

Volume 16-17 of the Stud Book, which covered 1919 to 1921, had an astonishing entry of 473 Dales ponies: 27 stallions and colts, 398 pony mares, 45 cob mares and 3 geldings; plus 19 colts and 46 fillies in the new Youngstock Supplement for ponies of four years old and under against an entry of only 67 in the Fell section and plus six colts in the Youngstock Supplement. This indicates the status of both breeds at the time. However, it underlines the strength in numbers of Dales ponies following the First World War; even though many lay on foreign battle fields. Fortunately, by 1919, the need for the registration of Fell ponies was becoming better publicised under the banner of the recently formed Fell Pony Society.

Among the Dales entries is **Glengarry** (1019 Dales) formerly (Fell 640). Because he was of Fell height, he was registered in the Fell Stud Book before the Dales Stud Book opened and was transferred when it became possible. Foaled in 1911, he stood 13.1 hands in 1913 but was taller when mature. He was by British Boy (by Yorkshire Fashion) out of a grey pony mare by Blooming Heather. Bred by Thomas Glen of

Brackenber, Appleby; he was later owned by Mr John Relph of Turn Bank, Shap, who gained the NPS Mountain & Moorland Supreme Championship with him in 1916, winning a 50 guinea trophy presented by *Country Life*. On that occasion, Mr Relph received the trophy from Queen Alexandra. Glengarry held the Fell Premium for Appleby for 1914-1918 and thereafter held Dales Premiums for 1921 and 1922 for Durham & Northumberland.

Of the seven grey stallions and colts the most influential was entered as:

Teasdale Comet 904, grey. Foaled 1898. Height 14.2 hands.
Sire: Young Comet, dark brown, by Comet.
Dam: Fanny by Glengarry (1019 Dales), black, 13.1.
G.dam: Lofty.
Breeder: F.Gibson. Middleton-in-Teesdale.

The sire of his dam was given the number of Glengarry (1019 Dales) but, as he was not foaled until 1911, it was probably the earlier grey Glengarry.

Teasdale Comet was a renowned trotter with tremendous action and speed, the winner of many races, sometimes in harness but mainly under saddle. He was 24 years old before he was registered but he was a most prolific sire of registered Fells and Dales from 1900 to 1924. All extended Dales pedigrees of modern ponies carry his line. Two of his sons became notable Fell stallions, the black Pendragon Comet (974 Fell) and the brown Weardale Hero (607 Fell) foaled in 1902, the sire of Heltondale Victor (938 Fell).

Teasdale Comet was closely followed in status by his grey son, **Gentleman John** (907 Dales) winner of a Dales Premium for 1920-1921 for Swaledale. Entered in the same Stud Book are two of his grey grandsons, Hilton Passion 966, foaled in 1917, and Hilton Jock, foaled in 1918, both by Mountain Ranger (598 Fell) out of the 13.3¼, grey (2491 Fell) White Heather II, foaled in 1903, by Teasdale Comet out of Merrie by Black Jock out of Peg by Old England (2210 HHSB). White Heather was bred by Joseph Townson, of Broadless Gate, Middleton-in-Teesdale, and transferred to the Dales Stud Book in 1917 as (3627 Dales) White Heather V (later amended to II) with a height of 14.1. She was the winner of 142 prizes by 1913, which included first at the Royal Show, Newcastle in 1908; and the NPS mare premium for Middleton-in-Teesdale.

In the Fell section of the same Stud Book, Hilton Passion was also

Glengarry (1019 Dales) foaled 1911.

entered as Hilton Fashion 980, out of (3627 Dales) White Heather V. As Hilton Passion he was awarded the 1920 Fell pony premium for Middleton-in-Teesdale and was travelled by his owner Mr F. Watson; and as Hilton Fashion he travelled the same area for the 1921 and 1922 seasons. At the same time his full brother Hilton Jock was travelling as a Dales Premium stallion, in Durham, Weardale, Barnard Castle and Swaledale. Hilton Fashion later became the property of the Earl of Lonsdale and won a Silver Medal for the Best Mountain & Moorland Stallion and the Group Prize with two Fell mares, at the National Pony Show, London, in 1923. His only registered progeny were a dark bay Fell filly 5850 Sowerby's Fancy foaled in 1923, and a grey Dales filly 5949 Bluebell VI, foaled in 1925.

The beautiful but short-lived Dales colt, **Guy Mannering** (937), was foaled in 1919, by Linnel Comet out of (3369 Dales) Moscow Black Bess. He was bred by Matthew Dodd of Moscow, Gilsland and his first owner was Captain T. S. Christie who named all his Dales ponies after characters in the novels of Sir Walter Scott. Roy Charlton bought Guy

The Dales stallion Teasdale Comet when aged.

Mannering and he sired Linnel Squire (1263 Dales) out of (4532 Dales) Linnel Dame. His Fell registered progeny were the stallion Linnel Boy (1260 Fell) out of (3722 Fell) Linnel Fancy by Dalesman and the mare (4894 Fell) Linnel Coquette out of (2916 Fell) Linnel Flirt also by Dalesman; both were foaled in 1923.

The Dales stallion **Linnel Heather** 888, (Black Blooming Heather/Stonedress Polly) was transferred to the Fell Section in 1923. He sired the Fell colts Linnel Jet and Linnel Snip and the Fell fillies, Linnel Fairy and Linnel Nancy before changing owners and travelling as a Fell premium stallion in Middleton-in-Teesdale, in 1921 and 1922. He was one of the Championship group of Fells at the 1924 NPS Show, London, when exhibited by Mr Charlton, with two Fell mares. Shortly after this, he was sold to the Spanish Government for a high figure.

Another stallion who can be found in the lines of modern ponies is the 14.1, Brown Jock 973, foaled in 1916, by Bendle Squire, an outcross by Royal Ratho (12,338 CHSB) out of Heather Lass by Blooming Heather. (4228 Fell) Heather Lass was out of Premium Lass by Old

Mountain Ranger, bred by William Raine, Park End, Middleton-in-Teesdale.

Of the 389 Dales pony and cob mares of known breeding entered in this volume, only 32 were by Fell registered sires but these were all out of Dales or roadster mares. Of these 32, all but 7 had been foaled before the Dales Stud Book was opened. These were one by Dalesman, one by Glengarry, and seven by Mountain Ranger (598 Fell) by the 14.0 grey Park End King, out of the 13.2 grey Scordale Queen by Blooming Heather out of a mare by Old Mountain Ranger.

One of the most interesting mares registered at this time was

3775 **Robinson's Gipsy**, whole black. Foaled 1917. Height 13.0.
Sire: Glengarry (1019 Dales)
Dam: (2218 Fell) Queen of Hearts, brown, 13.2 by Dalesman (572 Fell) brown, 14.0.
G.dam: (1678 Fell) Fairy Queen brown 13.2 by Sir James.
Breeder: J .R. Robinson, Billy Row, Crook, Co. Durham.

Robinson's Gipsy became as famous as Stanhope Beauty and, like her, was bought by Roy B. Charlton and when exhibited at the National Pony Show, London, in 1923, won first and the Lord Arthur Cecil Cup for the Supreme Native Brood Mare. Sadly, all her progeny were registered as Fells. Together with Linnel Comet and Blackthorn, she helped to stir up the contoversy between the Fell and Dales Societies.

Mr J. W. Dalton, who was a founder member of the Dales Pony Improvement Society and later became President of the Dales Pony Society, entered two of his ponies now carrying the Snowhope prefix:

(3225)Snowhope Black Bess by Yorkshire Fashion was re-entered from Volume 15 with her prize list, 9 firsts, 7 seconds and 2 thirds in 1919 and 9 firsts 8 seconds and 5 thirds in 1920. Entered for the first time was (3225)Snowhope Topsy by Blooming Heather (325 Fell) out of Jess II by Little Wonder (Little Wonder II 25) out of Jessy by Black Jock; and her daughter (3787)Duet by Teasdale Comet. He also entered one of his best known mares, the beautiful prize-winning

4126 **Fairy Glance**, 14.2, dark brown with a white near hind hind coronet. Foaled 1915.
Sire: Beacon Swell
Dam: Sally of Sandwath by Yorkshire Fashion
G.dam: Molly Mist.
Breeder: George Haswell, Sandwath, Kirkby Stephen

It is a pity that there is no photograph of this lovely pony, but I am told that Fairy Glance was a particularly good example of the type of up to height Dales pony John Dalton was promoting. She was bred in the fashionable way: i.e. by a smart roadster or roadster-cross from a mare by the Dales cob Yorkshire Fashion out of a mare by Blooming Heather. The sire of Fairy Glance was a 14.3 chestnut roadster of which little is known. Beacon Swell was used with great success in establishing the type of improved Dales pony which the society was looking for. Fairy Glance foaled two colts, Snowhope Fashion in 1923 and Snowhope Hero in 1925 but no fillies. In 1926 she was driven to Hexham Show, where she was shown successfully but became ill on the drive home. She was taken out of the trap and rested in a field but despite all efforts to help her, she died of colic.

Mr R.L.Close of Hazelgill, Skeddale, Bowes, registered the first of his Dales ponies, Skeddale Jennie (3855), brown, 14.1 by Teasdale Comet, foaled in 1912 bred by Mrs Thomson of Cragg Top Farm, Barnard Castle, and Skeddale Maisie (3902), bay, 14.1 by Blooming Heather, foaled in 1910, breeder unknown. Skeddle is printed Sleddale in the Stud Book. The prefix was later changed to Hazelgill.

Also entered in this Stud Book was Stanhope Beauty's half-sister, who was so admired at the Dales Pony Society Spring Show of 1920, described as

> 'a rare stamp of mare which, though showing a strong cross, is an ideal mare to mate with a Dales sire'.

This was Harvest (3812)by Black Boy by Sir Harry out of Emma by Cross Fell Hero by Lothian Prince. It is possible that Black Boy and Young Sir Harry were the same, as both Stanhope Beauty and Harvest were bred by T. Dixon Hutchinson but entered into the Stud Book by different people. It was customary to call the sons of well known stallions by their sire's names prefixed with Young until they became Old ad infinitum regardless of the son's real name. Young Sir Harry was sometimes described as a Dales as was Yorkshire Fashion and Norfolk Cob, which probably meant that he was out of a galloway mare, and was therefore an outcross such as Lothian Prince, Silver Top and Bendal Squire (sometimes spelt Bendle).

Mr Joseph B. Metcalf of Park House, Marwood, Barnard Castle, also entered five of his Dales ponies. Among them was his foundation mare, the 14.2 black (3742)Marwood Topsy by Teasdale Comet out of Barney Topsy by Blooming Heather, together with her progeny. These were her black 1918 colt foal Marwood Bang (975) by Valence Heather and her daughters (3753)Marwood Beauty foaled in 1919 by Mountain

(3775 Dales) Robinson's Gipsy, foaled 1917.

Ranger (598 Fell); and the Dales cob (3696)Cockfield Topsy, a bay with white on four legs, foaled in 1917 by Black Blooming Heather (674 Dales). The other was the brilliant 14.1, grey (3601)Marwood Daisy, foaled in 1912, by Teasdale Comet out of Cockfield Daisy.

The aged mare (2359 Fell)**Maid of Honour** was re-registered as (3586 Dales) Westgarth's Maid of Honour by Real Fashion (605 Fell) out of Poll (Dales). Her sire was a trotter bred from the Ayrshire Champion line through Black Jock and Young Perfect. Real Fashion was a black pony with three white fetlocks; the winner of 16 prizes in 16 outings, which included a first at the Royal Show, at Newcastle in 1908. Maid of Honour, foaled in 1900, was entered in the Fell Stud Book by her breeder, Joseph Blackett of Lower Westgarth Farm, Butterknowle, Co. Durham. She won numerous prizes between 1900 and 1912 including a second at the Royal Show, Newcastle, in 1908. Between 1919 and 1921 she was entered in the Dales Stud Book at a great age by Thomas Blackett who had inherited the farm and ponies. Her breeding is given as out of Darky by Pride of the North out of Bella; the entry by her breeder is probably the correct one. In

1916 Maid of Honour foaled a filly by Teasdale Comet,the white-faced bay mare (3802 Dales) Spicy Story who inherited Real Fashion's three white fetlocks. Spicy Story, her full sisters (3587 Dales)Westgarths Actress foaled in 1919 and (3587 Dales) Westgarth's Sprightly Spark by Royal Ratho foaled in 1915 were also entered together with Sprightly Spark's 1919 daughter by Teasdale Comet (3788 Dales) Westgarth's May Queen with her full brother Westgarth Comet foaled in 1920. Westgarth's Maid of Honour can be found in the extended pedigrees of a number of modern ponies.

Seven of the 49 mares registered in the Fell section at the same time were sired by Dales or roadsters. Of these the only one foaled after the opening of the Dales Stud Book was (4036 Fell) Little Wonder II by the 14.2 brown Mettles Lad (Dales) out of (2336 Fell) Stanhope Gate Fanny by the outcross Little John (599 Fell). Mettle's Lad was by the 14.2 brown Meteor by Young Comet. His dam, Mettle, was by Teesdale Heather by Park End King out of Polly by Black Jock. In 1912, at the Durham County Show, he won first prize for the Best Foal most suitable for Artillery purposes and was bought by Major Upton of Ingmire Hall, Sedburgh in 1915.

Apart from the transferred Dales stallion, Linnel Heather, the following were also registered in the Fell section of Volume 16-17: **Kirkdale Hero** (968 Fell), by Black Boy (by Sir Harry) out of Jennie by Little John (599 Fell); Twilight III and **Pendragon Comet** by Teasdale Comet; **Heltondale Victor** and Udale Hero by Weardale Hero (by Teasdale Comet) and North Star III by British Boy (Yorkshire Fashion); Total Eclipse by one of the Comets; Shepster Boy by the chestnut roadster Beacon Swell out of a mare by Daybreak; Gameboy by Cock of the North (by Highland Duke by Sir Harry); Mina by Glengarry out of Shrike by The Mikado and three by the unregistered 14.3 black, Valance Heather by Blooming Heather. This left just three of pure Fell breeding and one unknown.

There was a Mountain & Moorland Youngstock Supplement for 1922, in which 19 Dales colts and 46 fillies were entered, plus 6 Fell colts, all without numbers. Some were later entered in the stud book proper but many disappeared without proper registration and some, for instance Batts Nancy by Black Blooming Heather, and the colt Pride of the Dales by Gentleman John, appeared as the dam and sire of youngstock without ever owning a number in the Stud Book proper. Among the five colts by Linnel Comet was the fourth son of White Heather II, the black Merry Boy III foaled in 1920. Three were sired by Gentleman John, seven by Black Blooming Heather and one each by North Star II, Highland Laddie III and Dalesman. The most interesting colt, **Stanner's Lad,** was entered by A. B. Coulson of Newcastle-upon-Tyne.

Stanners Lad, black, little white on both hind feet. Foaled 1920.
Sire: Linnel Comet (841 Dales)
Dam: (3339 Dales) Prospect Damsel, brown, by Silver Top (833 Dales)
by King's Pilot (14,726 CHSB), Clydesdale.
G.dam: (3241 Dales) Prospect Jean dark dun, 14.0 by King of the
Mountains, black (breeding unknown).
Breeder: J.R.Coulson. Stanners Burn, Falston, Northumberland.

Stanner's Lad was later entered in the Dales section as Blackthorn.
Roy B.Charlton was appointed secretary of the Fell Pony Society in 1926 and proceeded with great success to promote the Fell pony and stave off threatened extinction of the breed. He had also in 1925 and 1926 exported stallions to Spain, which had given a filip to breeding. It was said that if a pony won a Premium, he would be booked for Spain the following summer and there was concern that this would do the breed no good. When interviewed on the matter, Mr Charlton stated that

The Dales mare Marwood Daisy by Teasdale Comet, foaled 1912.

he was quite satisfied with the position. He had numerous beautiful yearlings and two year old colts at the Linnel stud to take the place of those which had gone; in fact, in 35 years he had never had a better lot. What was true of his stud was true of Fell pony breeding generally, because, encouraged by the War Office Premiums, and also by the keen rivalry of the past few years, breeders are now retaining their best colts entire. This of course, entails a good deal of extra trouble, for whereas youngstock ordinarily roam the Fells with their dams - a young mare may be found with three of her offspring at foot - a young entire has to be cared for in-hand.

The report continued that Mr Charlton had just sent four of the most beautiful ponies ever seen in the North of England to Spain in one consignment.

Three of these held premiums, two Fell and one Dales. All were black and of the same height and not one had a white hair on the leg. Linnel Boy, bred by Mr Charlton, is a young pony which this Spring travelled the Appleby district; he has the best of legs and feet and is a great mover. He comes of the famous Comet family, his grandsire being that noted breeding pony, Linnel Comet, himself descended from Comet, and is typical of the pronounced pony character for which this family has a reputation. His sire was Guy Mannering and his dam Linnel Fancy (by the famous old pony Dalesman, which held a record as a premium holder) was a prize-winner when the Royal Show was held in Darlington, and full sister to the great prize-winning mare, Linnel Flirt, winner of the Cecil Cup at the National Pony Show in London 1924 and winner at the Newcastle Royal in the previous year.

The other Fell Premium holder which Mr Charlton disposed of was Minstrel Boy, the property of Mr L.Rutherford of Black Cleugh Farm, Wearhead, Co.Durham. He is four years old, was bred by Mr J.W.Dent, Fair View, Middleton-in-Teesdale, and held the Middleton district premium this spring. Minstrel Boy is full of Blooming Heather and Little John blood - two names to conjure with in Fell pony breeding. His sire was Linnel Heather, which headed the championship group of mountain and moorland ponies at the London show in 1924, and was then sold to the Spanish Government. His dam, Monks Fanny, got by the fine moving pony Mountain Ranger, was successful both in the showyard and on the trotting track. She was a first prizewinner at Darlington Royal,took a third at the Newcastle Royal, and won the trotting at Middleton-in-Teesdale in competition with recognised trotting ponies.

The third pony in Mr Charlton's quartette was a two-year-old colt got by Glengarry and described by his owner as the 'best baby' he has ever possessed. The quartette is completed with the Dales stallion Linnel Midnight. He won at Hexham show last year and in the spring of this year he gained the War Office premium of £80 for the Hexham, Alston and Bampton district, this brings him into the only Dales pony breeding area of Cumberland. He is got by the same sire as Minstrel Boy viz. Linnel Heather, referred to above, and his dam, Noontide, was a Dales mare which was a great favourite in the Stanhope district, and whose sire was Teasdale Comet.

Linnel Boy (1260 Fell) was by Guy Mannering (937 Dales) out of (3369 Dales) Moscow Black Bess. Minstrel Boy (1456 Fell) was by Linnel Heather (888 Fell, previously Dales) by Black Blooming Heather (674 Dales) out of (3206 Dales) Stonedress Polly. The 'best baby' was Wait and See (1212 Fell) by Heltondale Victor (938 Fell) by Weardale Hero(607 Fell) by Teasdale Comet (904 Dales); out of Russet II by Glengarry (1019 Dales late Fell) by British Boy (574 Fell) by Yorkshire Fashion; out of Russet I by Dalesman (572 Dales).

It should not be surprising that the breeds were so intertwined and the fact that the process continued can be explained by a paragraph in the *Live Stock Journal* of December, 1926, on the appointment of Roy Charlton as Secretary to the Fell Pony Society, where the following comment is reported,

> When the Dales Pony Society started 10 years ago, for the purpose of preserving the breed as a pony breed, there were, in Mr Charlton's opinion, far too many half-bred animals in the Dales country, but with the help of Fell stallions they were now producing chiefly animals of real pony type. He is of the belief that it was uneccesary to have two Societies for the Fell and Dales ponies.

From the Fell pony view, this is a spectacular bit of propaganda, desperately needed at the time. It did no favour to the Dales breed without which the Fells may not have survived. The debt has never been acknowledged but that may have been principally because Fell enthusiasts could not accept the Dales as a different breed. This is understandable as both breeds had evolved from similar roots. Anything registered in the Fell Stud Book was accepted as a Fell, and the breeds had been very mixed.

In a paragraph on Dales and Fells at The Royal Show, held in Darlington in 1926, published in the *Live Stock Journal* of March, 1927 were the following words

> The Fell pony is more a product of Cumberland and Westmorland than of Durham and Yorkshire. He is not as stout as the Dales pony, and was not nearly so well represented in respect of numbers as the Dales pony. As Highland, Dales and Fell ponies are all registered by the National Pony Society, a judicious effort to introduce a Dales pony cross into the Highland might be attempted. There would in such a case be control and public registration, so that the effects might be closely scrutinised. Of the commercial value of the four types passed under

review there can be no question. Whatever is of commercial value should be sedulously cultivated.

The writer is unknown but the idea was common to many.

Acknowledging the indiscriminate entry of ponies into the Stud Books, the Councils of the Dales and Fell Pony Societies agreed that in future, entries of registered dams and sires should show breed and number, such as the Dales mare

3677 **Domino**, Black, white mark on head, white ring of white round right hind leg, tip white inside left leg. Foaled 1917.
Sire: Highland Laddie III (642 Dales) black, 13.3.
Dam: (3628 Dales) Dolly Blue, black, 14.1, by Real Fashion (605 Fell) brown, 14.0.
Grand-dam: Bluebell.

and the Fell mare:

4052 **Polly Flinders**, grey. Foaled 1917. Height 13.2.
Sire: Teasdale Comet (904 Dales) grey, 14.2.
Dam: By Blooming Heather(325 Fell) black, 13.2.

This practice was to last until 1948 but no serious attempt to separate the two breeds was made. The more powerful, trotter bred Dales continued to exert a great influence on the Fells.

The Dales Pony Stallion Show held at Bishop Auckland on April 6th,1922, was combined with the Annual General Meeting of the Dales Pony Improvement Society, and attracted the best attendance yet at both. Mr Norman Field of Lartington Hall, near Barnard Castle, was elected president. Eight very good stallions paraded and according to the local newspaper report of the show

> Three £80 Premiums were awarded as follows:-For Swaledale and Teesdale, Linnel Comet, the nine year old unbeaten champion and sire of some of the best stock in the northern section of the Dales pony district. It is a matter of great satisfaction that after four successful years in the Hexham Country, this good pony sire should have been recently purchased by the President of the Society, who resides in Teesdale, and is now taking up his first Premium there, where the introduction of new blood will do an immense amount of good.
>
> For Weardale, Hilton Jock, a four year old grey by the Fell pony Mountain Ranger, which was second to Linnel Comet for the championship cup at the recent London pony show. Hilton Jock's dam is Mr John Townson's nice little grey mare, White Heather, which won

at the Royal when last in Newcastle-on-Tyne. A hot competitor for this Weardale Premium was the jet black, four year old Stanhope Hero. This pony evidently had many admirers around the ring, and from what one could gather from the many enthusiasts who were intensely interested in the selection of the Premium ponies, it is likely that the black pony will be the more popular in the Dale.

For Derwent Dale and North-West Durham, Dalesman, the twenty-year-old black, owned by Mr John Relph of Turn Bank, Penrith. Dalesman is a famous pony, and like Linnel Comet, he goes into a country which is quite new to him. Derwent Dale is lucky to have secured this great old pony. He is sire of the very best of the ponies of the Eden Valley in recent years; they all have his remarkable bone and substance, and, all alike, go with great dash and courage. The Dales Pony Improvement Society is to be congratulated upon securing Dalesman.

Among other well known pony stallions which delighted at Bishop Auckland were Kirkdale Hero, Black Blooming Heather and Gentleman John. Kirkdale Hero was a stranger from Fell country. He is an extra good sort and is likely to be heard of again.

In 1924 a total of 220 Dales ponies were registered, 39 colts and stallions and 174 mares, 5 cob mares and 2 geldings. The corresponding Fell numbers totalled 88: 22 stallions and colts and 66 mares.

By far the most important addition to the Dales Stud Book at this time was the stallion **Dalesman**.

Dalesman (572 Dales), Dark brown, star, white near hind foot. Foaled 1902. Height 14.0.
Sire: Yorkshire Fashion, black, 15.0 (pure Dales cob).
Dam: Doll, brown, 13.2 by Reformer, brown, 14.0.
G.G.Dam: Old Doll of Spittals, by Little John (599 Fell), black, 14.0.
Breeder: R. Bonsfield, Whygill Head, Little Asby, Appleby.

Transferred from the Fell Section at 22 years of age, he had always been a popular sire of Dales ponies. In the above transfer entry from Fell to Dales, the sire of his grand-dam is given the number, colour and height of Merry Jock (849 Dales) foaled in 1907 and a son of Dalesman. Merry John was before the Fell stud book opened and from the Merry Driver line. Little John was given the number of Little John (599 Fell), which must be wrong as he was not foaled until 1894 and so was too young to have sired Dalesman's great grand-dam, which was probably Little John, the sire of Blooming Heather.

The aged Dalesman won at the Royal Show, Newcastle-upon-Tyne in 1923. It was reported in *The Herald* at the time in the following words:

It was a tribute to the stamina and excellence of that famous old stallion, Dalesman, that it should again head the aged stallion class at the Royal Show for its owner, Mr John Relph, Turn Bank, Newby, near Penrith. Now 21 years old, and bred by Mr R Bousfield, Whygill Head, Little Asby, Appleby. Dalesman is showing signs of age but is still remarkably fresh.

In 1934 he died at the age of 32 years. The following is an extract from his obituary, written by Roy Charlton and published in *The Herald*:

Dalesman - was he a Fell pony or a Dales? He was bred in the Fell country but because of his size, was registered in the Dales section of the National Pony Stud Book. He was just as valuable to the one breed as to the other; it was common at one time to have his progeny winning for both Fell and Dales at the same show! But in size, he was a Dales, standing 14.2 hands and sired by Yorkshire Fashion.

Dalesman combined real pony character with the weight of a cob. His abundant vitality was inherited by his offspring, as for instance, his grand-daughter Robinson's Gipsy. She was shown at the Royal Show, Newcastle, and displayed that 'vim' which was so characteristic of her. That good judge of horseflesh, Sir Merick Burrell, rode her that day; to a friend he expressed his delight at the splendid ride, commenting that he was surprised how easily the mare carried weight. Robinson's Gipsy won the pony riding class that day; six years later she was the winner at the Royal at Harrogate; and she was also twice champion brood mare of all the mountain and moorland breeds at the National Pony Show in London, these successes being in 1922 and 1923.

Now, to mention two daughters of Dalesman - Linnel Flirt and Linnel Fancy, both bred by Mr Henry Holme of Thrimby and later the property of the Mr R. B. Charlton, the Hon. Secretary of the Fell Pony Society. Following Robinson's Gipsy's London Show successes, Linnel Flirt stood in the same position in 1924. Her daughter, Linnel Fluff won the Sir Arthur Cecil Cup in 1932, and is now the property of H.M.The King.

Linnel Fancy, the other daughter of Dalesman, also became a first prize-winner in London, and, through her alone, Dalesman has become the fore-elder of such ponies as Linnel Brown Boy, Linnel Boy, Linnel Darkie, Linnel Snip, Linnel Gallant Boy and lots more, including at least four now in Spain.

Again, Linnel Lingcropper, champion stallion at London in 1931 and 1932 and winner of H.M.The King's Premium at Penrith last April, was Dalesman's great-grandson. This is dealing with Dalesman's progeny in one line only. What a task it would be to trace even all the notable ponies! Bess of Hardendale, a Fell pony mare of true type and one of Dalesman's daughters, is at the head of another family.

So far one has mentioned only Fell ponies, and these only in a limited circle. Dalesman had equally as many Dales pony descendants. Ouston Model, bred by the late Samuel Walton, Ouston, Whitfield, was a son

Mr J. Relph's Dalesman (572 Dales), aged 21 years.

of Dalesman. Ouston Model was a noted pony, and was eventually exported to Spain. Another Dales son of Dalesman was exported along with five Fell mares to set up a stud in Michigan, U.S.A.

One has perhaps, written enough; suffice to say that as long as Fell and Dales ponies have their supporters, the name of Dalesman will be recalled. This pony travelled from the inception of the Board of Agriculture grants; probably more than any other pony, Dalesman perpetuated true pony character in Cumberland, Westmorland, Durham and Northumberland.

Dalesman belonged to the veteran, Mr John Relph of Turn Bank, and he kept the old pony not only in the days of its supremacy but in its later years. Dalesman was never beaten in the show ring, so Mr Relph assures us; its last appearance was at the 1923 Royal - when the photograph we reproduce was taken.

Among other Dales stallions entered was the 14.0, Kirkdale Hero 968, transferred from the Fell Section. One of his prize-winning sons was also entered in this volume, Snowhope Fashion 1194, foaled in 1923 out of Fairy Glance, bred and owned by J. W. Dalton.

Two notable stallions by Linnel Comet were Alston Comet 1063, foaled 1919 out of the unregistered Belle O'the Burn (by Little John), and Blackthorn 1067, late Stanner's Lad.

Blackthorn became the subject of a letter published in *The Live Stock Journal* of May 1925, in answer to critics after he had been barred from receiving a Fell Pony Premium by the Fell Pony Committee. Writing under the pseudonym of 'Waskew Fell', Dr Gibson of Orton pointed out that it was time the rules and regulations for registration of Fell ponies were enforced, as he believed outside blood would do harm to the Fell pony. There was no trace of Fell blood in Blackthorn or his sire Linnel Comet, who was registered as a Fell and bred in Fell country; though his breeding gave him no claim to be classed as a Fell pony. Both Alston Comet and Blackthorn were exported to Spain and in 1926 won the King of Spain's Gold Cup for pairs at the Great Horse Show in Madrid. Blackthorn left only two Dales mares; Alston Comet left six Dales mares and four Dales colts: Blackburn Fashion, Highlands Comet, Redwing Comet, and Kirkhaugh Pride.

Four Dales colts carrying the Linnel prefix were entered in Volume 18 of the Stud Book, Linnel Squire, Linnel Dick, Linnel Hero and Linnel Midnight, foaled in 1924. Before he went to Spain in 1927, Midnight had sired the Dales mares Coanwood Diamond, Helbeck Fanny, Linnel Gipsy, Linnel Christie and Linnel Kielder out of Dales dams. His Fell progeny was the colt Linnel Flame, out of Linnel Flirt by Dalesman and the fillies Linnel Flora, out of Linnel Coquette by Guy Mannering, and Linnel Nina out of Linnel Nellie by Glengarry.

Another first class Dales stallion was Ouston Model (1215) (Dalesman /Lonning Natalie by North Star II 900), a handsome black Dales pony foaled in 1921. Ouston Model had travelled as a War Office Premium stallion in 1924 and 1926 in Cumberland and Northumberland. At the 1928 National Pony Show he was beaten into second place by Moor Bradley (1476 Fell) by John Bradley by Brown Jock (973 Dales), thus taking Reserve for the Linnel Cup for the large breeds Stallion Championship. He also went to Spain in 1927 but he left six Dales colts, four of which became stallions; the most influential were **Glenholme** out of Marwood Topsy and Sonny Boy II out of Westgate Jessie, but Bonnie Charlie II out of Duchy and the dun Frank II out of Creamy III both left registered progeny. In 1928, thirteen of Ouston Comet's daughters were foaled, including May Beauty out of Stanhope Beauty. He left good stock and was a sad loss to the breed.

The stallion **Prince Comet** (1153) (Comet IV/Polly by Blooming Heather), foaled in 1920 did stay in Dales country. Bred in Appleby by Mrs Charnley of the Nags Head, he was owned by William Hully of the Bousefield Stud, Orton, Westmorland.

Mr J. W. Dalton's homebred mare, Snowhope Dewy (Kirkdale Hero/ Dewdrop by Bendle Squire) was foaled in 1923. Bendle Squire was by the

Clydesdale Royal Ratho out of a mare by Teesdale Comet. Snowhope Dewy was one of the winners of the Mountain & Moorland Group prize at the National Pony Show, London in 1926 and took third prize in the class for Mountain & Moorland Mares in 1927, being beaten by the others in the Dales winning group, Dewdrop and Snowhope Beauty.

Two mares entered in the Dales Section with a change of name were Linnel Lassie (late Gowbarrow Lily) with a height of 13.3½ and 13.3 Linnel Lucy (late Gowbarrow Bluebell). They were both by Bampton Pride (867 Fell) by Heather's Model (381 Fell) out of Sally by Comet. William Dalton's Heather's Model was by Blooming Heather out of a bay mare by Little Wonder II (Wilson pony) out of a mare by Black Jock by Bewcastle Jock.

One of the Dales cob mares entered in the Sub-section of Volume 18, was the 14.2 grey mare Hummerbeck Beauty. Bred by Mr G. W. Bowbank of Hummerbeck, West Auckland, County Durham, she was foaled in 1919, by the Clydesdale Smart Buchclyvie (19,283 CHSB) out of Polly (Merry Jock/Wheatside Topsy). This mare was the founder of a family which consistently produced high quality grey mares, such as Grey Queen II, Lady Sheila and the unregistered Silver Queen, the dam of All Fours.

The Dales/Fell situation had not yet been properly addressed but the Fell Society was now in the competant hands of Roy Charlton who from now on now dealt with the publicity of both breeds and the numbers and status of the Fell pony began to rise.

11
FELL VERSUS DALES

◆

THE DALES/FELL DEBATE became very heated following the opening of the Dales Pony Stud Book. In 1923 the *Agricultural Gazette* published photographs of Robinson's Gipsy and Hilton Fashion, the winners at the National Pony Show of 1923. This promoted great argument at the next meeting of the Fell Pony Society, where there was also a discussion on the transfer of Fell stallions to the Dales Section. Mr Roy Charlton, who was a member of both Breed Societies and owner of Robinson's Gipsy, had written :

> I think it is quite wrong to say that Lord Lonsdale's grey stallion which won at London should be registered as a Fell pony, when his full brother is registered as a Dales and travelled last season with the Ministry's premium through the Dales Society. Surely these full brothers should be allowed to compete in the same show. Neither the Dales nor the Fell Society has anything to lose by accepting a registered stallion for competition. It rests with the judges which of the stallions should actually win premiums; but I think we shall all agree that the greater the number of ponies to pick from the better chance there is of getting the choice a district desires. We have on this side of the country quite a number of 13h.3ins. registered Dales stallions that would suit Fell country, and it is wrong that I should wait to see how big a pony, Linnel Heather, should grow before I register him. His parents were both Dales registered. He was little, so he went into the Fell section, and last year had your Middleton-in-Teesdale Fell pony premium. It would be far better for both societies if we accepted stallions, either Fell or Dales for competition for either Dales or Fell.

Dr R. W. Gibson said that Dales ponies could not exist on the fells under the conditions in which Fell ponies were kept.

Captain Wingate (Lowther Estate), the secretary to the society, said a true Fell pony could only be told by its breeding. He had been told by Mr Norman Field of Lartington Hall that it was absurd that they should have two societies, because the Dales and Fell breeds were the same. Captain Wingate said that he believed they were nothing of the kind.

Mr Henry Holme said the Dales breed was just in its infancy. Unfortunately, the Dales pony men could not be stopped from using Fell pony stallions, but they ought to be stopped from entering Fell ponies as Dales.

Eventually it was agreed that a pony already registered as a Fell pony should not be transferred to the Dales section of the Stud Book, nor should a registered Dales pony be eligible for the Fell section, and protest was made against the Dales Society registering pure-bred Fell ponies in the Dales section.

A report of the above discussion was published in the *Live Stock Journal* of April 1923. This was followed by an item by R. B. (Charlton) published in the *North British Agriculturist* on July 13th,1923. In it he wrote:

> In addition to having a common foundation, a certain amount of interbreeding takes place between Dales and Fell ponies, and, although each breed has a society catering for its interests, and, although each has a separate section of the National Pony Stud Book, it is not an uncommon thing for a really pure-bred animal of one breed to be shown as of the other breed. In fact, Mr Roy Charlton's mare, Robinson's Gipsy, which in fact is of Dales pony height, won the Lord Arthur Cecil Cup at the London Pony Show, being entered as a Dales pony, although she was bred in the Fell pony district and by a Fell pony stallion, Glengarry. At the same show Lord Lonsdale showed in his first prize Fell group, a stallion which has a full brother entered in the Stud Book as a Dales stallion, while Linnel Heather, bred from Dales parents, has held a Fell pony premium. But whether Dales or Fell, these mountain and moorland ponies are a credit to their native districts, and worthy of inspection at Newcastle by all lovers of Britain's native pony breeds.

Few Dales or Fell men entirely agreed with this outlook and the disagreements rumbled on until they became quite acrimonious. The argument was continued in the *Live Stock Journal*, beginning in February 1925 with the following letter:

> Sir, - The three photographs of Fell pony sires (Wait and See (Heltondale Victor x Russet II by Glengarry), Linnel Glen (Glengarry x Flora III) and Linnel Heather reproduced recently in the Live Stock Journal are the type of pony favoured by Fell pony breeders and are bred on orthodox Fell pony lines. It is true that there are other ponies approaching these in type but which can easily be distinguished by the initiated as not ponies but dwarf horses with a preponderance of cart-horse blood in their veins. These are reversions to a Fell pony type in the breeding of a bigger type of pony than that which has its habitat on the North Country Fells. The Fell pony has been used as a foundation stock to breed Dales from, and which was of more use to the Dales

farmer, owing to its size, than the pure Fell, which is able to stand the rigours of the bleak inhospitable Fells, winter and summer, whereas the Dales pony or small horse would soon succumb. The pure Fell pony is partly descended from the old celtic pony, crossed with the old Border Galloway and infused with a dash of old-fashioned Hackney blood, through Old Merry Driver. Many of these ponies so bred, though only 13 hands in height, could trot a mile in three minutes on the highway, carrying 12 stone, e.g. Merry Driver by Old Merry Driver trotted ten miles against Mousetrap for £50 a side, beating him and going the whole distance in 33 minutes, carrying 12 stone. Other famous ponies were Atkinson's Doll and Heather Belle, Little John, Merry John and Grey Bobby - all with Merry Driver blood in them; Bennett's Little Fan, who trotted against Steel Grey, and won, and many others from whom are descended the best and purest Fell ponies. Another infusion was Highland pony blood through Glengarry, a 13 hands pony, about 1858.

Mr Roy Charlton's black pony mare, which is registered and has recently been shown as a Dales, and which you have depicted in the Live Stock Journal, is a Fell pony bred on much the same lines as two of the Fell pony sires shown, and should have been registered as a Fell. What the Dales Pony Improvement Society is, no one connected with Fell pony or Mountain and Moorland pony breeding exactly knows. Some are bred on Fell pony lines, some are dwarf horses with outcrosses. The best of them possess some Fell pony characteristics, but when turned out on the Fells to 'fend' or pick up a living for themselves, they are soon found stretched out or are down at the farm fold-gate, whereas the Fell ponies belonging to breeders of the old and pure type are never seen near the homestead, even in the depth of winter.

The Dales Pony Society are, it is true, making a praiseworthy effort to breed a useful class of animal, but they are a young society, and when formed had a very hazy idea of what a Dales pony was, or should be. They had no knowledge of a Fell Pony Society formed many years before theirs, nor even of sections set apart for Mountain and Moorland ponies in the National Pony Society Stud Book, and knew nothing of the history of the Fell pony; nor were they old enough to remember the little trotting steam engines of fifty years ago; nor had they travelled or wandered on the bleak Fells of Westmorland and Cumberland and seen the hardy ponies on their native ground. They had got hold of ponies purchased at Brough Hill Fair which had been introduced into Northumberland, and had marvelled at their strength and endurance, and decided to form a society to preserve this type, ignorant of the fact that breeders and admirers of the type had been working hard to preserve the foundation stock from which the Brough Hill pony has been bred. Indeed, as one of the 'promoters' remarked, they had been snowed under, so far as Fell pony lore was concerned. It is a compliment to Fell pony breeders to find that the Dales pony men are scrapping their first idea of a Dales pony and are claiming not only the Fell pony type as their ideal of a Dales pony, but are going in strongly for Fell pony blood as well to manufacture their improved Dales pony.

The Dales Galloway of the old type was certainly bred from a Fell pony, and the best of them were like their smaller relatives, noted trotters. Many of them owed their trotting capabilities to a horse of Border Galloway descent, the noted Old Comet. This breed of Dales horses is known as the 'Comet' breed. Several sons of Old Comet were used as sires, and many of their progeny were sold for high prices. Comet descended sires are much in request at this day, and if Dales pony men would, instead of poaching on the preserves of the Fell Pony Society, cross their registered mares with sires full of 'Old Comet' blood, and increase the height of their Dales and call them Dales horses, not only would their nomenclature be more correct, but they would have in breeding a highly valued animal for military or general purposes, even though it were a cross and newly manufactured breed as it is at present. Yours etc. `Waskew Fell'

'The Glengarry' referred to is either full brother to Highland Laddie, the galloway /roadster which won the Cup for the Best Pony Sire at The Royal Show, Chester, which may have had some Highland blood or the galloway/roadster cross by Merry John by Merry Driver. The horse of Border Galloway descent' was the trotter from Wales, almost certainly Trotting Comet (1411 HHSB):

The answer to the letter from 'Waskew Fell' appeared in the next edition of *The Live Stock Journal*, in these words:

Sir, - I should be obliged if you would allow me space to reply in defence of Dales ponies to 'Waskew Fell's' letter, which appeared in your issue of February 27th. The letter referred to is most interesting, and is evidently written by one who has the welfare of Fell ponies truly at heart. I admire his enthusiasm, and agree with him that the Fell pony is the most wonderful of all our small native breeds of British Mountain and Moorland ponies. I, however, cannot allow his whole hearted condemnation of the larger pony, the Dales, to pass unchallenged. 'Waskew Fell' appears to be thinking of what has happened over the past seventy years only, whereas it is an acknowledged fact that there have been semi-wild native ponies on both sides of the Pennine Range, possibly as long as there has been semi-wild ponies in the New Forest, and they are mentioned in King Edward I's time.

The ponies of the West side of the great backbone of the North of England are named Fell ponies, and those on the East side, Dales ponies. I feel sure 'Waskew Fell' will agree with me when I say that these ponies were originally one and the same. Teesdale, Weardale, East and West Allendale and Tynedale were busy centres of lead mining ages before there were railways by which to transport the lead ore to the ships in the North-east coast seaports, and Dales ponies were used in hundreds for carrying the lead upon their backs on those great journeys, over rough tracks, which are still shown on the Ordnance Survey Maps as 'lead roads'. These roads never had a wheel over them.

Dales ponies were used over a very long period for this purpose, right up to within living memory of the older of our Dalesmen. These ponies had to work hard, and would be fed for hard work; that care and attention would have a natural tendency to increase their size. They were as surefooted as goats, and were bred to get over the ground quickly. It is from this stock that our present day Dales ponies descend, and not from the Fell pony, as stated by 'Waskew Fell.'

Within the last two years the British Army has purchased in the dales of Northumberland and Durham, upwards of 200 Dales ponies, all over 14 hands, and not exceeding 14 hands 2 inches. All were over five years of age, weighing half a ton and with a girth of 68 inches and able to carry 21 stone on a mountain.

General Bate, the Army buyer, who is judging the Mountain and Moorland classes at the London Pony Show this week, wouldn't look at an animal which showed the slightest sign of a carthorse cross. Every animal he has purchased is a truely bred Dales pony. The Dales Pony Society, which 'Waskew Fell' accuses of having 'a very hazy idea as to what a Dales pony was' and which was established in the year 1916, has now over 700 members, each paying an annual subscription of 5s.,and has roughly 800 Dales ponies registered in the National Pony Society's Stud Book. The poor old Fell Pony Society, which was established some thirty years ago, by sound good fellows like Dr.R.W.Gibson of Orton, Tebay, and the late Col.Wingate Saul, is sadly in need of some young blood to help Dr. Gibson today. I think our friend 'Waskew Fell' should think all this carefully over, and then perhaps he will agree with me that the present-day Dales pony is so much of a military and general purpose animal that breeders are having the greatest difficulty to keep pace with military and general purpose demands.

It always strikes the writer as the strangest state of affairs that the breeders of Fell ponies are invariably content to give all their ponies away to dealers at places like Brough Hill Fair, instead of the breeders finding a direct market themselves. The Fell Pony Society should take a leaf out of the Dales Pony Society's book upon sales for their ponies.

There again I say the Fell pony men are dead asleep. Breeders of Fell ponies do not trouble to register their young eligible Fell ponies, and members of the Fell Pony Society Committee seem to forget that it is their duty to get such entries. The result of this is proved by the registration of Mr Roy B. Charlton's mare Robinson's Gipsy, the subject of these letters in The Live Stock Journal.

I agree that this mare, probably the greatest north country mare living, was bred in Fell pony country from Fell pony parents, and if she had been registered before she came to maturity I have no doubt she would have been accepted for the Fell pony side of the Stud Book; but she happened to be one of those unfortunately neglected ponies, sold as a two year old for an old song in Penrith Auction Mart. The purchaser, Mr Robinson, took her into Durham County, and when she reached the age of four years, he submitted her to Dales Pony Society inspectors, who rightly measured her 13h.3ins. One inch beyond the Fell pony maximum height; and there she is, one of the foundation stock mares for the new register of pedigree Dales ponies.

Let us turn to the three Fell pony stallions, the photographs of which were shown in The Live Stock Journal and which 'Waskew Fell' says 'are the type of pony favoured by Fell pony breeders and are bred on orthodox Fell pony lines'. One of the three, Linnel Heather, the pony which headed Mr Roy Charlton's championship group of Mountain and Moorland ponies at the London Show a year ago, is by Black Blooming Heather by Blooming Heather (Gibson's of Widdy Bank-in-Teesdale). The dam of Linnel Heather is Stonedress Polly (Dales) by Highland Laddie III by Little John. Everyone of the above named ponies were bred in the Dales and not Westmorland or Cumberland, the home of the Fell pony. Linnel Heather is from registered Dales parents, and was actually registered himself by Mr Roy B.Charlton as a Dales pony. Mr Charlton sold him as a three year old. The new owner won an £80 Ministry Premium with him through the Fell Pony Society, so it is necessary to forget that he was a registered Dales pony and have re-registered him as a Fell pony. He is now called an orthodox Fell pony.

Let us go one more year back at the London Pony Show, and we find a pony named Hilton Fashion, owned by Lord Lonsdale, heading the winning Fell pony group. Hilton Fashion was bred by Mr John Townson, of Hilton Moor, West Auckland, Co.Durham. His dam is the famous prize-winning registered Dales pony mare, White Heather. This mare won the Dales pony brood mare class so far back as 1908 in Newcastle. Hilton Fashion's full brother is a registered Dales pony, and has had more than one Dales Pony Society premium.

No, Mr.'Waskew Fell', there are any number of truly bred Dales ponies in the Dales today. Before concluding, I want to refer to just a few of the fast trotting 'Fell' ponies 'Waskew Fell' is so proud of - and he has good reason to be proud, if he would only give the name 'Dales' a fair crack of the whip. He mentions Atkinson's Doll and Heather Belle. Does he know that Mr Dent's brown pony of Baldersdale was the dam of both these famous trotters? Baldersdale is right down Teesdale near Cotherstone, in Dales pony country, and we claim these ponies as Dales ponies, and not Fell ponies.

The fact of the whole matter is that the ponies were originally identical, but known by different names. The two districts are so near together there was bound to be overlapping and crossing of one family with another. The Fell Pony Society got some twenty-five years start of the Dales Pony Society. They not only registered the ponies of Westmorland and the West Country, but they poached in the Dales, registering very many of our purely bred Dales ponies in the Fell section of the Stud Book. 'Waskew Fell' wishes to say that these ponies have always been Fell ponies. Little John and his full sister Weardale Polly (surely the latters name speaks for itself?), and Little John's son, Old Blooming Heather, were all Dales ponies. Some thirty years ago Blooming Heather's round was from Langdon Beck, in Teesdale, over to St. John's Chapel, in Weardale, down the dale to Stanhope Town over night, then across and up Teesdale through Middleton Town then home. Yet they got him a Fell number in the Stud Book and persist in their arguments that the registration made him into a Fell pony. Please, 'Waskew Fell' let us get right down to it. I contend that originally the ponies were one and the same breed of semi-wild pony, which was indigenous to the Pennine Range and the surrounding Fells and Dales; that the different conditions under which the ponies have been kept and the purposes for which they have have been required over a very long period, have set the Fell pony at a height of 13 hands to 13h. 2in., whilst the Dales pony stands a hand higher, and, although built on heavier and stronger lines, he is equally a pony all over. Yours etc.,

`Crossfell'

'Waskew Fell' was Dr R. W. Gibson MD and 'Crossfell' was R. B. Charlton. The May issue of the *Live Stock Journal* published a reply from 'Waskew Fell' reiterating his beliefs along with the following item:

A YORKSHIRE OPINION

In the Dales of North Yorkshire and Durham, within the past two years, the Army has purchased almost all the suitable material that it can lay its hands upon, so that amongst hill farmers in those parts the breeding of pure stock is exciting much more attention than it used to do, says 'The Yorkshire Post'. In a recent article in the 'Journal' of the Ministry of Agriculture on this breed of pony, Mr Roy Charlton speaks of it as the most saleable kind of horse that the North of England is producing today.

'The outer world' he says 'appears to have discovered the Dales pony only recently, and they are being sold as deer-stalking ponies for Scotland, and the Spanish Government is buying Dales stallions. They really are booming.'

The Fell pony of the Lake District, for instance, lives a wild and exposed life, and Mr Charlton says it is rarely called upon to do any work, the mares paying for their rough keep in the produce that is sent periodically in droves to local horse fairs. On the other hand, the Dales pony does a lot of work for its owner on the farm. Consequently, it is better fed, and in course of generations it has developed on sturdier and stiffer lines. Certainly, the specimens to be seen at local shows impress one with their spirit and the embodiment of strength in a small compass.

This exchange of ideas and theories is open to criticism on quite a few points but the most interesting thing about it is that Dr R. W. Gibson MD, of Orton, Westmorland was a member, and later the representative, of the original Fell Pony Committee, and a Council member of the Fell Pony Society. Roy B. Charlton was a founder member of the Dales Pony Improvement Society, the strength of which, during the early years, was largely due to his great talent for publicity. This, however, was not to last much longer as he was beginning to change his allegiance, as instanced in the following report in the *Live Stock Journal* of May 1926:

> Mr R.Charlton, now a Council member of the Fell Pony Society, as well as the Dales Pony Improvement Society, gave a talk on Mountain and Moorland Ponies to the pupils of the Cumberland and Westmorland Farm School, near Penrith, in March 1926. The meeting was an open one and several leading Fell pony breeders were present.
>
> Speaking of the Fell and Dales ponies, he confessed that today he was more keen on the Fell than he was on the Dales. He believed they should do more to let the world know the type of pony they had, advertise the breed more and let outsiders who bought ponies from them breed as they liked; but he pleaded that they, as breeders of Fell ponies in Fell pony country, should stick to the pure pony at home.
>
> He also stated that his opinion was that the Dales and Fell ponies, and also the Galloway ponies, were of the same breed, full of pony blood, and he added that the Fell pony remained the purest. Some people argued that the Dales was not a pure pony breed. He did not agree. He did agree that Clydesdale blood had been introduced, and that it had done a tremendous amount of harm, but apart from that, there were still pure Dales ponies. He went on to say that the main object of the Dales Pony Improvement Society was to wipe out the stallion with carthorse blood in him.

In November 1926 Mr Charlton gave an illustrated talk on British Breeds of Ponies, at Alston. When speaking of the ponies of northern Britain, he remarked that there was a striking similarity between the Highland and the Dales. In the Highland breed, as in the Dales of a few years ago, there were too many signs of Clydesdale blood, which led to nothing but trouble. When the Dales Pony Society was started 10 years ago there were far too many half-bred horses knocking about; now, with the help of stallions of Fell blood, they were back to true pony type. Personally, he preferred the Fell, his ideal being under 14.0 hands, but men like John Dalton, who aimed at producing a bigger animal of pony type, had done wonderfully. The old Galloway of south-west Scotland had almost passed away. It was the same type as the Dales, and not many years ago, Mr Matthew Marshall won at Stranraer with a mare that was a pure Dales pony. He continued by saying that he was now of the opinion that it was unnecessary to have two societies for Fell and Dales - there was a difference in height but the blood was intermingled - and he considered it was a bad rule which prevented such ponies as Alston Comet and Blackthorn from holding Fell pony premiums because they happened to be registered in the Dales section of the Stud Book.

In December 1926 Roy Charlton became the secretary of the Fell Pony Society, a post he occupied until 1934, and directed his considerable energies towards saving the threatened Fell pony breed from extinction. He remained a council member of the Dales Pony Improvement Society and became President for 1931, but the Dales pony never again enjoyed his full support. He dealt with publicity for both breeds and from hence forward Dales ponies were treated as an addendum to the Fell pony and it became the practice to speak of the two breeds as one, 'the Fells and Dales'. The Dales were described as too full of Clydesdale blood to be anything other than a small carthorse. The known Clydesdale blood was limited to Royal Ratho (Bendle Squire), Royal Lothian (Lothian Prince) possibly Sir Harry (Young Sir Harry, Black Boy and Highland Duke), one mare each for Carlatton, and possibly Royal Treasure and Black Samson (Norfolk Cob) plus Hummerbeck Beauty by Smart Buchlyvie. Some Clydesdale blood had also gone into the Fells.

Dales Ponies were at this time becoming increasingly popular and the very successful Dales Pony Improvement Society became complacent. The pony was still supreme for light trade work and as the power unit of small hill farms, but there was a veiled threat from the increasing number of motor vans and lorries.

In 1922 the Board of Agriculture ceased awarding Premium Grants for pony breeding. For some years the War Office had been considering the quality of their army horses. With pressure from the National Pony Society Council, the War Office was now prepared to support a move to get more native pony blood into their troop horses and offered four War Office Premiums of £80 per stallion to replace those of the Board of Agriculture. Dales stallions which held War Office Premiums from 1923 were Hilton Jock, Kirkdale Hero, Ouston Model, Stanhope Hero, Alston Comet, Brown Jock, Snowhope Fashion, Lord Dundas, Linnel Midnight, Lord Dewdrop, What's Wanted and Glenholme.

Sadly, horse breeding in general was about to enter the hard times of the Depression and the War Office began to run down the cavalry in favour of motorised divisions. This resulted in War Office Premiums being discontinued from 1930.

12
THE INTER-WAR YEARS 1926-36

THE DALES PONY ENTRY in the Stud Book for 1925 to 1927 was 216 plus two Dales cobs and one gelding, against a total entry of 119 Fell ponies. Fell numbers were improving as those of the Dales were falling. Of the 50 Dales colts registered 6 became stallions holding War Office Premiums in 1929-1930. These were Hazelgill Chief 1308 (Black Blooming Heather/Skeddale Scamper), Kirkhaugh Pride 1445 (Alston Comet/Kirkhaugh Model), Searchlight 1490 (Ouston Model/Starlight XII), Snowhope Hero 1427 (Kirkdale Hero/Fairy Glance), Rigg Comet 1433 (Linnel Comet/Grange Fashion) and the grey, Hilton Comet 1469, (Mettles Lad/White Heather II), foaled in 1916, the older half brother of Hilton Jock and Hilton Fashion. Other colts which became successful entires were Linnel Nigger 1316 (Dalesman/Ouston Peggy), Bonnie Blooming Heather 1324 by (Glengarry/Batts Nancy) and the black Tweddle Hero 1343 by Glengarry out of the roan mare (5166 Dales) Roanie. William Hully of the Bousefield Stud entered a colt bred by S. A. Moffat of Orton, Tebay, which shows that the Comet influence had not abated - the dark bay Bousefield Enterprise 1400, foaled in 1922, was by Comet by Young Comet by Old Comet by Daddy's Lad; which was by Young Comet by Old Comet!

Only 14 of the 160 Dales mares were by Fell stallions which were all, with one possible exception, from Dales lines. Of these 14, three were by Linnel Greybird (breeding unknown), three by Pendragon Comet by Teasdale Comet, three by Little John II (1329 Fell) by Pendragon (767 Fell) by British Boy by Yorkshire Fashion; one each by Brown Heather (1210 Fell) by Valence Heather (Dales), Heather Jock II (1211 Fell) by Black Blooming Heather (674 Dales), British Boy by Yorkshire Fashion, Blooming Heather II (Blooming Heather/Queen of the Dales by Black Jock); Heltondale Victor by Weardale Hero by Teasdale Comet and Goldsborough (1231 Fell) by Just-in-Time by Bendal Squire. The Dales influence is clearly evident in the Fell sires used on the Dales mares.

Dales mares of note are the black, Snowhope Dewdrop

(5012)(Kirkdale Hero/Dewdrop), bred by John Dalton and foaled in 1924. (5131)Snowhope Beauty, by an un-named sire by Yorkshire Fashion out of (5447 Dales)Greenside Beauty by British Boy (574 Fell) by Yorkshire Fashion; she was black with a star and white hind fetlocks, foaled in 1922, bred by John Winder of Ravenstonedale and owned by John Dalton. One of Stanhope Beauty's daughters, (5525)May Beauty by Ouston Model 1215, foaled in 1927 is included; and Stainton Grey (5465) by Gentleman John (907 Dales) dam unknown, which became the foundation mare of the Burdon ponies bred by Harry Barron. Another was the black (5623)Kexwith Darkie by Linnel Comet (841 Dales) out of a dam of unidentified breeding, which appears in many modern extended pedigrees. Richard Watson's lovely grey mare (5472)Glenholme Supremacy (Hilton Jock/Glenholme Success) and (4504)Kielder Damsel II by Linnel Greybird (984 Fell) of unknown breeding, out of Prospect Damsel by Silver Top (833 Dales) out of the dark dun Prospect Jean are all to be found in Volume 19.

Among the 43 Fell colts and stallions registered at the same time are Glengarry Again (1461 Fell) by Glengarry (1019 Dales) out of Batts Nancy (Dales Supp.1921) by Black Blooming Heather (674 Dales) and Linnel Boy (1260 Fell) by Guy Mannering (937 Dales) out of (3722) Linnel Fancy by Dalesman (572 Fell). Eleven are either by or out of a Dales pony, for example Linnel Mite (1460 Fell) out of (5460 Dales) Linnel Dolly by Dalesman and Minstrel Boy by the transferred Dales, Linnel Heather (888 Fell). Another 13 Fell colts carry a good infusion of Dales blood in the third generation, for example Fair View Victor (1530 Fell) by Walthwaite Ranger (1157 Fell) by Troutbeck Swell (758 Fell) by Dalesman (572 Dales); out of (5453 Fell)Fair View Zeb by Linnel Heather (888 Fell ex Dales) by Black Blooming Heather (674 Dales) out of (3206 Dales)Stonedress Polly.

Included among the 88 Fell mares are 56 carrying strong Dales influence; to name but a few: Bretherdale Don by Dalesman out of Fair View Zeb by Linnel Heather, Fanny out of Lucy by Lingcropper II (now Linnel Comet), Ladybird X out of (4532 Dales)Linnel Dame, Linnel Dolly by Dalesman out of Potter's Dolly by Norfolk Cob and Linnel Frolic out of Linnel Coquette by Guy Mannering.

One of two mares of out-cross breeding which were entered was the mare Holwick Maid (5052 Dales) by Satire (18911 CHSB) a Clydesdale which travelled in Cumberland in 1919, out of a mare by Flashlight (7811 HHSB), foaled in 1898, bred and owned by John Wannop of Westheral, Cumberland. Holwick Maid was bred by John Graham of Hethersgill, Carlisle, and owned by The Countess of Strathmore and Kinghorne. Neither the foaling date nor the breeding of Satire and

Flashlight were given. No known progeny were ever registered. The second was the mare(5218) Mickley Queen, foaled in 1917 by Sir Gilbert, the Wilson pony by Sir Horace out of an un-named Dales mare. She became the dam of the colt Mickley King (1362 Dales)in 1925.

The colours of the 214 Dales ponies entered still show an interesting variance: 79 were brown or dark bay, 64 were black, 40 were grey, 22 were bay, 3 were roan: (5166 Dales) Roanie (Teasdale Comet/Roanie of Wadsworth by Real Fashion out of a mare by Blooming Heather) and her daughters, (5837 Dales) Tweddle Beauty by Glengarry and (5473 Dales) Tweddle Fashion by Brown Jock (973 Dales). The only dun, with a black list, was 5168 Mousie by Glengarry out of a mare by Blooming Heather.

At the National Pony Show in 1925, the four-year-old Dales stallion Linnel Nigger was second in the Dales, Fell and Highland stallion class. At the same show in 1926, the Dales mares Snowhope Beauty (Yorkshire Fashion/Greenside Beauty), Snowhope Dewy (Kirkdale Hero/Dewy) and Lucky Star III (Linnel Comet/Homage) took first prize for the best group of three. The 1927 Group of Three was again won by the Dales, this time by Mr John Dalton's trio of mares Snowhope Dewdrop (Kirkdale Hero/Dewdrop), Snowhope Beauty and Snowhope Dewy. The same three mares stood in the same order in the first three places in the Brood Mare class.

This report was published in the *Live Stock Journal* of April 23rd, 1926:

> The dashing, vigorous Dales pony was seen to advantage yesterday at Bishop Auckland, on the occasion of the annual selection of premium stallions for the various districts - four premiums being offered by the War Office to the value of £80 each. The event was organised by The Dales Pony Improvement Society. There was a fair entry, and the quality of the animals, which were true to the pony type, was very well maintained. In the field adjoining Gaunless Auction Mart, a representative attendance of the public assembled to witness the animals showing their paces, including War Office and Ministry representatives.
>
> Mr J. W. Dalton's young stallion Snowhope Fashion, which was awarded the Weardale premium, has been a prominent winner and is descended from well known prize-winning stock, his sire being Kirkdale Hero and the dam being the well known Fairy Glance, winner of numerous prizes at the leading shows of late years.
>
> Ouston Model, a jet black five year old, shown by Mr J. H. Johnson of Crook, was put up for sale by public auction at the Gaunless Mart, and sold for 41 guineas. Brown Jock looked well. He got the Barnard Castle premium after a successful year in the Weardale area. Weardale Perfect, one of last year's winning stallions, had met with an accident

and was therefore unable to compete.

The premium winners were selected for the following districts:-

Barnard Castle and Swaledale:- Brown Jock, 10 years old, sired by Bendal Squire out of Heather Lass by Blooming Heather, owned by Mr J J Beadle, Middleton-in-Teesdale. Reserve:- Hazelgill Chief, a four year old sired by Black Blooming Heather out of Sleddale Scamper, owned by Mr W W Watson.

Weardale:- Snowhope Fashion, three years old. Reserve:- Tuer's Spring (860 Fell) by Dalesman out of a mare by Blooming Heather, owned by Mr J. Tuer of Penrith.

Hexham and District:- Hazelgill Chief. Reserve:- Merry Jock, also owned by Mr W W Watson.

North-West Durham:- Ouston Model. Reserve:- Hilton Fashion, owned by Mr F James, Riding Mill.

A total of 131 ponies were entered in the Dales section of Volume 20 of the Stud Book (1928-30), whereas 70 ponies were entered in the Fell section. Among the 27 Dales stallions and colts was the 14.1 Black Diamond, foaled in 1925 and bred by Ralph Kirkbride of Whygill Head, Appleby. His breeding was unusual, he was by the unknown Staggs Fell Hero by Young Surprise out of a 14.2 black Dales mare by Sir Harry II, Grand-dam by British Boy by Yorkshire Fashion. The breeding of Young Surprise is not stated, but if it was Clydesdale then Sir Harry II was likely to have been Sir Harry II (1167 HHSB) who was bred at Selby in Yorkshire and went to Scotland, rather than Young Sir Harry or Black Boy.

One of the 13 grey ponies in this volume was the colt Hilton's Wonder by Hilton Comet (1469 Dales) out of (6015 Dales) Westgate Black Bess by the Hackney Norfolk Swell (545 HHSB) otherwise known as Perfection (545 HHSB). Also registered was the strawberry roan colt Tweddle Star (1672 Dales) foaled in 1928 by Linnel Midnight out of Roanie, her third roan foal.

Seven Dales colts were entered from the Linnel Stud including Linnel Romany 1624 (Linnel Nigger/Robinson's Gypsy) foaled in 1926 and later exported to Spain; two sons of Stanhope Beauty, Linnel Success 1710 by Linnel Brown Boy (1523 Fell) and Linnel Surprise by Bonnie Blooming Heather 1324. Three were by Linnel Midnight out of Dales mares and Linnel Pretty Boy was by Linnel Raven (1602 Fell) out of (4318 Dales) Fenella II. Linnel Raven was by Teasdale Comet.

Included among the entered Dales mares were (5897)Linnel Gipsy by Linnel Midnight and (5902)Linnel Roma by Linnel Nigger, both out of (3775 Dales) Robinson's Gypsy. Others by Linnel Midnight were (5888)Linnel Christie out of Fenella II (4318) and (6077) Linnel

Mr John Dalton's winning group, 1929: (left to right) Snowhope Perfection, Snowhope Beauty, Lord Dewdrop (N.P.S. Pony Show, London), 1929.

Kielder out of 3339 Prospect Damsel, daughter of the dark dun (3241)Prospect Jean by Silver Top (833 Dales).

Entered in the Fell Section were Linnel Flame by Linnel Midnight (1261 Dales); Linnel Dandy (1616 Fell) and Linnel Harvester (1620 Fell) by Tweddle Hero (1343 Dales) and Linnel Lingcropper (1621 Fell), Linnel Natty (1622 Fell) and Linnel Sportsman (1625 Fell) all by Linnel Boy (1260 Fell) by Guy Mannering (937 Dales).

In the Fell Section were the mares (5887 Fell) Linnel Bunty by Tweddle Hero (1343 Dales) out of (4177 Fell)Bess of Hardendale by Dalesman (572 Dales); (5896 Fell) Linnel Flora by Linnel Midnight (1261 Dales) out of (4894 Fell) Linnel Coquette by Guy Mannering (937 Dales) and (5900 Fell) Linnel Nina by Linnel Midnight (1261 Dales) out of Linnel Nellie by Glengarry (1019 Dales).(6076 Fell) Linnel Frisk was also out of Linnel Coquette and (6078 Fell)Linnel Nin was out of (5901 Fell)Linnel Nellie . Linnel Rhoda was out of (5013 Fell) Rhoda VI by Linnel Comet (841 Dales). Linnel Nigger (1316 Dales) also sired (5852 Fell) Gowbarrow Belle and Brown Jock (973 Dales) sired (6047 Fell)Polly of Craigmore.

At the National Pony Show of 1928, Ouston Model stood second in the large breed stallion class, and the Dales Group was second in their class but the 13-year-old Dales mare, Stanhope Beauty, took first place and the Lord Arthur Cecil Cup in the Brood Mare class.

Mr John Dalton took all the honours at the 1929 London Show, the Dales stallion, Snowhope Hero (Kirkdale Hero/Fairy Glance) stood top of the Stallion class, with Lord Dewdrop (Kirkdale Hero /Dewdrop) standing third. Snowhope Beauty won the Brood Mare class and, together with Lord Dewdrop and Snowhope Perfection (Dalesman/ Perfection), stood first in the group class.

Following the purchase of the eight Dales stallions by the Spanish Government, further consignments were taken of 12 Dales-bred registered Fell stallions, two sons of Linnel Heather - Linnel Snip and Minstrel Boy - plus Linnel Boy, Linnel Glen, John Bradley, Wallthwaite Ranger, Wait and See, Blencathra, Jacks Delight, Linnel Moor Boy, Bousefield John Bull, Good Hope and Moss Crop II. They went into the mountainous areas of north-eastern Spain, behind San Sebastian, as improvers for army pack pony stock. They ran with Asturian and Garrano mares, the modern representatives of their ancient forebears which would have been ridden along Hadrian's Wall and the Roman roads of Britain. When Roy Charlton was in the area some years later he saw many Spanish mares supporting black foals.

The army had been taking ponies in considerable numbers over the years and the council of the Dales Pony Improvement Society voiced their unease, following which no more ponies were taken from the dales until the Second World War. Only 48 Dales ponies, including 6 cobs, and 51 Fells were entered between 1931 and 1933 in Volume 21. Of the 5 Dales stallions entered in the Dales section the most influential was James Akrigg's **Black Prince II** 1809, foaled in 1929 by Black Diamond out of a Dales mare by Sir Harry, grand-dam by Young Comet, great grand-dam by Merry John, fourth dam by Little John. Black Prince II was black with a star, stripe and snip with a white hind pastern, bred by Simon Calvert of Greenses, near Muker in Swaledale. The only other stallions to leave progeny were George Wearmouth's dun Frank II (1781) by Ouston Model (1215 Dales) out of his dun mare Creamy III (4273); and the brown, Prince Royal (1773)(Dalesman/Princess XIII by Black Blooming Heather), who displayed a star, stripe and two white hind coronets.

Among the 37 mares only (6197)Calva Beauty by Mountain Boy (1401 Fell) by Pendragon Comet and Thomas Stainton's (6206) Tebay Blossom by Mountain Ranger (598 Fell) by Park End King, were got by Fell sires. 6254 Elegance III is said to be by Tyron Rufus which is probably Tyrone Rufus (4050 HHSB) mis-spelt, out of (4780 Dales) Endurance by Young Sir William by Sir William by Billy Bounce, of

Snowhope Purple Heather, champion at the Royal Show, 1935.

roadster descent. An interesting entrant is G.W. Bowbank's (6439) Grey Queen II by Brown Jock (973 Dales) out of (4692 Dales) Hummerbeck Beauty by the Clydesdale, Smart Buchlyvie (19,283 CHSB). This very good mare was held in high regard and scooped many prizes. There was also (6246)Lucy VII who was foaled in 1914 by Highland Duke by Sir Harry, who was one of the last known Clydesale outcrosses.

Of the six Dales cobs in this Volume, four were of unknown breeding, (6273)High House Bet was by Royal Ratho (12,338 CHSB) but the sixth entry was undeniably interesting. The 14.3, grey (6274 Dales) White Lees Jean , foaled in 1912, was by Meteor by Young Comet, out of Janet by Prince Stockwell (5761 HHSB) out of an unknown Highland mare. Prince Stockwell stood at Haltwhistle, Northumberland from March, 1897. His sire Stortford Prince (3988 HHSB) was by the famous **Dangelt** (174 HHSB) out of (1645 HHSB) Lady Lucy by Knapp (399 HHSB) by Shepherd F.Knapp, foaled in 1857, his dam was a mare by Whalebone

(The Clark Horse) a son of Sherman by Justin Morgan , the foundation stallion of the Morgan Horses. The sire of Shepherd F. Knapp was the Eaton Horse, who goes back to Jary's Bellfounder (55 HHSB) who was exported and became a foundation sire of the American Trotters, with both Shales and Fireaway lines. Prince Stockwell's dam, (653 fsHHSB) Magdalen, was by Stockwell, a winner of the 2,000 Guineas and the St Leger and one of the most successful racehorse sires of his day. Stockwell came from the Eclipse line which goes back to the Darley Arabian. No Dales progeny was registered from White Lees Jean, bred by Messrs. Lowdon of Blanchland, Shotley Bridge but there is always a possibility that something of hers came through the grading-up register in later years. It remains a mystery why she was registered as, a Dales cob at the age of at least 19 years.

Among the 12 Fell Stallions entered in Volume 21 was Linnel Nero (Linnel Darkie/Rhoda IV by Linnel Comet (841 Dales)),Linnel Smasher (Linnel Darkie/3775 Robinson's Gipsy), three with Dalesman as grand-sires and one by Heltondale Victor by Weardale Hero by Teasdale Comet.

Among the 36 Fell mares were the Dales mares (5902 Dales) Linnel Roma (Linnel Nigger/Robinson's Gipsy) and (5897 Dales)Linnel Gipsy (Linnel Midnight/Robinson's Gipsy) now transferred to the Fell Stud Book and re-entered as (5902 Fell) Linnel Roma and (5897 Fell) Linnel Gipsy. The latter's daughter (6381 Fell) Linnel Gipsy Queen by Linnel Brown Boy (1523 Fell) a grandson of Dalesman, was also entered. One of (3331 Dales) Stanhope Beauty's daughters, Linnel Belle II (6477 Fell) was also entered, with her dam's number changed to (3331 Fell) though she was never transferred. Six of the other mares were out of Dales mares and 20 had a Dales sire or dam or both in the third generation. The Dales influence on Fell breeding was of significant but unmentioned value between the wars.

Volume 22 of the NPS Stud Book covering 1934 to 1936 had a healthier Dales entry of 87 ponies. The most important of the 19 stallions and colts was the 14.2 brown, seven-year-old **Snowhope Purple Heather** 1929 by Mountain Jester (1409 Fell) out of Jess by Pendragon Comet (974 Fell) out of a mare by Beacon Swell out of a mare by Yorkshire Fashion. He was bred by Mr R. G. Spenceley of Howsyke, near Leyburn and foaled in 1929. His sire Mountain Jester was a 13.3 black pony by Mountain Ranger (598 Fell) out of Darkey II, by Lothian Prince out of Darkey by Merry Hero (327 Fell) out of Polly by Mountain Hero. His dam Jess was a very good mare by Pendragon Comet (974 Fell) by British Boy by Teasdale Comet. Purple Heather was bought as a three-year-old by Dick Cowperthwaite who said he was the best Dales pony he had ever seen. He travelled him very successfully for a few years before selling him to John Dalton, who registered him with his Snowhope prefix. In his very old age, the stallion was grazing in a field next to some pit ponies which broke through to attack him. Sadly, the old boy did not recover from his injuries. As Snowhope Purple Heather he became a particularly notable stallion and is to be found in the pedigree of every Dales pony alive today. Two other Snowhope stallions were also entered, the brown, Snowhope Lad (1879) (Snowhope Hero/Snowhope Beauty) foaled in 1931 and Snowhope Perfect 2020 (Snowhope Purple Heather/Snowhope Perfection), foaled in 1936.

The three-year-old colt, Dales Fashion (Black Prince II/Grange Fashion) was exported to Melbourne, Australia in July 1936. Other colts which became successful stallions were Blackton Glory (Glenholme/ Gloaming II by Glengarry), Prince Comet II (1933) (Black Prince II/ Kexwith Darkie by Linnel Comet), and the grey Danny Boy (1975) (Wheatside Favourite/Dolly Grey III). Both Prince Comet II and Danny Boy had three white fetlocks. The three-year-old brown colt Unicorn (1976), was by the 15.2, dark bay general purpose horse Wheatside Hero, out of a mare by Daddy's Lad. He stood half an inch over 14.2 hands and older breeders have often said that he was an exceptionally good stallion. Unfortunately he was cut before his stock was old enough to show his potential. Sonny Boy II (1877) by Kirkhaugh Pride, out of the roan Dales cob mare, (4982) Jeanie, was described as hackberry brown, a dappled dark bay. Of the other 12 colts, those by or out of Fell ponies were Forester VI (1926) by a two-year-old Fell colt out of a Dales mare by British Boy; Linnel Whiskey (2000) by Linnel Smasher and Linnel Laird (1999) and Lartington Heathercropper (1885 Dales) by Linnel Lingcropper. Forester VI sired only the grey filly, (7674 Dales) Polly Dyke out of a mare by Gentleman John (907 Dales).

Among the Dales mares entered in Volume 22 were (6919 Dales)Linnel Molly and (6920 Dales) Linnel Susan both by Linnel Smasher (Linnel Darkie/ Robinson's Gipsy) out of Dales mares; Linnel Darkie was a grandson of Dalesman. (6660 Dales)Rosgill Peggy by Heltondale Victor out of a Dales mare by Glengarry out of a mare by Dalesman; Rovegill Bonnie by Pendragon Comet by Teasdale Comet; Hazel V by an unregistered Black Prince by Silver Top (833 Dales) out of (4497 Fell) Hazel III by Highland Fashion (612 Fell) by Yorkshire Fashion out of a mare by Swaledale Comet by Norfolk Cob; and Jean X by a dark chestnut, Lord Derby out of a Dales mare. Ten registered mares and one gelding measuring 14.3 hands, should have been entered in the Cob section, together with Cragg Fashion 14.3½ hands and

Brownie X, 15 hands, but this system seems to have lapsed.

Twenty-six Fell colts were entered, all by Fell sires which all had some infusion of Dales blood with 15 out of dams of Dales extraction. The entry of Fell fillies include (6695 Fell)Linnel Brown Girl by Alston Comet (1063 Dales); (6669 Fell) Linnel Crosby by Glance Again (1677 Dales); (6673 Fell)Linnel Marina out of (3775 Dales)Robinson's Gipsy; and (6671 Fell)Linnel Firespark out of Harvest(3812 Dales). Nineteen others were by Linnel Lingcropper, 10 by Linnel Smasher and six by Linnel Gallant Boy, all carrying recent Dales blood. Others were out of Dales dams and grand-dams.

Brown remains the predominant colour: of the 87 ponies in Volume 22, 34 were brown, 25 were black, 16 were grey, 11 were bay and one was dun, the gelding Linnel David by Linnel Midnight out of (5404 Dales) Kielder Damsel II, the great, grand-daughter of the dun, Prospect Jean by Silver Top.

Premium awards for 1934-1936, were made up from grants from the War Office and the Race-horse Betting Levy Board. Premium Dales stallions were Black Prince II, Sonny Boy II, Snowhope Purple Heather and Danny Boy. They each travelled a district in Swaledale & Bowes, Alston & District and Stanhope & Westgate, covering 117 mares in 1934, 120 in 1935 and 179 in 1936.

13
THE SECOND WORLD WAR,
1939-1945

ONCE AGAIN THERE WAS A DEMAND for Dales ponies and breeders set about providing them. Mr William Patterson, who had been secretary of the Dales Pony Improvement Society since its establishment, took over as Treasurer and Mr J. B. Hinds became Secretary between 1940 and 1942. Renewed efforts were made to rustle up entries and 246 ponies were registered in the Dales section plus 12 re-entries and one transfer from the Fell Stud Book; Teesdale Ella was re-registered as a Dales at a great age, having been foaled in 1910 by the Dales stallion North Star II 900 (Rutherford's) out of the unregistered mare Magic. Of the total entries only 41 were actually foaled between 1937-39, 92 were foaled between 1930-36, 95 between 1920-30, 6 between 1900-19 and 4 were entered as aged; 16 were re-entries. Due to war conditions the Stud Book for 1937 to 1939 was not published until 1940.

Of the 20 Dales colts entered, the most influential was **Mountain Heather II** (2227) (Snowhope Purple Heather/May Blossom IV), foaled in 1936 and owned by Mr Thomas V. Emerson of the Wheatside Stud. He was a lively brown pony, bred by T. Hanlon of Gibbert Hill, Howden-le-Wear. His dam was by Black Blooming Heather out of Jenny Lind II (Highland Laddie III/Polly by North Star). It is told that in the general euphoria after winning a Dales championship for the first time, the Hanlon brothers were showing Mountain Heather off in Yarm when the stallion became so exuberant he lashed out and kicked in the plate glass window of a shop. The grey Brussleton Boy (2152) (Danny Boy/ Brussleton Folly by Black Blooming Heather), foaled in 1937, also became a popular stallion; Brown Prince (2130) (Black Prince II/4697 Limelight II by Linnel Comet) and Black Duke (2294) by the unregistered Black Oak by Black Diamond (1625 Dales) out of Betty by Teasdale Comet also appear in modern pedigrees.

Of the 225 mares and one gelding, 97 were of unknown breeding.

Nine were by known Fell stallions from Dales lines with one exception, (7226 Dales)Botany Lass by Mountain Ranger (598 Fell) out of an unknown mare. The sire of the 13.3 Mountain Ranger was the 14.0 grey Park End King, which was said to be by 'Comet', probably the grey Teasdale Comet. The dam of Mountain Ranger was the grey Scordale Queen by Blooming Heather.

The Dales mares with viable bloodlines are (7078) Brussleton Folly by Black Blooming Heather, the dam of Brussleton Boy and (7511)Brussleton Judy by Prince Comet II (1933 Dales) and(7474) Burdon Heather (Snowhope Purple Heather/Stainton Grey) the first to carry this prefix which Harry Barron brought to the fore in the 1960s. Another was 7032 Generous Gift by the unregistered 15.0 brown Wheatside Favourite out of Stanhope Beauty.

The colours of the 246 ponies entered between 1937 and 1939 were 94 black, 79 brown, 44 bay, 29 grey, 3 roan and 1 dun. The roans, (7516)Ivelet and (7579)Ouston Blossom of unknown breeding but Taffy(7366) was by Hilton Jock out of a mare by Daddy's Lad. The one dun, (7520) Dapper Filly was by Unicorn (1976) out of (6267) Lily IV (re-entered with George Wearmouth's prefix as Briscoe Lily in this volume) by the black Glenholme (1571) out of the dun Creamy III. Dalesmen habitually refer to both dark bay and bright bay as dark or light brown. If browns and bays are added, brown was still the predominant colour, as it was in the Scotch galloways.

One of the 22 Fell stallions and colts entered in the same years, Linnel Buster II was out of (5887 Dales) Linnel Bunty by Tweddle Hero (1343 Dales); Fell Model was by Black Diamond (1635 Dales) and Linnel Border Lad and Linnel Kielder were out of (5404 Dales) Kielder Damsel II from the line of Silver Top and the dun Prospect Jean. All the other colts and all of the 19 Fell mares in this Volume could boast of one or more Dales grandparents or great-grandparents.

Premiums were again awarded out of grants made by the War Office and the Racehorse Betting Control Board; the value of each grant was three premiums of £55 for 1936, three of £59.3s.4p. for 1937, four of £38.15s. for 1938 and four of £75 for 1939. Dales Premium stallions for 1937-1939 were Black Prince II, Unicorn, Prince Comet II, Snowhope Purple Heather, Blackton Glory, and Greenside Reformer. Travelling in allotted areas of Swaledale & District, Barnard Castle & District, East Durham, Weardale & District, Stainmore & District and Derwent Valley, they covered 135 mares in 1937, 290 in 1938 and 246 in 1939.

Volume 24 of the Stud Book (1940-43) held only 71 Dales pony entries, including the last to be entered in the Dales Cob Section, the 15 hand Kitty Grey II. The many mares, including young ones, which were taken for town work rarely returned and the few that did were usually without their registration papers and the number of registrations in all breeds was dropping. The National Pony Society had recieved a total entry of only 615 ponies, covering all pony breeds entered in the Mountain and Moorland section of Volume 24 of the Stud Book, compared with 1,134 entries in 1937-1939. In the Preface of the Volume 24 is the following appeal from the National Pony Society.

> It is earnestly hoped that members will keep the Society informed of any alterations or additions to entries and to enter all eligible stock. It is obvious that immediately after the war here will be a tremendous demand for horses and ponies, and apart from the fact that registered stock will always command higher prices, breeders surely have a responsibility to future generations to maintain the continuity of the pedigrees of the various breeds of ponies, which have been established in this country with so much forethought and expense in the past.

Only eight stallions or colts were entered of which 2321 **Black Jock II** was the most influential. A 14.2 black pony with a star, he was foaled in 1937 Black Prince II (1809 Dales) out of (5533 Dales) Rookby Kate by Pendragon Comet (974 Fell) by Teasdale Comet (904 Dales). His Grand-dam was (5532 Dales) Rookby Lass, foaled in 1914 by Brown Prince (before Dales registration) out of a mare by Teeswater Swell. Of the others only Brownberry II (2405), Oakley Prince (2427) and Raven Comet (2391) are to be found with registered progeny.

Among the 61 mares entered are the foundation mares of several important families. The first of Mr Bayles's Ackram ponies makes an appearance with the black mare (7748)**Ackram Polly**, foaled in 1936, by (1365 Dales)Black Diamond II together with (7747)Ackram Topsy, foaled in 1932, (by a Dales stallion out of a Fell mare) and her daughter, (7749)Ackram Lady, foaled in 1941 by Mountain Heather II(2227 Dales). These ponies used to horse the Bayles' smart Ice-cream vehicle and were a familiar sight around West Auckland and Barnard Castle. Two of William Iceton's mares by Blackton Glory (1895 Dales) were entered, (7807)Blackton Beautiful, out of 6197 Calva Beauty by Mountain Boy (1301 Fell)by Pendragon Comet by Teasdale Comet, and (7806)Blackton Glamour out of (5007)Glimmer by Goldsborough (1231 Fell) by Just in Time by Bendle Squire by Royal Ratho (12,338 CHSB) out of unregistered stock. Willy Iceton's farm at Blackton was eventually drowned by the new Reservoir in Baldersdale and he had to move lower down the dale. All his ponies worked on the land, gathering bracken and hay on sledges, tedding, gathering hay with sweeps, leading hay, (carting) and jagging (carrying) burdens of hay to sheep in the winters. The bay mare (7805)Briscoe Polly II, foaled in 1940 was another of the dun, Creamy III's foals. One of Hilton Jock's last foals, (7694)Grey Jean, foaled in 1936, was also entered.

Mr George H. Hodgson of Ivy House Farm Hilton, later to become President of the Breed Society, entered his first Dales mare, (7870)**Hilton Betty,** foaled in 1931. Black with a blaze and a few grey hairs in her near hind coronet, she was of unknown breeding. George often told of going to Yarm Fair where his grandfather bought his first Dales pony. The 18-month-old filly cost £8.10s. He considered himself to be very lucky as few youngsters had such a luxury during the great depression. It was the start of his lifelong interest in breeding and showing his Hilton Dales ponies. The mare worked on his farm and founded a line of grand ponies which continues through Hilton Gemini.

The family and forebears of Thomas Valentine Emerson had bred Dales ponies for many years. When they moved to Wheatside Farm, West Auckland, they took over the Wheatside prefix and entered Wheatside Beauty(7817), black with a star and three white fetlocks, foaled in 1937 by the unregistered Wheatside Favourite out of an unidentified Dales mare; her daughter by Mountain Heather II was the famous **Wheatside Perfection** (7855), known by the pet name of Fecky, a 14.2 black with a star and two white fetlocks, foaled in 1940. Her name can be found in the pedigrees of all Dales ponies today as the dam of the stallion Wheatside Perfect. In the showring she was never beaten. Wheatside Queen II (7816) was the other entry, a dark bay by Snowhope Purple Heather out of a Dales mare, the previous Wheatside Queen (5636)(Glengarry/Wheatside Topsy)was entered in 1927 by William Holmes who then owned Wheatside Farm.

The Dales section had many dams entered without numbers, such as the (7867 Dales) Glenwhelt Black Bess and (7869 Dales) Glenwhelt Blossom both out of May Blossom which should be (3611 Dales) May Blossom IV; and Sweet Bloom III out of Sunbiggin Betty, which should read (7540)Sunbegin Beauty. Also Polly Dyke by Forester which should be Forester VI (1926 Dales). This may have been due to records being destroyed but general lack of time or care in recording details was beginning to cause confusion.

Only What a Jem (7696) was by a Fell sire who carried a Dales lines through Robinson's Gipsy and Dalesman. Ackram Polly and Ackram Topsy with unknown Fell dams are the only others with possible Fell influence entered in this Stud Book.

There had been sustained effort to breed more ponies and a good number of foals must have been born and the future of the breed ensured. It had been a boom time for pony breeding with everything selling. Horse power had kept the Home Front going when petrol was

Black Prince II foaled in 1932.

rationed and horses had not yet been surplanted by tractors on the land and in the forests. Railway dray horses had not yet been superseded by lorries. Canals were of the greatest importance, where one horse could move tons of coal at a steady pace for great distances. Remount officers were searching for weight carrying ponies for army pack work and Mountain Artillery needed them to take the place of mules which had to be imported from overseas. Clydesdale and Cleveland Bay sires were used on Dales mares to breed active vanners particularly for railway express parcel delivery vans. It was a heartening wartime sight to see these well turned out horses rattling through city streets at a spanking trot, drawing the heavy four-wheeled vans in LMS, LNER and GWR livery. The number of pure-bred mares may have accommodated the burden of the cross-breeding but unfortunately they too were bought up by tradesmen coping with wartime transport and little petrol.

Up to 1940, the National Pony Society had been run from their office at 12, Hanover Square, London, which was also the headquarters of the Hackney Horse Society. During the London blitz the offices were destroyed by bombing with the subsequent loss of many records. Wartime difficulties had not helped the efficiency of small societies and non-working ponies were not allowed rations of feed, so surplus ponies were put down. This did not much affect the Dales as, with few exceptions, all ponies worked including the brood mares.

Only 47 Fell ponies were entered in Volume 24. None of the 13 stallions and colts were by Dales sires but all could show varying degrees of Dales blood in their pedigrees, for example Linnel Romany II by Linnel Gallant Boy (1704 Fell) out of (5902 Fell)Linnel Roma by Linnel Nigger (1316 Dales) out of Robinson's Gipsy. Linnel Romany had double doses of Dalesman, Yorkshire Fashion and Norfolk Cob plus Glengarry in his pedigree. Three of the 22 mares were by Black Prince II (1809 Dales). Two more were by Linnel Duke (2145 Dales) and Snowhope Heather (1663 Dales). Nine had Dales grand-dams. The numbers were made up by 12 re-entries.

The grants for Dales stallion premiums were now only being awarded by the Racehorse Betting Control Board and supplemented by £35 pounds annually from the Dales Pony Improvement Society, which together gave four premiums to the value of £30 each for the years 1940 to 1943. The army was now motorised.

The Premium stallions were Blackton Glory, Greenside Reformer, Prince Comet II, Unicorn, Glenholme Surprise, Mountain Heather II, Brown Prince, Danny Boy, Black Jock II, Brownberry II and Raven Comet. They travelled the same districts and covered 235 mares in 1940, 109 in 1941, 105 in 1942 and 119 in 1943.

The peaceful sight of horses working or grazing in fields had been commonplace for generations; the belief that it would last forever was taken for granted. The National Pony Society was wrong, there was to be no further demand for horses or ponies and within a few years they had nearly all gone. It was some years before they began to slowly reappear in the guise of leisure horses and ponies; though a few native ponies, Highlands, Fells and Dales among them, continued to work in their usual roles.

14
POST-WAR DIFFICULTIES

---◆---

ONLY 50 DALES PONIES were entered in Volume 25 of the Stud Book (1945-47) against 123 in the Fell section and some Dales/Fell crossing was still going on. The eight colts were all by Dales stallions, one each by Snowhope Purple Heather 1929 and Prince Comet II 1933, two by Black Jock II 2321, three by Mountain Heather II and one by an unregistered son of Black Diamond 1635 named Herbert.

Of the 42 Dales mares only 5 were by Fell registered sires; (8140) Bleathgill Gipsy by Pendragon Comet (974 Fell) out of a Dales mare(unknown) , (8145)Dene Polly by Linnel Prim (2360 Fell) out of the 14.2 bay (8144 Dales) Dene Molly, Ghyll House Peggy by Purple Heather (1216 Fell) out of the unregistered Darkey, and her daughter Newlands Beauty by Coronation Boy (2043 Fell) which had two lines to Teasdale Comet through Heltondale Victor and one through Pendragon Comet. The other sires all had recent or earlier infusions of Dales blood.

Fell registered progeny of Dales sires at this time were the gelding, Birkett Bank Jackie by Black Prince II (1809 Dales), Birkett Bank Little Fan and Birkett Bank Perfection by Dalesman out of Fell mares by Dalesman. Fell entries carrying Dales lines were Linnel Dame by Linnel Lingcropper (Guy Mannering/Linnel Fancy by Dalesman out of (7624 Fell) Linnel Damsel out of (5404 Dales) Keilder Damsel II and Dene Shepherd Boy (2621 Fell) by Linnel Radiant (2399 Fell) out of Dales) (8144Dales)Dene Molly, now re-registered as 14.0 bay (8334 Fell)Dene Molly.

Although there was general agreement that cross-bred Dales and Fells should be registered in the dam's Stud Book, the progeny of the Dales mares Robinson's Gipsy and Linnel Dale, Dell, Dinkie, Coquette, Lady (by Sir Horace) and Linnel Belle II (out of Stanhope Beauty) had all been absorbed into Fell stock. Of the 30 Fell colts entered in Volume 25 all but one had Dales grand-sires or dams or both. All the 101 Fell mares of known breeding had Dales forebears in at least one line. Notable entries being Dalemain Romola by Linnel Gallant Boy out of (5902 Fell)Linnel Roma(Linnel Nigger/ Robinson's Gipsy, both Dales)

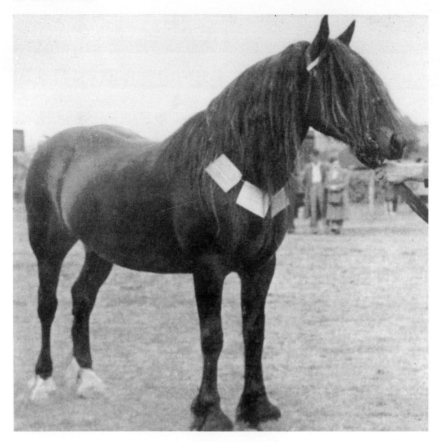

Mr J.W.Dalton's great prize-winning mare, Snowhope Heather Belle, foaled 1940.

which had been transferred from the Dales Stud Book in Volume 21, together with (5897 Fell)Linnel Gipsy (Linnel Midnight/Robinson's Gipsy, the dam of (6841 Fell)Dalemain Gipsy Queen (late Linnel Gipsy Queen) and (1760 Fell)Windsor Gipsy(late Railton Gipsy Black Princess) by Linnel Gallant Boy.

An interesting entry in the Highland Pony Section of the same volume was the mare 8406 Iona VI, foaled in 1942. Her dam was the unregistered mare, Peanut by Snowhope Lad (1879 Dales) out of White Spot by Mountain Ranger (598 Fell). It is possible that Snowhope Lad was the Dales pony used by the Earl of Ancaster when he was experimenting with a 'Dales' sire at his Glenartney Forest Highland Pony Stud around 1937. The pony was not named but was of good quality as the following description shows: 'This pony stands over fourteen hands high with great bone, fine long riding shoulders with a long rein and small pony head, and also a very correct mover.'

Only two Dales stallions entered in this Stud Book come through into modern pedigrees. One is the 14.2 black **Newlands Prince**(2478) (Prince Comet II/Generous Gift) foaled in 1942. His dam by the unregistered Wheatside Favourite was one of the four Dales offspring of Stanhope Beauty. His line runs through Wharton Beauty into Stainton ponies. The other stallion, **Mountain Prince** (2651)(Mountain Heather II/Ackram Polly), foaled in 1945, a black with a star and two white fetlocks, became the sire of Bousefield Dalesman, Midnight Star, Stainton Prince and some very good mares.

During the years from 1948 to 1952 , 93 Dales ponies were registered, 5 in 1948; 8 in 1949; 3 mares in 1950; one mare in 1951 and one colt in 1952. Only 8 ponies were foaled during these years. The others were all foaled during or before the war.

Of the 183 Fell ponies registered at the same time 50 were foaled in 1948; 48 in 1949; 12 in 1950; 14 in 1951; 6 in 1952 but none in 1953. This shows a sharp downturn in the fortunes of both breeds.

Two colts which produced no progeny and the filly (9418)Glenwhelt Jewel were by Linnel Romany II, a grandson of Linnel Roma by Linnel Nigger (1316 Dales) out of Robinson's Gipsy. They were the only ones sired by a Fell registered pony.

The Dales influence was now well disseminated throughout the Fells but Dales-bred stock continued to be entered in the Fell Section. One in particular was the stallion

Master John (2883 Fell). Black, white off hind heel. Foaled 1946. Height 14.0
Sire: Black Jock II (22321 Dales)
Dam: Dainty Molly(unregistered) by Seldom Seen (1628 Fell) by Pendragon Comet (974 Fell) by Teasdale Comet (904 Dales)
Breeder: Mr James Wilson of Kirkby Stephen

Master John passed into the ownership of Mr John Baxter of Guardhouse, Threlkeld. He was awarded a Fell Premium in 1952 and was the last Fell registered stallion to travel on foot. He sired 46 Fell ponies including the stallion Johnnie Walker, later exported to Canada. He also sired Wharton Master(4714 Fell), Guards Model(13708 Fell), and Merry John III(3709 Fell), which, together with their sire, were used on a few Dales mares during the mid-1960s. Master John was undoubtedly more Dales than Fell.

The Fell mares Lanquitts Betty, Brafell Madge II, Udale Dinah II,

J.W. Dalton with Horsley Miranda, bred by W.J. Dalton, foaled 1945, winner of Dales championship at the National Pony Show, Malvern, 1967.

Udale Lady Atkinson III and Udale Poll and the colt Lanquitts Pride, foaled in 1949, all by Black Jock II (2321 Dales); Dene Darkie by Black Prince II (1809 Dales) Peggy 25th and Town End Jewel by Rising Star (1403 Dales) were also entered in this Volume.

The Dales section of this Stud Book was full of errors and missing registration numbers. The distinguishing bracketed number and breed was discontinued in both Dales and Fell sections. Many ponies entered in the Dales Section were of unknown breeding, either unregistered or having lost their identification certificates. How many of these were actually out of or by registered stock will never be known, because during these years many ponies were sold without papers into markets flooded with redundant working animals.

One of the two Dales stallions of importance in this volume was **Lummas Comet** 2740 (Black Jock II/Lummas Beauty by Prince Comet II) foaled in 1945. He stood 14.1 and was black with a star and three white fetlocks and bred by John Robert Longstaff of Lummas House, Marske, Richmond, Yorks. Comet and his dam, (8700)Lummas Beauty out of an un-named Dales mare, were among the first ponies to carry the Lummas prefix; the lines from these ponies are strongly represented today by both the Lummas and Lowhouses ponies.

The other stallion was All Fours 3264, foaled in 1949, bred by G. W. Bowbank. He was a brown stallion standing 14.1 with an elongated star running down his forehead. His entry is incorrect, his sire being given as Hilton Jock 965 by Purple Heather, and his dam as Silver Queen. It should read:-

Sire: Snowhope Purple Heather 1929
Dam: Silver Queen by Hilton Jock 965

Silver Queen was probably an unregistered daughter or grand-daughter of Hummerbeck Beauty (Smart Bychlyvie/Polly by Merry Jock), perhaps a half-sister or daughter of Grey Queen II (Brown Jock/ Hummerbeck Beauty) foaled 1927 or the grey Lady Sheila (Snowhope Fashion/Hummerbeck Beauty), foaled 1929. All Fours can be found in the tail female lines of modern ponies.

The 14.3 black Prince Charles of Middleton 2748 (Blackton Glory/ Lady Charlotte of Middleton by Prince Comet II) got a few foals during these years but most disappeared; there is a possiblity that some came through into the grading-up register of 1964. Only one of his daughters, Lady Helen of Middleton (9020) was registered.

Snowhope Purple Heather was still getting foals during these years - his last two were born in 1949. His 28 daughters included Wheatside Queen II, White Lees Success, Snowhope Heather Belle and the remarkable Horsley Miranda who astonished spectators at the NPS Show in 1967 by winning the Dales Championship in a good class at the age of 22 years. Sadly she left no registered progeny to continue her line.

Besides Snowhope Purple Heather the most popular sires of these years were Black Jock II, Mountain Heather II, Newlands Prince, Mountain Prince, Prince Comet II, Lummas Comet and Blackton Glory. Stock by Sonny Boy II, Unicorn, Hazelgill Startler, Rising Star, Prince Charles of Middleton, Danny Boy, and Brownberry II were also entered in this Stud Book. The unregistered Black Oak by Black Diamond was also getting registered foals.

A good choice of unrelated stallions was then still available but registration was hit and miss, geldings and colts were often sold without registration forms. Fillies were sometimes sold with registration forms which were never returned by un-informed owners. The travelling fraternity have always appreciated smart trotters and were keen buyers of good Dales ponies; particularly as they are also well capable of horsing caravans in hilly country. The much fancied piebalds which are shown off at Appleby Fair are mostly Dales bred.

Two of Mr George Hodgson's mares were entered: Hilton Nancy (Prince Comet II/Hilton Betty) and the well-known **Hilton Beauty** (10123)(Mountain Heather II/Hilton Nancy). Beauty was a prolific prize-winner in hand, as a brood mare and under saddle, and also worked about his farm. The last of the long line of Hilton ponies, Hilton B'George was foaled a few weeks after Mr Hodgson's death in 1997.

Norman Field MFH, of Lartington Hall, Barnard Castle, had registered the bay cob, Cockfield Topsy 3696(Black Blooming Heather/Marwood Topsy), in 1919. He was elected President for 1922 and at about the same time bought the stallion Linnel Comet. He served on the Dales Judges Panel from 1925. The first pony to carry his prefix was Lartington Fairy (Linnel Comet/Wellhope Gipsy) foaled in 1922. He followed Lord Barnard as President in 1939 and remained in office throughout the war years, struggling to keep the society on an even keel as the ponies and members disappeared. In this volume he entered four more of his mares Lartington Lichen, Lartington Stonecrop, Lartington Sundew and Lartington Valerian.

Volume 27 of the Stud Book covering 1953-54 revealed a sad state of affairs, with only four Dales mares entered. Two were owned by John Dalton, Horsley Jennie II by Horsley Hero (2966 Fell) by Heltondale Victor out of the unregistered Horsley Jennie, and Snowhope Heather Belle, foaled in 1940 out of Snowhope Perfection. The others were Walter Tuer's Mystery VI, foaled in 1943, dam of unknown breeding and Hollin Hill Beauty, foaled 1943, bred by the Secretary of the Society, Mr F. F. Collingwood; all by Snowhope Purple Heather.

No Dales were entered in Volume 28 of the Stud Book for 1955-1956 and it appeared that extinction was about to overtake the breed. Happily, in 1980 all these entries were found in the office of the National Pony Society. They had been processed but the entries had never been published in the Stud Book due to the many discrepancies in the registrations; no doubt due to a breakdown in administration during those very difficult years. Some of the entries had been duplicated with different names, and a few were later entered in the Fell Section, but the 57 eligible ones were published retrospectively in Volume 1 of the Dales Pony Society Stud Book when it was opened in 1982. In 1956 this number of registrations would have looked healthy. Sadly, only three of the ponies appear in later pedigrees, most disappeared without leaving registered stock. Survivors without certificates may have been collected into the grading-up register, after inspection, when it was instituted in 1965.

Among the 'lost' entries was that of **Bousefield Dalesman 3592** (Mountain Prince/Greenside Queen), a name which comes into all modern pedigrees. He used to be entered on pedigrees as of unknown breeding until 1982.

BOUSEFIELD DALESMAN 3592. Foaled 1950. Black with a faint star and white inside hear hind pastern, a few white hairs on near shoulder.
Sire: Mountain Prince 2651.
Dam: 7856 Greenside Queen, black, 14.2 by Black Duke 2294
G.dam: 5466 Greenside Pride, dark brown, 14.1 by Pendragon Comet
    (974 Fell) by Teasdale Comet.
G.g.dam: Brown mare by Brown Prince (2131 Dales)
G.g.g.dam: Mare by Tees Water Fashion (Dales)
Breeder: Mr W. Dixon of Greenside, Ravenstonedale
Owner: Mr W. Hully of the family which bred so many Comets.

BLACK DUKE (2294 Dales), Black with a star and stripe. Foaled 1936, Height 14.3
Sire:Black Oak (unregistered) by Black Diamond (1635 Dales), black,
    14.1
Dam: Betty by Teasdale Comet (904 Dales) grey, 14.2

Bousefield Dalesman sired only Hilton Betty II, Wheatside Polly, Wheatside Polly II, Heather Patience and the stallion Wheatside Perfect - what a selection of grand ponies!

An interesting colt entry was the stallion Wheatside Laddie (Mountain Heather II/Wheatside Queen II), foaled in 1952. Bred by T. V. Emerson, he was purchased for export by the Government of Pakistan in 1955.

One important entry was that of the mare Bowburn Silver Star by Mountain Prince out of a mare of unknown breeding, and her daughter, **Bowburn Silver Star II** by All Fours, foaled in 1955, from which comes a line of grey ponies. Ackram Polly II 10703 was also entered and lost, resulting in two Ackram Polly II's instead of II and III.

Mr G. Slack of Stoneriggs entered the mare Mountain Lookout which Mrs Glenda Spooner bought in foal to Lummas Comet, for the Ponies of Britain Club. This brown mare was by Mountain Prince out of an unregistered mare named Spy Cop who had no further registered progeny.

The entry in the 1957 Stud Book was of only nine ponies. None of the three entered colts became stallions. The brown colt, Sprig O' Heather (Wheatside Pride/Oakley Heather Bloom) foaled in 1956, was

The champion stallion Grey Bobbie (1966-1989), seen at Appleby Fair.

bred by Mr T. W. Coulthard and was another purchased by Mrs Glenda Spooner for The Ponies of Britain Club.

It became more difficult for the Dales Pony Improvement Society to keep going in the absence of a good market and the continuing wholesale destruction of equines. Particularly unhelpful was the adverse propaganda which some equestrian writers were producing at the time. The Dales pony was continually described as 'a miniature cart-horse with straight shoulders, and as such would inevitably find it hard to survive as it was not a breed which could be ridden.' Later it was suggested that they might find a useful niche as trekking ponies. As some writers did little research, these descriptions have continued until very recently. It never seemed to occur to them that ponies that could produce fast trotting times under saddle must have free shoulder action. Neither did they understand that the Dales pony was bred on very similar lines to, and for the same reasons as Welsh Cobs, which were generally lauded for free action.

The origins for this lay in breed descriptions publicised by the Fell Society, which persistently spoke of both breeds as the 'Fell and Dales', and still implied that the Dales was a Clydesdale/Fell cross which had degenerated into a ponderous draught horse. This came from clever publicity at the time when the Fell pony was disappearing and the Dales was still in its hey-day but it proved as damaging to the Dales breed as it was helpful to the Fells.

Unhappily, the death of the President, Captain Norman Field, in 1956 did not help matters. Mrs Olive Field realised that the situation was getting out of hand and called a meeting to try to save the society. It was not possible for them to take over the Dales Pony Improvement Society, but the NPS gave permission for the establishment of a new society to be named the Northern Dales Pony Society, with articles of memorandum based on those of the original society. The new society was to administer all future entries in the Dales Section of the Stud Book.

On February 9th, 1958, the Northern Dales Pony Society was founded at a public meeting at Barnard Castle. There were to be representatives in Teesdale, Baldersdale, Arkengarthdale, Stainmore, Westmorland, County Durham and elsewhere as decided by the council. The council consisted of the President, Mrs Olive Field of Lartington Hall, the Vice-President, Mr W. Wilkinson of Spanham, the Treasurer, Mr Leaman Wall of Raygill and the Secretary, Mr P. W. Nixon of Barnard Castle. Some of the older Dales breeders were unwilling to change their allegiance from the original society, but could now only register ponies through the new society.

The NPS Stud Book, Volume 30 (1959-60) has a Dales Section entitled

Mr Thomas Denham riding his champion mare Molly Steptoe at N.P.S. show, Malvern, 1969.

The Northern Dales Pony Society. There was an entry of 24 ponies. Of the four colts only the grey Spanham Mr Pigg 4097(Brussleton Boy/ Spanham Madge II) and Wharton Heather 4011(Brussleton Boy/Intake Polly) became stallions. The colour varience remains much the same: of the 24 ponies there were 12 black, 6 brown, 2 bay and 4 grey.

Mr T. W. Coulthard of West Auckland entered the mare **Oakley Foundation** of unknown parentage. She became a prolific prizewinner in her day and became the dam of stallions Oakley Dalesman, Oakley Spartan, Oakley Matchmaker and some lovely mares, among them Oakley Sparkle and Oakley Fragrance.

Three Lartington fillies were entered by Mrs Field plus the re-entry of Lartington Valerian (Lummas Comet/Lartington Lichen) with a new number. Mr Wilkinson entered three Spanham mares including the brown **Spanham Lucy Glitters** (All Fours/Stang Betty) who became the foundation mare of Mr Reid of Robertland's line of 'Surtees' ponies, some roan and all by Spanham Mr Pigg. The last of her line is the bay roan stallion Wharfedale Prince Regent by Stainton Prince. His dam was the incredible roan mare, **Robertland Miss Bussington**, a wonderful performance pony who died recently at the age of 28 years. Otherwise she left some excellent part-bred hunter stock and some pure-bred geldings. The roan line continues through the daughters of Prince Regent who is still active.

Mr J. W. Longstaff entered two mares - Lummas Ruby (Mountain Heather II/Lummas Beauty) foaled in 1940, and her daughter by Lummas Comet, **Lummas Topsy**, foaled in 1956. Mr R. Close entered **Hazlegill Darkie**, foaled in 1947 of unrecorded breeding, who became his foundation mare. Miss Helga Frankland entered her first mare under the Needlehouse prefix previously used by her father, Dr E. P. Frankland. This was Needlehouse Burnet by Mountain Prince out of an unregistered pony. The Needlehouse ponies still live in Ravenstonedale, the latest one being Needlehouse Rowan, foaled in 1994.

The filly entered by Walter Tuer, **Wharton Beauty**, was another famous mare and few ponies could beat her in her prime. Bred by Mr A. Metcalf and foaled in 1954, she was by Mountain Heather II out of an unregistered daughter of May Beauty (Ouston Model/Stanhope Beauty) by Newlands Prince. Owned by Mr Joseph Hall, she founded the Stainton line of ponies. Among her 20 foals were the stallions Stainton John II and Stainton Bobby and a line of powerful mares which included Ewebank Beauty and continues through Raygill Diamond and Stainton Diamond. The stallion **Stainton Commando** was her great-grandson. She had her last foal, Stainton Saul, at the age of 28 years and died in 1982.

One mare entered in Volume 30 who found fame is **Masie** (Mountain Prince/West Silver Star), foaled in 1952. She grew to be a very good stamp of mare, 14.2, black with a narrow blaze and a white off hind fetlock. She was the choice of Glenda Spooner to represent an ideal Dales pony for the Beswick Mountain & Moorland pottery model pony series, manufactured by John Beswick Ltd of the Longton, Stoke-on-Trent. Mr Reggie Summerhayes, a horseman of great distinction, had suggested the idea of a series of model British pony breeds and acted as consultant with help from Mrs Spooner of the Ponies of Britain Club. Some very good models of Champion ponies were produced and are now valuable as collector's items. Unfortunately, the revitalised Dales Pony Society issued a rule in 1964 that barred ponies displaying a blaze or any white on forelegs from the Stud Book proper and they were relegated to the grading-up register. As can be imagined, this caused a certain amount of contention in later years but the pony was a good one and represents the type of Dales pony which abounded in the mid-twentieth century, when white markings were of little account.

The Ponies of Britain Club also entered the two fillies Brickett Sunstar (Lummas Comet/Lartington Sundew) given to Mrs Spooner by Mrs Field and Brickett Shooting Star, the foal from Mountain Lookout. No pure-bred stock was registered from either but they produced some first class cross-bred stock.

Brickett Sunstar was put to the Thoroughbred Ardencapel in 1961 and produced Sun of Arden. This gelding had a most versatile career. He carried his owner, Mrs Aglen, and her daughter hunting and competed successfully in many Pony Club events. He was a member of the Linlithgow & Stirlingshire Pony Club Inter-branch Team for seven years and competed in Area Trials where he won the Junior title twice and the Senior title once. His team won the Area Trials and in 1968 were runners up for the Championship. In 1968 after only a week of training with Richard Stillwell, he came third in the Finals of the Spillers Combined Training Event. Of him, Richard Stillwell remarked, 'He has the temperament of a lamb and the courage of a lion.' In 1970 he won the Greatheart Cup for Dressage at Stoneleigh. Throughout he remained as sound as a bell.

Sunstar next produced a filly to Ardencapel, which was sent to the Queen's Thoroughbred, Night Watch, and produced a colt foal. The mare was small but later proved a great success as a Polo Pony. In 1968, Sunstar produced another colt, the 16.1 Arden Sunflash. In the ownership of Dr P. Hayward of Edinburgh, he competed successfully in one day events, dressage and combined training. Sunstar's last foal was Mrs Jan Robertson's grey mare, Ascot Sunnydale, by the Queen's Thoroughbred, Sanbal. Sunny was a very successful performer gaining a first in the 15-hand Hunter Pony class at the South of England Show, winning in Novice and Open Pony Club Horse Trials and the Bisley Pony Club Dressage Championship. Ascot Sunnydale was one of the first entries in the Dales Part-Bred Register when it opened in 1983; her daughter, Ascot Dazzledale by Catherston Dazzler, was also entered in 1989.

Volume 31 (1960-61) had Dales ponies entered for the second and last time, under the short-lived Northern Dales Pony Society title. It contained two stallions, Midnight Star 4134 by Mountain Prince 2651 out of (7523 Dales) Stennerskeugh Dolly by Pendragon Comet (974 Fell). The second was Wharton Guardsman, a grandson of Master John, foaled in 1958 by Guards Model (3708 Fell) out of a mare of unknown breeding.

Of the 12 mares entered, only Beauty XIV by Mountain Prince 2651 out of a mare of unknown breeding has a continuing line through Pepita May and Stella May.

15

A NEW BEGINNING
IN A NEW AGE

$\blacklozenge$

1962 WAS A TURNING POINT in Dales pony history. It was the year the
Dales Pony Improvement Society and the Northern Dales Pony Society
were pulled together under an 'umbrella'. Elected representatives of
both societies met at Bedale Rectory on September 17th, 1962, under
the chairmanship of the Reverend J. Massingberd-Munday.

The representatives from the Dales Pony Improvement Society were
Mr John Dalton (Snowhope), Mr George Hodgson (Hilton), Mr Peter
Lawson (Cleveland), Mr Norman Bayles (Ackram) and Miss Margaret
Emerson (Wheatside). Representing the Northern Dales Pony Society
were Mrs Olive Field (Lartington), Mr R. Beadle, Mr R. Close
(Hazelgill), Mr Walter Tuer (Wharton), Mr W. Wilkinson (Spanham)
and Mr Leaman Wall (Raygill).

It was unanimously agreed that both societies would unite under
one umbrella society, to be called The Dales Pony Society. Each branch
for the time being should retain its distinctive administration for
membership which in either society should constitute membership of
the Dales Pony Society. Sadly, the minute book for the Dales Pony
Improvement Society disappeared at this point, and has, so far, never
been found.

The Dales Pony Society should have three executive officers not
connected with either branch of the society, for a period of three years
in the first instance. By which time it was hoped that both societies
would have drawn together and have a common membership and
organisation. The Reverend J. Massingberd-Mundy was unanimously
elected chairman with Captain Miles Stavely and Mr Ken Easby
consenting to serve as executive officers. Ken Easby continued to act
as Treasurer and commentator at the breed shows until his death in
1987.

The Dales Pony Society was to be the unit for all registrations and
the organisation of the Spring Stallion Show, for which both societies

would combine. The late Miles Stavely gave the both the 'umbrella' and the new society tremendous encouragement and support. He urged them to look to the future and promote the ponies in an active way and advised the new council to get the ponies into the major show rings as a good shop window was neccessary to display the quality of the ponies.

The Dales section of Volume 32 of the Stud Book (1961-62) was entered under the title of The Dales Pony Society, with a note to the effect that it was formed in 1962 under an umbrella society which covered the Northern Dales Pony Society and the Dales Pony Improvement Society.

Of the three colts entered two became stallions; Lord Rupert 4285 (Black Jock II/Sweet Bloom III) and the brown Spanham Heather Lad 4225 (Mountain Heather II/Sweet Lavender II). Lord Rupert, foaled in 1950, was black with a star and three white coronets. His dam was by Snowhope Purple Heather out of Sunbegin Beauty, a black mare with a blaze and one white fore fetlock, foaled in 1932. Sunbegin Beauty was by the Clydesdale, Royal Ratho, out of Sally of unknown breeding. Lord Rupert became the sire of Raygill Julie, a champion brood mare of the 1980s, Stella May, Trimdon Star and Galphay Supreme. The latter is a Section C mare with a remarkable performance record but with no filly to replace her. Lord Rupert also sired three other Section mares, all with continuing lines.

Spanham Heather Lad was foaled in 1958. His dam was by Mountain Prince out of Stainton Mary. This was an earlier Stainton prefix than that used by Mr J. Hall, belonging originally to Mr William Thompson of Great Stainton.

Of the 18 mares entered, the filly Brickett Beauty (Spanham Heather Lad/Blackton Beauty) was the last Dales to be registered by the Ponies of Britain Club. Blackton Bonnie was bought, in foal, by Mrs Spooner to save her from slaughter. She was later put to Ardencapel and produced Jim Dale. In 1971 he was placed in every event he entered with a record of seven firsts and eight seconds in Combined Training, Hunter Trials and Show Jumping and in the Tetrathlon Team which was first in the Area Trials for Linlithgow & Stirlingshire and qualified for Stoneleigh.

The well named mare Robertland Lady Scattercash (Spanham Mr Pigg/Spanham Lucy Glitters) foaled in 1960, was the first of David Reid of Robertland's 'Surtees' ponies. Four other entered mares were of unknown breeding and one was out of a registered mare by an unregistered sire. The bay mare Wharton Lady was by Wharton Guardsman out of (12332 Fell) Lowhouse Madge of unknown breeding,

Mr H. Barron's great mare Heather Mixture III, foaled 1950, driven by Mr Gordon Thompson.

foaled in 1954. Lady's line continues through Murton Princess, Stoneriggs Princess, Stoneriggs Duchess and Stoneriggs Merry Lady. The bay Lartington Starwort (All Fours/Lartington Valerian) was the last to carry this prefix.

The first meeting of The Dales Pony Society was held on March 5th, 1964. The chairman reminded the meeting that the NPS would recognise only one Dales Pony Society, and on this would depend the Stud Book and the premiums. He also expressed the hope that in future the two branch titles would become of less importance and the focal point would be the well-being of the Dales pony and the Dales Pony Society. All sides saw the wisdom and obvious advantages of this. Mr Peter Lawson was appointed Secretary and was very active in getting things moving at a good pace.

During the following year the questions of new membership, subscriptions and badges were discussed and it was decided to fix the subscription at 10/- per annum. It was also agreed that the progeny of any registered Dales pony mare covered by a Fell stallion during 1963,

1964 and 1965 should be accepted into the Dales Pony Stud Book. This was due to the dearth of good unrelated stallions.

A newsletter was produced and the Spring Stallion and Breed shows organised with social events arranged to pull the membership together. A society badge, depicting the mare Wheatside Perfection, and a Society Tie and Car sticker designed by Mrs Lawson depicting Burdon Winsome, were offered for sale to members. Following the resignation of Mr Lawson, George Hodgson took on the office of secretary, which he held until appointed president in 1982.

A projected 'Points of the Dales Pony' chart to be printed by The Farmer & Stockbreeder was being pursued and it was agreed that the pony to be used should be the champion pony at the next Spring Stallion & Breed Show. Unusually, the champion proved to be a yearling filly, Burdon Winsome. There was much discussion on the use of an immature animal for the venture. Some thought that as Mr Barron, who owned the filly, also owned a champion brood mare, Heather Mixture III, she should be used instead. Eventually photographs of both were used, with the mare added to show the mature animal. The photograph of the same yearling filly was on the huge display boards in the Indoor School at the British Equestrian Centre for over 30 years and has undoubtedly given many viewers an odd idea of a Dales pony.

The 1963 Stud Book, Volume 33, contained a new look Dales section containing this new description regarding colour.

Colour - Black predominant, grey and brown also found. Only a white star or white snip allowed on head and only white coronet on legs.

Of the 26 ponies entered the most important was the stallion **Wheatside Perfect** (4355) (Bousefield Dalesman/Wheatside Perfection) foaled in 1956. Bred by Thomas V. Emerson, he became a dominant sire of modern Dales ponies; very few ponies alive today fail to show his name at least once in their pedigree. There were also four colts foaled in 1962 of which the grey **Hett Real Fashion** 4365 (Wheatside Perfect/Bowburn Silver Star II) bred by S. Bell and owned by William Watt was the only one to become a stallion.

Among the 21 mares entered, 11 carried the Wheatside prefix, the oldest was Wheatside Rose (Black Jock II/Wheatside Queen II) foaled in 1945, followed in age by Wheatside Polly out of Wheatside Queen II foaled in 1953 ; Wheatside Dolly foaled in 1956 and Wheatside Beauty II foaled in 1957 out of Wheatside Rose, all by Mountain Heather II. Wheatside Fashion went to Mr Peter Lawson from which he bred the Cleveland ponies. The others were spread over the intervening years. Mr George Hodgson's Hilton Betty II(Bousefield Dalesman/Hilton

Nancy) foaled in 1955 and Hilton Dawn (Wheatside Perfect/Hilton Beauty were also entered. Hilton Betty was won numerous prizes in-hand and under saddle and shared the farm work with Hilton Beauty. She also produced a string of good foals carrying the Hilton prefix. She died at the age of 28 years in 1983. Hilton Dawn became a foundation dam of Mr Thomas Ramshaw's Wolsey ponies. The remarkable roan mare Robertland Miss Bussington (12604) was also entered.

The first Dales Pony Society Spring Stallion & Breed Show, incorporating the Dales Pony Improvement Society and the Northern Dales Pony Society, was held in the Auction Mart Field, Barnard Castle on the third Wednesday in May 1963. It was an ancient custom to hold the Stallion show on Hiring Day. This later became Market Day, which allowed farmers to look the stallions over when they came into market. In the old days their paces were shown off in the main street.

The premium awards were £30 each for 4 stallions, £10 each for 2 two-year-old colts and £5 each for 2 yearling colts. The judges were Captain Miles Stavely and Mr John Dalton.

There were 38 entries with 20 forward. In the stallion class, Wheatside Perfect stood first above Lord Rupert and Spanham Heather Lad. Four of the eight brood mares were forward, all top class ponies with formidable prize-winning records. Placed first was T. Couthard's famous Oakley Foundation, above G. H. Hodgson's Hilton Beauty, T. V. Emerson's Wheatside Polly and A. Metcalf's Wharton Beauty. Only three yearling fillies were forward, Mr Harry Barron's Burdon Winsome taking the Championship. The two-year-old class was won by T. V. Emerson's Wheatside Heather Queen. The geld mare and gelding class was won by G. H. Hodgson's Hilton Betty II taking precedence over T. V. Emerson's Wheatside Heather and P. A. Lawson's Wheatside Fashion.

The new beginning looked hopeful. The next few years would decide whether the reconstituted society was going be successful in regenerating interest in the threatened breed, which, for the first time in a long history, was having difficulty in finding a niche.

16
THE DALES PONY SOCIETY

◆

IN 1964 A LETTER FROM MRS GLENDA SPOONER arrived informing the council that Mr David Reid of Robertland had donated a Cup for the Best Schooled Dales Pony at the Ponies of Britain Show, Kelso. She also pointed out that there was concern for the future of the breed if Dales ponies were not allowed to canter and gallop in ridden classes, as all the other Mountain & Moorland ponies did.

This would be a complete break with tradition. Although free moving Dales ponies had always been comfortable under saddle, they were bred specifically as stylish harness ponies with high knee and hock action. However, it was agreed that in future such classes should be included at the breed shows and competitors encouraged to school their ponies to a good show standard. Today, at Breed Shows, the very popular traditional ridden classes (walk and collected and extended trot) are still retained together with conventional ridden classes.

Of the 15 ponies registered in 1964, Volume 34, only Bess of Bleachgreen, out of a dam of unknown breeding, was by Wharton Guardsman (4154 Dales) by Guards Model (3708 Fell), a grandson of Black Jock II. The others were all by Dales stallions. Only two of the four colts became stallions, T. M. Robinson's black **Trimdon Comet** (4460) (Lummas Comet/ Lartington Rowan) foaled in 1963 and Thomas Coulthard's **Oakley Dalesman** (4448) (Wheatside Perfect/Oakley Foundation) who became a sire of great importance getting some very good mares and seven stallions; which included Oakley Spartan, Oakley Free & Easy, Storm Boy of Oakley, Burdon Freestep, Kirkleatham General, Heather's Son and finally the Devonshire bred Tamarvale Durham Lad foaled in 1988. Oakley Dalesman died in 1989 aged 25 years. Trimdon Comet is represented today by the families of Wensleydale Pride and Rose of High Croft, a Section D mare with an extended family of some quality which has reached the Stud Book proper.

Among the 11 entered mares was **Queen of the Heather II** (All Fours/ Queen of Heather) foaled in 1953, and her daughter Heather's Beauty by Wheatside Perfect, foaled in 1962. Queen of the Heather II is remembered

Master John (2883 Fell) by Black Jock II (2321 Dales) with Walter Tuer.

for her speed and action as a harness pony; it is said that she was so keen she would trot on the spot if held up. She was the dam of the stallion Heather Boy II and the lovely Dales mare Ackram Daisy II and grand-dam of Heather's Son. Queen of the Heather II's line is viable and continues through some excellent mares. The other mare of interest is Burdon Winsome, the champion Dales as a yearling filly. She was always handsome but was not an outstanding brood mare.

Volume 35 for 1965 held 31 entries, some still living in 1994. Only 4 of the 10 entered colts became stallions. The most influential was J. R. Longstaff's **Heather Boy II**(4523) by Wheatside Perfect, who was foaled in 1963 and spent his long life at Lummas House, high above Swaledale. Heather Boy's last foal was born in 1991, the old fellow died in 1992. His progeny have passed on the true, sharp Dales action of his dam. The second colt became influential by accident: Stainton John (4522) was out of Wharton Beauty (11719 Dales) by Master John (2883 Fell) by Black Jock II. As a yearling he sired Stainton John II out of his own dam. Stainton John spent much of his long life working for the Epsom Group of Riding for the Disabled as a gelding. The third colt, Hilton Saturn 4535 (Wheatside Perfect/Hilton Beauty) sired a few nice foals including Daisy Hill Donna and the splendid Section D mare Parkside Beauty before he was also gelded. The fourth colt was **Stainton Prince** 4532 by Mountain Prince out of the unregistered mare, Bousefield Maid, foaled in 1963. In a letter to the secretary of the society regarding the registration of Stainton Prince, his breeder, Mr Moses Hully of the Bousefield Stud, which was started in 1898, based on Comet II, wrote: 'I have signed the registration form for the pony which I bred, but sorry to say I don't know this mare's breeding. I bought her on performance not on her breeding.' Stainton Prince became a foundation sire of Mr Ernest Blockley's Hodgson Lane ponies. He left some very good mares and ponies, who are noted for pony 'spark' and great activity.

Among the 20 mares only Cleveland Delight out of Wheatside Fashion was by a Fell sire, Blake Beck Boy, which carried Dales influence in his tail male lines to Teasdale Comet and Just-in-Time by Bendal Squire.

The Supreme Champion
Dales Pony Stallion

4532

"STAINTON PRINCE"

Min. of Ag. Licence No. 1749D

Ackram Daisy II was foaled in 1964 by Wheatside Perfect. At the age of 30 years, she was still enjoying an occasionally drive with her owner Mr Stanley Bracken. She died in 1994 following an attack by another mare. Her line is continued through her only daughter Low Oaks Judy and subsquently her grand-daughters Scandlebeck Dawn amd Adamfield Treasure. Ackram Daisy II was said to be very similar to John Dalton's famous mare Fairy Glance. Another notable entry was Ewebank Beauty (Wheatside Perfect/Wharton Beauty) foaled in 1962. She became the foundation mare of the Raygill and Brimfield Studs and was dam of the prizewinning mare Raygill Julie. In the ownership of Mrs Jane Gowland, Ewebank Beauty won the veteran class at the Breed Summer Show in 1984 at the age of 22 years, still displaying unblemished limbs.

The filly Owler Bar Venus (Spanham Heather Lad/Lummas Topsy) bred by Mr J. R. Longstaff was foaled in 1962. She went to Mrs Ted Hill in Derbyshire and became the dam of some good hunters used by hunt staff of the Barlow Hunt.

The first ridden Dales pony class was held at the Spring Stallion and Breed Show of 1965. The class was well received, a spectator remarking to the chairman 'that the days of the muck cart and mowing machine Dales was gone and the Society was right to promote the pony for riding.'

The 15.0 hand height limit for mares was ended in 1965. Any bred before 1964 were allowed the old limit if from fully registered parents. In August of the same year the secretary, Mr Peter Lawson, also recommended that a grading-up register for inspected mares should be instituted. This would ensure that three generations would pass before entry into the Stud Book proper of any unregistered mares. It was also agreed that foals by registered Fell stallions be accepted into the Dales section of the Stud Book for a further three years.

The Fell stallions used all had infusions of Dales blood to some degree and Master John and Stainton Prince were half Dales out of mares of unknown breeding. Wharton Guardsman was by a son of Master John out of a dam of unknown breeding. Wharton Master and Merry John III were by Master John out of mares with strong Dales influence.

At a Council Meeting in 1966, Mr T. Denham told the council that he had inspected a pony which, though very good, had a white stripe down its face and in his opinion should be registered in the grading-up section. The rules and regulations of the grading-up register did not include recommendations regarding colour or markings. After long discussion between those who liked white markings and those

Mr T.W. Coulthard driving his champion mare Oakley Foundation, foaled 1953.

who liked whole black, it was suggested by the secretary that acceptable markings should be a white star or a snip on the nose and white up to the coronets of the hind legs only. This was later amended to:- 'Colours black, brown, bay or grey with white markings only as a small star on face, snip on nose and up to the fetlocks on the hind legs only.'

The rules for the grading-up register are:

'Mares and fillies which are not eligible for the Stud Book Proper may be entered in the Register provided:-

SECTION D Passed by two inspectors as being true to type, height, and colour.

SECTION C By a registered sire and from a Section D dam and passed by inspectors as being true to type, height and colour.

SECTION B By a registered sire out of a Section C dam and passed by inspectors as being true to type, height and colour.

Mr Peacock driving the impressive trotting mare, Queen of the Heather II, foaled 1953.

SECTION A   By a registered sire out of a Section B dam and and passed by inspectors as being true to proper type, height and colour; fillies eligible for stud proper. Colts do not have stallion status.

NOTE: If the progeny of fully registered parents or of Section A mares exceed the height of 14.2 hands or display incorrect white markings, they will be down-graded to Section B.

The rule on markings may seem strange for a breed struggling for its existence, and which had always carried white markings. The idea behind the rule was to preclude ponies with suspected recent Clydesdale blood from the Stud Book. White markings on Dales ponies are rarely above the fetlocks or down the face, whereas Clydesdale white often includes a ratch (blaze) and runs up to the body. The rule has proved to be ineffectual as all Dales stallion lines carry at least one

Ackram Daisy ridden by Stanley Bracken (right) *at Breed Show in 1973.*

white fore-foot in their genes as do many of the mares, and lines carrying a star and snip will also throw an occasional stripe. Research has shown that the percentage of ponies carrying either a blaze or white fore-feet has not changed since 1916, in spite of over 40 years under the rule.

Volume 36 (1966) had 40 ponies entered, including 9 mares in Section D of the new Register. Five of the 12 entered colts were by Fell sires. However, only Kexwith John 4645 (Master John/Kexwith Blossom) the resident stallion at Kexwith, Marske-in-Swaledale for over 20 years, left a continuing line.

Master John also sired two of the mares: one was John Dalton's Snowhope Heather Belle III out of Snowhope Heather Belle II; unbeaten in her day but leaving only one fading line. The other was the Section B mare Needlehouse Blaeberry, who does have a continuing line through Dr Helga Frankland's Needlehouse ponies which live in Ravenstonedale.

Wharton Guardsman sired four mares, Wolsey Empress and Wolsey Princess, both out of Hilton Dawn, with one line continuing through Princess; Hett Katy out of Bowburn Silver Star II, her line coming through Hett Shamrock and Hett Sally, and lastly, Molly Steptoe's daughter Elsie's Surprise, who from the age of four years was owned by Mrs Joyce Bellamy of Croydon. She became very well known in London, representing her breed at many displays, including two at the Royal Mews. 'Elsie' died in 1991 aged 25 years, leaving only one gelding.

Blake Beck Boy (2842 Fell) sired Hilton Carousel out of Hilton Beauty, who became foundation mare of Mr R. Graham's Durham line of ponies. No stock was registered from any of the other mares.

Linnel Fox (4926 Fell) sired Kexwith Beauty and the Section D mare Rosaline, each with a continuing line.

The slow upward movement of numbers of registered Dales ponies continued in 1967. Volume 37 held 18 Dales pony entries; two of the eight colts, Cleveland Dauntless out of Wheatside Fashion and Bantry Playboy out of Prospect Beauty II, were both by Blake Beck Boy(2842 Fell). Cleveland Dauntless sired a few registered progeny; his line is tenuous. Bantry Playboy, though long-lived, sired only one registered gelding.

Four of the 10 mares were by Fells, but only the sisters Bleachgreen Dawn and Bleachgreen Hinny (Wharton Guardsman/Bess of Bleachgreen) and Hillbro' Rebecca (Blakebeck Boy/Dolly XXIX) have continuing lines.

Numbers doubled in 1968 when 36 Dales ponies were entered in Volume 38 of the Stud Book. Two of the eight colts were by Fell sires but only Hilton Merry Beau (Merry John III/ Hilton Beauty) black with a long snip and a star, became a stallion. He was used by Mr A. Slack on his Stoneriggs mares but apparently he disappeared from the Fell in 1976 and was never seen again.

Three of the colts became popular stallions. **Grey Bobbie** 4881 (Hett Real Fashion/Grey Queen IV) was foaled in 1966, bred by Mr R. Corner. Grey Bobbie was a prolific sire with a propensity to produce twins which continues to run in his line. In the year of his death, 1989, he got the twins Rosebarr Grey Bobbie and Rosebarr Grey Rosie out of Dartdale Dawn (Hett Shamrock/Hollywell Lane Jane). **Hett Shamrock** is the son of Grey Bobbie; Hollywell Lane Jane was by Stainton Prince out of Durham Bell by Grey Bobbie. Other known twins are Hilton Gemini and her stillborn sister (Copelaw Quickstep/ Hilton Maytime by Grey Bobbie) and Abigale and Dolcie of Meadow Hill (Grey Rupert by Grey Bobbie/Doris of Castle Hill). A pair were foaled in 1992, by Raygill William (Ashwood Black Prince/Raygill Emerald) out of Lambton Rose (Copelaw Quickstep/Lambton Beatrix). Lambton Beatrix is by Hett Randy (Grey Bobbie/Wolsey Countess). In 1994, Mrs Jan James's Highcroft Grange Blossom (Grey Bobbie/Kerry's Gentle of Highcroft) slipped twins.

Stainton John II (Stainton John/Wharton Beauty) took over stud duties at Stoneriggs after Merry Beau disappeared and has since stood in Lancashire and in Lincolnshire. He died in 1994, his last foals were

A Dales yearling filly, the late D.R. Hibbert's Slaypits Cilla.

registered the following year.

Lanquitts Lad (Wheatside Perfect/Dolly XXIX), bred by Mr R. Tunstall, took over stud duties at Wheatside when his sire retired. He lived on there in retirement until well over 30 years of age.

Among the 12 mares was **Sally of Hodgson Lane** (Wheatside Perfect/Wheatside Heather Queen), the foundation mare of Mr E. Blockley's prizewinning Hodgson Lane ponies. The only Fell-bred filly to have a continuing line was Cleveland Delarne (Blake Beck Boy/Wheatside Fashion) through her daughter, Cleveland Dena.

Of the 14 Section mares the only Fell-bred mare to have a continuing line was Mr R. Corner's black Village Star (Section B) by Wharton Guardsman out of Grey Queen IV. Three more of Mr Corner's mares were entered in the grading-up section, all grey and all stemming from Silver Queen, the unregistered grey mare by Hilton Jock, but by different Dales sires.

Mrs Jane Gowland's Gipsy of Pembroke and Mrs P. Paull's Catriona III, both inspected mares, were also entered in this grading-up section. These two mares kept the Dales flag flying in the Mountain & Moorland classes at major shows in the 1960s and 1970s. Gipsy had no progeny but Catriona's daughter by Hodgson Lane David, Sunglow Karalina, came onto the show circuit at the age of 11 years with great success. At the NPS Show, 1985, she won the Ridden Dales class, the Trophy for the Best Schooled Dales and the Linnel trophy for the Best Ridden Dales, Fell and Highland and was second in the Novice M & M Working Hunter Pony class. In 1988 she repeated her success at the NPS Show, winning the Susan Spencer Cup for the second time and also qualifying for the Mountain & Moorland Ridden Championship Final, Olympia. The Sunglow Stud continues to produce good quality performance ponies from this line.

In 1969, 32 Dales ponies plus 24 Section mares were entered in Volume 39. Of the 15 colts, 6 were by Fell or Dales/Fell sires, of which only **Hodgson Lane David** (5022) (Stainton Prince /Hett Rose) left a continuing line. Bred by Ernest Blockley and owned by Mrs P. A. Paull, he was often the only Dales stallion shown in southern classes in the 1970s. The Dales bred colts who became stallions were T. W. Couthard's Oakley Spartan 5039 (Oakley Dalesman/Midnight of Oakley) and Miss E. E. Redfern's home-bred **Heather's Son** (5026) (Oakley Dalesman/Heather's Beauty), a popular stallion owned by Mr G.L.Wall and based at Raygill.

Three of the 11 mares were by Fell or part-Fell sires, but none has a continuing line. Among the other mares there are sound lines from Burdon Mixture (Oakley Dalesman/Heather Mixture III), Hett Susan

(Wheatside Perfect/Battle Heather Belle), Wheatside Princess (Lanquitts Lad/Wheatside Heather Rose) and Wheatside Rose III (Wheatside Perfect/Wheatside Rose).

The society had the survival of the Dales pony in hand, and although the numbers were slow to pick up, the quality of the mares was generally of a good standard. More colts were being registered but there was still concern about the shortage of good unrelated stallions.

THE TURBULENT DECADE

Twenty-one ponies were entered in Volume 40 (1970) of the Stud Book. Among the 10 colts was Harry Barron's **Burdon Freestep** 5427 (Oakley Dalesman/Heather Mixture III) foaled in 1970. He was the sire of many excellent ponies including Hodgson Lane Fair Grand and Hodgson Lane Kitt. Only two other colts became stallions, Kirkleatham General 5307 (Oakley Dalesman/Oakley Mettle) sire of Daisy Hill Star and four Whitworth mares; and Raygill Supreme 5272.

Of the 12 entered mares, one well remembered is Thomas Coulthard's brilliant little **Oakley Sparkle** (Oakley Spartan/ Oakley Foundation) who really could move as if on wheels. The only mares by Fell sires had no registered progeny.

The grading-up section held 12 mares in Section C and 27 in Section D. Three Stoneriggs mares were entered in the Stud Book, Stoneriggs Duchess out of Wharton Lady, Stoneriggs Gem out of Spanham Bright Eyes and Stoneriggs Princess out of Murton Princess, all by Mountain Prince. Seven more were entered in Section C and nine in Section D. Also entered in Section D were 3 full sisters of Stainton Prince, consigned to Section D under the grading-up rules: Bousefield Heather, foaled 1969, Bousefield Queen, foaled 1968 and Hillhead Beauty, foaled 1964.

The lone gelding registered in this Stud Book, Speedy of Smallpage of unknown breeding, deserves mention as he was the stablemate of Donna of Smallpage by Prince Consort out of the unregistered Trixie. Both were owned by Mr and Mrs B. Spencer of Halifax and shown by their daughters Christine and Susan throughout the 1970s. They were excellent representatives of the breed, carrying on from Gipsy of Pembroke and Catriona III, competing and winning in performance classes at most of the major shows. Tragically Susan was killed in a road accident, but her memory is kept alive by the Susan Spencer Memorial trophy which is awarded annually at the National Pony Show to the Best Schooled Dales pony, and also by the Susan Spencer Native Pony Show held each year near Halifax.

In 1970, the council ruled that a pony eligible for registration in the Fell Stud Book would no longer be registered in the Dales Stud Book, and also that Section D of the Grading-up Section would be closed at the end of 1971. It was also agreed that in future colts from Section mares would be registered. The Council of the National Pony Society was not in favour of the proposal to register colts from Section mares, perhaps not fully understanding the desperate shortage of unrelated stallions. The Council of the Dales Pony Society therefore agreed to register colts from Section mares only after castration. With hindsight this appears to have been a rather short-sighted move as many of the grading up mares were of excellent quality and may have carried good bloodlines from the past.

Volume 41 of the Stud Book (1971) held 18 entries with 4 mares in Section B, 3 in Section C and 16 in Section D. One of the entered colts, Bracken Boy of Lunesdale (Heltondale Sonny Boy/Spanham Bright Eyes), was the last Dales stallion reputed to be by a Fell sire. He lived until 1989 and sired a few mares and some registered part-bred stock. Heltondale Sonny Boy comes from lines through Heltondale Victor to Teasdale Comet. Of the other five colts only the dark brown Hett Randy 5577 (Grey Bobbie/Hett Susan) sired registered Dales progeny, among them some very good mares. Waltroyd Black Storm 5511 (Stainton Prince/Marshes Blossom) had a short, very successful show career but only left two geldings before he died. The grey Barmston Lad (Grey Bobbie/Barmston Lass) made his name as a a spectacularly beautiful grey driving stallion who also carried a side-saddle. Unfortunately he was not eligible for breeding registered stock as he was out of a Section B mare, which had a white foreleg.

Of the 7 mares entered, the best known is the many times champion brood mare, **Raygill Julie** (Lord Rupert/Ewebank Beauty), foaled in 1971 and bred by Mr G. L. Wall, Chairman of the Dales Pony Society at the time. Raygill Julie produced the colts Raygill Jubilee, Raygill Rupert, Raygill Jet, and Raygill Caviar in 1991 also the fillies, Raygill Duchess, Gemma, Countess, Ruby, Betty and Holly (Sec. B). She produced her last foal, the colt Raygill Victory in 1995. The beautiful grey Heather Bloom (Grey Bobbie/Heather's Beauty) foaled in 1970, produced her last filly foal in 1985.

Four Section B mares were entered in the Stud Book proper in error. One was Barmston Lass (Blake Beck Boy/Hett Daisy) foaled in 1966; she left a good line of mares besides Barmston Lad. Her daughter Barmston Queen was winner of many Championships, the last at the Annual Summer Breed Show in 1993, aged 19 years. The others were Eskrigge Katey (Stainton John II/ Hazel of Gastle Gill), Hett Betty (Trimdon Comet/Bowburn Silver Star II) and Hodgson Lane Mary II (Stainton Prince/Sally of Hodgson Lane). All these mares were well-bred but were mis-marked under the new rule.

Although 57 ponies were registered in 1972, 44 were in the grading-up section, 4 in Section B, 16 in Section C and a final 18 in Section D. The grading up register was closed on December 31st, 1971; a total of 81 inspected mares had been registered since 1965.

Of the 13 colts, 5 became stallions. These were **Hett Shamrock** (Grey Bobbie/Hett Katy), Prince of Colliery (Grey Bobbie /Hilton Carousel) and three sons of Stainton John II: **Stoneriggs Alick** out of Spanham Bright Eyes, **Stoneriggs Banner** out of Stoneriggs Gem and and **Stoneriggs Bobby** out of Bleachgreen Dawn. Alick and Shamrock were still siring stock at the age of 25 years. Stoneriggs Bobby went to Mrs Delia Weedon in Sussex where he stood for some years until his death.

Of the 22 mares, two were by Stainton Prince: Hodgson Lane Rosemary out of Sally of Hodgson Lane and Brymor Mimi out of Prince's Grace, both prolific prize-winners with three generations of active progeny coming on. The grey Heatherdowne Princess (Grey Bobbie/Grey Queen IV) became the dam of some very successful performance ponies which include the grey gelding Rebel of Burnaby and the very successful bay mare, Abdylane Nancy, which qualified for the Mountain & Moorland Ridden Championship, Olympia, five times. Hilton Maytime (Grey Bobbie/Hilton Beauty), Trimdon Mischief (Heather Boy II/Trimdon Star) and 6 Wheatside mares are also among an entry of exceptionally good mares.

The question of the 15 hand ponies came up at the AGM in 1972, when it was pointed out that the Dales Pony Improvement Society had had a Dales cob section in the Stud Book in the past. In reply the President, J. W. Dalton said that he feared the NPS might not agree to it but the question should be reconsidered at a later date. The over-height mares have continued to be registered and bred from providing a most valuable gene pool and helping to correct any Fell influence on height.

Registration numbers were up in 1973 to 64 entries in the Stud Book and 28 in the grading-up section. Of the 12 entered colts, Hilton Heathcliffe (Burdon Freestep/Hilton Beauty) sired one registered gelding and Stoneriggs Combine (Hilton Merry-Beau/Stoneriggs Princess) sired two Stennenhalle section mares; Village Boy (Heather Boy II/Grey Princess) sired Haswell Outlook and Village Queen among others.

Of the 23 mares, 6 were by Stainton Prince. These were: Hodgson Lane Delight out of Sally of Hodgson Lane, Low Brook Dawn out of Wheatside Pride, Waltroyd Blossom out of Marshes Blossom, Waltroyd Beauty out of Stainton Midnight, Ashwood Princess out of Wheatside Pride and Gallowgate Medina. Also entered were the grand mares Wolsey Lady Sara (Grey Bobbie/Hilton Dawn) and Heather Mixture

IV (Grey Bobbie/Heather's Beauty). All these matrons are past prizewinners, in-hand or in performance classes up until 1994. Another, Stoneriggs C-H-S (Hilton Merry-Beau /Murton Princess) became one of the the foundation mares of the Akehurst Stud, producing many foals. Hillbro' Little Dolly (Stainton Prince/Dolly XXIX), Kexwith Black Bess (Heather Boy II/Kexwith Black Beauty) and Village Princess (Heather Boy II/Grey Princess) are all formidable brood mares, who continued to throw excellent foals until very recently.

The next Stud Book, Volume 44-45-46, which covered 1974 to 1976, had 149 Dales ponies entered, with 59 in the grading-up section, but it was not published until 1978. The NPS had entered the registrations under a confusing new system which omitted white markings. Twenty-five of the Dales entries were foaled between 1962 and 1973.

Five of the 44 colts became successful stallions. These were Ashwood Black Prince (Burdon Freestep/Lowbrook Dawn), Grey Rupert (Grey Bobbie/Spanham Heather Queen), Oakley Matchmaker (Oakley Spartan/Oakley Foundation), Stainton Bobbie (Burdon Freestep/Wharton Beauty) and Stoneriggs Dice (Hilton Merry Beau/Stoneriggs Gem).

Of the 55 mares, many are well known in showing classes, such as Copelaw Mettle (Burdon Freestep/Wheatside Princess), a successful competitor in Combined and Show driving for Miss Susan Bailey. **Ackram Rose** (Heather Boy II/Queen of Kirkleatham), one of a magnificent Tradesman's pair which belonged to Mr J. W. Dickinson. Robin Wells and Moggy Daniels's **Ashwood Delight** (Stainton Prince/Village Lass) who has won numerous Championships, in-hand and under saddle and has twice qualified for Olympia. **Barmston Queen** (Grey Bobbie/Barmston Lass) has collected many brood mare championships; **Sunglow Karalina** (Hodgson Lane David/Catriona III), a brood mare and past Olympia Qualifier; and that great performer **Galphay Supreme**, Rosemary Walker's habitually unshod Section C mare, an Olympia qualifier and winner of numerous prizes in all disciplines.

Registrations for 1977-78 were entered together in Volume (47-48) of the Stud Book. These numbered 128 among which were 17 geldings. The Section ponies could not be identified from fully registered ponies and there were numerous errors which gave rise to later problems regarding stallion eligibility.

Of the 32 colts, 10 became stallions, among them Breed Champions **Copelaw Quickstep**, (Stoneriggs Alick/Wheatside Princess) and **Raygill Jubilee** (Heather's Son/Raygill Julie). **Trimdon Morning Star** (Village Boy/Trimdon Star) was another good stallion who sired some nice ponies before being cut.

Mr R. James' prize-winning performance mare, Abdylane Nancy.

Many of the 79 entered mares are well known, among them **May Queen IX** (Heather Boy II/Lummas Pearl) the other of the pair of mares driven to Mr J. Dickinson's trade wagon; Raygill Duchess (Heather's Son/Raygill Jewel) who hunted regularly with the Bedale, and Eskrigg Donna (Heather's Son/Eskrigge Jess), a performance pony of considerable ability. Other renowned brood mares are Dougie Hibberts **Rosie of Slaypits** (Lanquitts Lad/Wheatside Rose III), the foundation mare of the Slaypits ponies; Whitworth Sarah (Kirkleatham General/ Whitworth Queen), Wolsey Lady Caroline (Hett Randy/Hilton Dawn), Black Velvet of Akehurst (Burdon Freestep/Black Silk), Burdon Lucinda (Stoneriggs Alick/Burdon Mixture) and the Section mares Highcroft Grange Beauty (Copelaw Quickstep/Kerry's Gentle of Highcroft) and Village Queen (Village Boy/Village Star). The latter has had many triumphs under saddle and is a past qualifier for the Mountain & Moorland Ridden Championship Final at Olympia.

The Chairman of the Dales Pony Society Mr Brian Moore was keen to see more progress in 1978. Premiums were raised to £50 each for three stallions and all prize money was raised. The first independent Dales Pony Society Annual Summer Show was held in Barningham Park, near Barnard Castle, by kind permission of Sir Mark Millbank. The society is lucky to have such a beautiful park as the venue for the show, thanks to the continuing support of Sir Anthony Millbank.

Volume 49-50 of the NPS Stud book for 1979-80 was produced in the same form as the previous two. The Dales section had again amalgamated the 94 fully registered and section ponies with no markings given. The numbers were healthy but the registrations confused.

Of the 35 colts entered **Oakley Free & Easy** (Oakley Dalesman / Romany of Oakley) was the only stallion to leave much stock. Brown Boy (Village Boy/Lingfield Queen) left one good mare, Village Dancer, out of Trimdon Black Velvet, before he was castrated. Both these stallions were out of Section B (mis-marked) mares wrongly entered in the Stud Book. The council wisely allowed them to be left entire as both were correctly marked, but refused stallion status to a full brother of Oakley Free & Easy because he had a lock of white hair on a fore-foot.

Of the 59 mares entered, 11 should have been in Section B and 9 in Section C. The better known of the Section A mares include Hodgson Lane Fair Grand (Burdon Freestep/Hodgson Lane Rosemary), Hodgson Lane Kitt (Burdon Freestep/Hodgson Lane Delight), Millgate Rosie (Lanquitts Lad/Wheatside Rose III) and Village Princess II (Oakley Dalesman/Village Princess).

The decade had been one of much turbulence as various means of financing and running the Society had been tried, tested and changed. Despite the difficulties the Council had finally got to grips with the problems and was rewarded by a steady rise in the numbers of registrations, show entries and members. There was still little known about the ponies away from their northern breeding grounds and it was difficult for potential buyers to find a good Dales pony and to buy it if they did. A few owners had been flying the flag in the south and Midlands but it was a rare occasion when one or two appeared at major shows. The Rare Breeds Survival Trust held a watching brief over their progress and placed the Dales pony in Category 2,'Rare'. At the end of the 1970s the Dales Pony Society was considered by outsiders to be very parochial and disinterested in the equine world outside the north east. In fact the society was quietly reviewing the slow recovery with a view to stabilization and further developement without upsetting the status quo.

J. Dickinson and Sons' mares Ackram Rose and May Queen IX, the winners of many championships particularly in tradesman's classes.

17
THE WATERSHED

◆

IN 1980 THE COUNCIL OF THE SOCIETY was approached by Mrs Delia Weedon, breeder of the Akehurst ponies in Sussex, who wished to form a Dales Pony Enthusiasts Club. This was agreed and the club was joined by 40 other Dales pony owners. This has given southern pony owners a chance to enjoy various activities together and has given support to the parent society such as the club's donation of £100 to the Midlands and South Dales Pony Show, for Merit Awards which allow stallions and colts from the Midlands and south to be inspected for a type of Premium. The awards are made by two Dales pony inspectors. The trophy for the Breed Olympia Qualifier was also donated by the Enthusiasts Club which also offers rosettes, runs an independent show and a Points Award Competition.

The 1981 National Pony Society Stud Book (Volume 51) carried 66 Dales pony entries but these were the last. The new format of their Stud Book had omitted important details, such as sections and markings. The Council of the Dales Pony Society therefore decided the time had come to produce an independent Stud Book. The difficulty of communication between members in distant parts of the country and the council was acknowledged and a newsletter was once more published; this has grown into a bi-annual magazine known as the *Dales Despatch*. To help breeders find good homes for their stock, publicity was improved and up-to-date sales lists produced.

All 88 ponies in Volume 1 of the Dales Pony Society Stud Book (1982) were entered with the last two digits of the year/number, i.e. 82/1 **Raygill Gemma** (Heather's Son/Raygill Julie), who became the foundation mare of Richard and Freda Longstaff's stud in Middleton-in-Teesdale. Gelding entries numbered 23 of which 6 were re-entries, a great improvement on previous registrations. Colours showed a black dominance, with 59 black, 22 dark bay and bay (brown) and 7 grey. Among the 49 ponies transferred to new owners were Robert Wall's Raygill Beauty (Heather's Son/Ewebank Beauty) in foal to Ashwood Black Prince, Langrigg Jenny (Heather's Son/Stoneriggs Ephie) bred

ABOVE *(Left to right) Mrs Sue Peckham on Wharmton Brigadier, Anni Sommers on Yartleton Comely and Mrs Jan James on Highcroft Grange Beauty.*

BELOW *Mr W. Watts' champion stallion, Hett Brown Boy.*

by Mr Earnest Coulthard and Stoneriggs Dianne (Stoneriggs Alick/ Stoneriggs Princess) bred by Mr Arthur Slack, who were all exported to Mrs Carol Eames in France, where the Arc-en-Ciel (Rainbow) stud was founded. The society continued giving Premiums to deserving stallions who were presented at the Spring Stallion show. These depend on finance available from the Racehorse Betting Levy Grant, and are awarded to yearling and two-year-old colts, and junior and senior stallions. The ponies are inspected by a panel of inspectors before judging begins and the awards are not made known until the show is over. As the class winners are not always Premium winners, particularly among the youngstock where promising but backward colts may well get an award though standing near the bottom of the line. Premiums are also awarded to brood mares and promising fillies.

In February, 1981 President John W. Dalton, MBE, died at the age of 89 years. He had showed ponies for his father at the age of 11 years and when 13 years old he had ridden his Dales pony to Crook Show and come home with a rosette and an enduring enthusiasm for the breed. John Dalton had been influential in fixing the breed standard and was known as the breeder of the renowned Snowhope ponies. He was the last of the founder members and had served on the first council of the Dales Pony Improvement Society. A member for 64 years, he had been President for the last 20 years and in 1979 he was awarded an MBE for services to the Dales Pony Society.

The next President, George H. Hodgson, farmer and breeder of the Hilton ponies, was appointed at the AGM in November. He had served on the council as member, chairman and secretary. He was a benign and popular President who quietly influenced decisions to modernise the society. From the time in 1933 when he was given his first Dales pony he enjoyed an abiding passion for the breed. He loved showing, in-hand and under saddle and the flame of his zeal was never dimmed. His favourite riding mare, Hilton Maytime, died aged 25 years, shortly before his own death in 1997. One of the most enjoyable activities of the society, the President's Ride, was started in 1982. The first ride took place in North Yorkshire at the end of the season in September, organised and led by the assistant secretary, Penny FitzGerald. Fifteen ponies and riders followed a route from Oxhill through Osmotherly to Kepwick. Then up over the shoulder of Black Hambleton and back via the Cleveland Way and the old drove road to Slapestones and Sheepwash. The 21 miles were covered in good time with a break for lunch. Rosemary Walker's Galphay Supreme (Lord Rupert/Elizabeth of Hodgson Lane) was, as always unshod. All arrived back in good order in time for tea. The President, who had joined the riders on his mare Hilton Maytime, gave all the participants a commemorative rosette, and was heard to say, 'I have really enjoyed myself today, this is better than showing, it's as good as a day's hunting.'

There was much light hearted discourse over tea with some good ideas tossed around. Suggestions for sponsoring the ride and perhaps establishing a Performance Show came from the younger element, who showed signs of taking a tentative hold of the reins. Meanwhile, one of the older riders was heard wondering whether he could drive his horsebox home standing up! The ideas were later put to the Council and it was agreed that in future the President's Ride would be sponsored and the money put towards a Performance Show.

A sub-committee of younger members was approved and the Dales Pony Performance Show was established. It was first held at Top Farm Museum, West Harwick, West Yorkshire in 1983. There was an entry of 19 ponies to compete in Novice, Open and Part-bred Sections. This was a success, the friendly, helpful atmosphere ensured that the novice riders and ponies were able to learn a great deal in the small informal classes. The Performance Show committee moved the next show to the Great Yorkshire Showground, Harrogate, thanks to the support and help then given by the showground staff. This move was undertaken with some trepidation in case the cheerful atmosphere was dissipated on the larger ground but happily this was not the case. This show has continued to be a well attended, cheerful event, particularly good for novices, both equine and human, and is well worth a visit. It is both competitive and fun and is good example of what a mountain and moorland show should be. Owing to increasing costs and double booking in 1998 the show moved again and is now held at Clifford Moor Farm, just south of Wetherby. The numbers competing have risen to over 40.

When the Ministry of Agriculture & Fisheries ended their Stallion Licensing Scheme the Dales Pony Society Council produced an independent one. The first five Dales stallions were licensed by the society in 1983, after passing a rigorous veterinary examination for hereditary defects. The council ruled that from 1984 no stallion would be licensed under the age of three years. As Dales ponies mature late and have a long life span, it was considered wise to give colts more time before serving as stallions. Foal registrations were to be free to breeders if registered in their foaling year. The problem of unregistered geldings was also addressed as many unwanted colts were sold without registration in spite of a good demand. With the National Pony Society giving so much encouragement to Mountain & Moorland ponies with the Ridden and Working Hunter Pony Championships, more people were looking for active registered native ponies. Because Dales mares were rarely sold for performance and

Dales ponies and riders enjoying a President's Ride.

registered Dales geldings were so few, the Council decided that for the time being geldings would be registered free.

Eighty ponies were registered in 1983 which included the first two French foals. Five stallions were licensed and 41 ponies transferred to new owners. In response to requests from pony owners in the south, a Part-bred Dales Register was opened in 1983. This was limited to the youngstock of Dales stallions only, until breed numbers were large enough for exclusion from the Priority List of the Rare Breed Survival Trust. Exceptions were made for Part-bred stock from Dales mares foaled before 1985 and from part-bred Dales mares. Originally native and heavy horse crosses were not eligible, the preferred youngstock to be from Thoroughbred, Cleveland Bay, Hackney, Hunter or Sports Horse mares. This was later extended to any part-bred stock by a Dales Stallion. Since the register opened the highest number entered in a year so far has been 14. The most popular cross is from Thoroughbred or Hunter mares which produce excellent riding horses. The next in popularity is from coloured (piebald or skewbald) mares, a traditional cross which produces the coloured trotters for driving, seen in great numbers at Appleby Fair in Cumbria and much beloved by travellers and gipsies as not only can they trot, they can also pull the caravans.

Stud Book entries in 1984 numbered 89 including 11 geldings and 4 re-entries. Twenty-three ponies were transferred to new owners and 6 stallions were licensed, one being the brown **Haswell Outlook** (Village Boy/Lummas Betty II) bred by W.T. Kitching from the Heather Boy II line. Mr Peter Lawson's last homebred foal, Cleveland Dalesman (Lanquitts Lad/Cleveland Dalarne), went to Mr W.S. Noble who bred the Heltondale Fell ponies and who had bought a batch of good Dales mares, the progeny to carry his Highhouse prefix. Cleveland Dalesman comes from the line of Blake Beck Boy (2842 Fell): he sired two geldings and 85/46 Highhouse Honey out of 82/91 Lowmoat Heather.

In 1984, the council reluctantly parted with tradition and changed the day of the Spring Show which was always held on the Auction Mart Field in Barnard Castle on the third Wednesday in May. This used to be the day of the Hiring Fair for farm workers and later became a market day. There was much argument for and against the move to a Saturday, but numbers both of exhibitors and spectators had risen and there was no room left for expansion on the Market Day because market livestock lorries also needed space to park. In the end the change (to a Saturday) proved to be a success with more room for the ponies, their transport and spectators.

Only 54 ponies were entered in 1985, including 6 geldings and 8 re-entries, but 72 ponies were transferred to new owners. Four were entered in the Part-bred register. Black Star of Arc-en-Ciel was among the 11 stallions licensed, of which Dennis Urwin's black **Stainton Commando** (82/60) (Copelaw Quickstep/Stainton Princess) bred by the late Joe Hall and Mr Tommy Ramshaw's **Raygill William** (Ashwood Black Prince/Raygill Emerald) bred by the Wall family were probably the most important. Mr W.S. Noble's **Waterside Prince** (Burdon Freestep/Hodgson Lane Rosemary) bred by Mr Walter Heap was also licensed and went first to the Highhouse stud.

Since 1977 the Rare Breeds Survival Trust has held a watching brief for Dales ponies and now promoted them out of Category II (Rare) into Category III (Vulnerable), as the number of breeding mares has grown. A breed is considered safe once it holds 1,000 breeding mares. Not all mares are brood mares and it seems more relevant to monitor the numbers of foals produced each year.

A milestone was reached in 1986 when 110 ponies were registered, the highest number since 1940. Five were entered in the Part-bred Register and 60 ponies were transferred to new owners. Nine colts were licensed, one being Millgate Major (Stoneriggs Alick/Wolsey Marchioness) bred by William Gaskin of South Yorkshire, who went to Mr L. Bell of Moneyreagh, Northern Ireland, where he undertakes

Mr W.E. Eastwood's brown stallion, Dartdale Bobbie, three times supreme
champion at the Dales Pony Society (DPS) spring stallion and breed show.

work about the farm, mowing, ploughing and carting besides his stud
duties. Another was the bay **Dartdale Bobbie**, (Hett Shamrock/Stoke
Heather) bred by Mr W. Eastwood in Kent, who took a hat-trick of
Championships at the DPS Spring Stallion Shows of 1995, 1996 and
1997. In June, the first DPS Driving Rally took place from Hett Village
with a good turnout. This has also become an Annual event, organised
in different venues throughout the North Yorkshire, Cleveland and
County Durham and hosted by members of the society. Another
popular scheme started in 1986 is the Annual Points Award Scheme,
organised by Mrs Jill Graham. The first winner was Miss Phillipa Booth
with the gelding Robbie of Lowside (Wheatside Perfect/Trimdon
Mischief). They gained 3,220 points, mainly in Driving events and most
from FEI Combined Driving Competitions.

The total number of entries in 1987 was 74, which included 12 mares
from Wheatside. Only 6 geldings were registered with 5 re-entries. Four
stallions were licensed and 55 ponies were transferred.

Eighty-one ponies were registered and 82 were transferred to new
owners in 1988. Seven stallions were licensed, one being Mr R. Corner's
Black Robbie (Hodgson Lane Prince II/Wheatside Perfection III) bred

by Mr D. Crow. This versatile stallion won the Overall Championship at the DPS Summer Show in 1990, and won in-hand, driving and under saddle, gaining the breed qualifier for Olympia in 1994. He has also been driven in tandem and pairs, ridden side-saddle and been hunting with the Fitzwilliam in Cambridgeshire. In 1998 he went back to the Corner family to await export to Denise Dunkley in Canada. Other stallions registered this year were: Melvyn Thompson's brown **Millgate Baron** (Stoneriggs Alick/Wolsey Marchioness) bred by William Gaskin, Champion at the 1989 Spring Stallion Show; Mrs Weedon's **Lummas Rambo** (Heather Boy II/Lummas Star) bred by J.R. Longstaff. Though not much to look at when young, he became the sire of some good ponies and was noted for getting fillies. Sadly he died at the Westwick stüd in Co. Durham in 1997 getting his last foals in 1998.

Dales ponies had enjoyed good publicity during the same year, with Mr J. R. Longstaff's gelding, **Raygill John** (Heather's Son/Raygill Julie) being chosen as the new Blue Peter pony for Riding for the Disabled. He replaced the first Blue Peter pony, the Connemara, 'Rags'. The significance of the choice of a sensible weight carrier was that many who had joined Riding for the Disabled as children were growing heavier as they approached maturity. The request gave the Council of the Dales Pony Society some difficulty as ponies were being snapped up immediately

Mrs Stocker's Gullivers Poppy Cracker at the Blackmore & Sparkford Vale P.C. one-day event.

R.Corner with the champion stallion Black Robbie bred by D. Crow.

they came on the market. At the time there were some good young colts about but the required pony had to be a good specimen of the breed; over 4 years old and preferably unbroken, with free action and no vices; with a good temperament and steadiness. Raygill John was certainly imperturbable having been brought up at Lummas House near an army firing range above Swaledale. He was chosen out of three possibles available at the time and had continuing exposure on television for many months. He was given the stable name 'Jet' by the popular vote of the Blue Peter audience and now works for the Barrow Farm Riding for the Disabled Group under saddle and in harness.

Registrations rose to 146 in 1989. It was a particularly good year for fillies which numbered 71 and with 105 ponies transferred to new owners. Nine stallions were licensed, the most notable being J.R.Longstaff's **Lummas Prince II** (Heather's Son/Lummas Daisy) who took the Championship at the 1994 Spring Stallion Show; another was the late J.R. Forster's **Burdon Ace** (Stoneriggs Dice/Burdon Lucinda) bred by Mr Harry Baron, who has since gone to Germany. Ten geldings were registered with 10 re-entered.

The results of 10 years' hard work by the council had put the society on a firm threshold for future expansion with registration numbers growing annually and an enthusiastic and supportive membership.

18

INTO THE LAST DECADE OF THE 20TH CENTURY

◆

A TOTAL OF 109 PONIES were registered in 1990 including 7 geldings with 14 gelding re-entries; 106 ponies were transferred to new owners and 10 stallions were licensed. There are now a number of stallions serving in various parts of the country and it is impossible to name them all. Miss Doris Kleffken who had been working as a Veterinary Surgeon in England bought Slaypits Princess (Raygill Jubilee/Rosie of Slaypits) and Slaypits Tilly (Slaypits Black Magic/Byway Surprise), bred by Douglas Hibbert, and took them to Germany when she returned. They have become the foundation mares of the Archenoah (Noah's Ark) stud. The forthcoming integration of Stud Books within the European Common Market scheduled for 1992 caused great consternation among the Mountain & Moorland Breed Societies, particularly those with feral herds of ponies. The council got down to the business of giving the Dales breed a safe entry into the EEC. The monthly meetings went on into the night as every aspect of the European requirements were discussed and the Society Rules and Bye-laws were scrutinised, tightened and a new Rule Book issued to all members.

The Ministry of Agriculture, Fisheries and Food oversaw the implementation of the new legislation regarding the harmonisation of Stud Books throughout Europe and laid down criteria for the Mountain & Moorland Breed Societies which allowed them to become Mother Stud Book Societies. These belong to the country where the breed originates; any other stud book of a breed in Europe is known as a Daughter Stud Book. The Dales Pony Society was fortunate in having few ponies in Europe, all registered in the Mother Stud Book. It was necessary for breed societies to have officially recognised 'legal personality' to control the Mother Stud Book, which meant they had overall command of all rules and regulations for their breeds. The Dales Pony Society had to become a company limited by guarantee in order

Miss S. Dickinson showing the gelding Warren Lane Jupiter, bred by Mr C.W. Smith.

to comply and so become able to issue Passports for every registered pony. The EEC regulations were meant to facilitate free trade in equines in Europe. Readers will not be surprised that this caused great confusion and worry to the council with no apparent benefit, as trade with Europe had been non-exsistent and only recently become minimal. Work now had to begin on redrafting the recently updated Rules of the Society to fit the requirements of incorporation. The very long drawn out affair was not completed until 1998 when the new company was registered. However it is doubtful if the work would have been completed yet had not the Treasurer of the Dales Pony Society, Ian Graham of Halifax, fallen off a ladder and fractured his arm. The enforced time off work enabled him to give all his attention to the job and the council was lucky to be able to rely on his expertise.

1991 was a better year with 115 stud book entries including 10 geldings with 19 re-entries. Licensed stallions numbered 16 and 103 ponies were transferred to new owners.

While the council was worrying through the problems of harmonising the Stud Books the ponies were extending their influence. Dales ponies moved into the New World in 1991 after the Dales gelding

Brimfield Beau (Ashwood Black Prince/Ewebank Beauty), bred by Mrs Jane Gowland in Co.Durham, fixed the interest of his new owner Mrs Denise Dunkley from Canada, in the breed. This led her to buy the black yearling colt Treskewis Tom (Waterside Prince/Lummas Pearl II), bred by Mrs J. Thomas in Cornwall, and the two-year-old Dartdale Freddie (Hett Shamrock/Stoke Jennie) bred by Mr W. Eastwood in Kent. They were exported to Canada, together with the eight-year-old brown mare, Cragside Queen (Copelaw Quickstep/Daisy Hill Star) and her filly foal Stonygill Mountain Ash by Wheatside Mountain Heather IV, bred by Mr F. Clark in Co.Durham; the Section B yearling Akehurst Promise (Lummas Rambo/Akehurst Primrose) and the foal Akehurst Maytime (Lummas Rambo/Akehurst May Blossom), bred by Mrs D. Weedon in Sussex; two foals bred by the late John Forster, Copleylane Ruby and Copleylane Amy, and the yearling filly bred by Miss E. Heywood, Stoneygill Heather all from Co.Durham with the yearling filly Sowermire Louise (Haswell Outlook/Wolsey Jane Ann), bred by Mr Michael German in Lancashire. These ponies, accompanied by the much loved Brimfield Beau, went with Mrs Dunkley to Canada where they became the foundation of the successful Canadale Dales Pony Stud in Ontario. More Dales pony studs are now being established in Canada.

In 1991 Mr and Mrs Charles Parker of Ingleton, North Yorkshire bought two geldings, five-year-old Raygill Harry (Tudor Scott/Raygill Sapphire) and four-year-old Hollingside Quickstep (Hilton Choirester/Hollingside Beauty) bred by Mr H. Robson, for an experiment using Dales ponies in his forestry work. The following year he bought the gelding Escowbeck Star (Kexwith John/Langrigg Diana) bred by Mr P. Hodgson of Morcambe, Lancashire,to join his team of snigging ponies. The venture into forestry with Dales ponies was very successful. Charlie Parker had been a forester for some years before trying Dales ponies as his traction units. He found them all that was desired for clearing trees in trappy hillside woodland known as 'snigging'. This was usually done with heavy horses but Charlie has found the ponies much nippier; they work loose headed and draw the logs at a trot which helps to tighten the chains on the swivelled swingletree, thus keeping the log ends free from snagging in the earth. They wait at the logging station for the timber to be released and are led back to the next load. They are very good at negotiating the unstable load down steep slopes, through surrounding trees and undergrowth at speed. Escowbeck Star once pulled 24 tons of timber out in one day. Together with the other ponies, they are driven to a flat cart when delivering fencing posts and also ridden on pleasure rides and love hunting; where the Master was

One of Mr C. Parker's 'snigging' ponies - Raygill Harry working loose-headed.

once heard to say of them 'he had never seen anything so hairy go so fast!'

The Parkers launched The Working Dales Centre at Ingleton in 1998 where they demonstrate the ponies' versatility. It also allows visitors to meet the only roan Dales stallion, Wharfedale Prince Regent (Stainton Prince/Robertland Miss Bussington) bred by Miss Margaret Harvey in West Yorkshire), his mares and some of his roan progeny.

The gradual rise in registrations suffered a jolt in 1992 when only 98 ponies were registered, including 8 geldings with 17 re-entered. Eleven stallions were licensed and 78 ponies transferred. The lower number of entries this year reflected a lack of confidence in the market. The majority of Dales pony breeders have a healthy fear of having to winter more stock than can be managed. The northern breeders had suffered very badly from the disaster of the 1950s and have found it hard to believe that the market for Dales ponies was sound. Some still find it difficult not to undervalue gelding status colts, which a few years earlier would have been sold unregistered at sales. In January the two-year-old colt Sandtoft Star (Raygill Thomas/Cass Melody) bred by the late Jeffrey Helliwell of South Yorkshire, went to Doris Kleffken in Germany, where he was one of the very few which passed the rigorous test for a German stallion licence. Later in the year Beamish North of England

Museum bought the Dales mares Colliery Queen II (Stainton Commando/ Colliery Queen) bred by Dennis Urwin and Westwick Dawn (Ashwood Black Prince/Rose of Westwick) bred by David Eccles, both of County Durham. The ponies are used for the 1820 exhibit at Pockerley Manor, Beamish, as nineteenth-century pack ponies.

1993 was much more encouraging with 138 ponies registered, including 24 geldings plus 16 re-entered, 110 ponies transferred and 8 stallions licensed. Then came the problem of Passports which were to replace the Certificates of Registration and include information regarding vaccinations, health checks, transfers and exports plus a diagram of identity which included five distinguishing features such as whorls in the coat. This gave the council great cause for thought as Dales ponies were registered with a three-generation pedigree and a description of colour and markings given by the breeder. The standardisation of such descriptions was a virtual impossibility as they differed from breeder to breeder, some being very accurate and others vague in the extreme. Whorls are hard to find on a lively foal and then have to be transferred to a diagram, as are the important white markings. All options were considered and it was decided accurate markings could probably only be obtained from a veterinary surgeon which would be prohibitively expensive. The practices of hot branding, freeze branding and micro-chipping were considered, hot branding being the most tempting. It was obviously going to be advantageous to have positive identification of ponies as much time was spent by the council in trying to trace ponies and prove identification. Micro-chipping was eventually chosen as a cheaper option. The Micro-chip Marketing Company had produced a plan for chipping the ponies and completing the identification form at the same time, thereby relieving breeders of a difficult task. This system was adopted in 1998 and is now considered satisfactory. All foals are now micro-chipped as a requirement of registration and backed up by a DNA sample of hair. All this involves necessary changes for the long established breeders who now have to get application forms in early and handle foals well in preparation for the chipping. The great majority of foals are not disturbed by the process. The cost of chipping, currently £22.50, was a worry as the previous loss of unregistered colt foals was well remembered. The council therefore decided to refund the cost of micro-chipping colt foals to the breeders. Fortunately extra money was allocated and from the much appreciated Race Horse Betting Levy Board grant.

Annual registrations continued to improve and a highpoint was reached in 1994 when 164 foals were registered including one in Northern Ireland and three in France. The gelding numbers were stable

The late President, Mr G.H. Hodgson, showing his home-bred mare, Hilton Maytime.

with 23 registered and 14 re-entered and 93 ponies transferred. Licensed stallions numbered 15 including one in Canada and one in France.

In 1994 the Auction Mart in Barnard Castle needed extending so there would no longer be room for the Spring Stallion and Breed Show, which had been held in the Auction Mart field since 1963. The support given by the Directors of the Mart to the vital stallion and breed shows was crucial to the regeneration of the breed and had been much appreciated. The new venue remains within the town on the Desmesnes, by kind permission of the Teesdale District Council. This is a quiet, open space bounded by the River Tees and the move so far has been a success.

During 1993 Mr and Mrs Steve Barker arrived from America specifically to look at Dales ponies and meet breeders. In 1994 they imported Mr Donald Crow's colt foal Castle Hill Rob (Stoneriggs Alick/ Castle Hill Polly II) and the filly foals Lummas Beauty III (Ashwood Black Prince/Lummas Star), Lowhouses Amanda (Lummas Prince II/ Lowhouses Anna) from the Longstaffs of Teesdale and Sowermire Diane (Moorend Jock/Wolsey Jane Ann) bred by Michael German in Lancashire. All travelled safely to Oregon, where they have become the foundation of the Bloomingdales Pony Stud, with the Prefix Redprairie, the first in the USA. All the Redprairie stock is registered in the Dales Pony Stud Book.

In Germany the three year old Castle Hill John II (Stoneriggs Alick/ Castle Hill Beauty) was licensed by The Dales Pony Society and then underwent a rigorous testing for a German stallion licence. He passed with flying colours, standing top of a line-up of his section, which was otherwise made up of 23 Welsh and Shetland ponies. He then went to undertake his duties at Dr. Doris Kleffken-Weiderhold's Archenoah stud in Greven, in place of Sandtoft Star who had suffered a fatal colic.

At home, Miss Zana Jackson had bought the three-year-old gelding Moorend Jack (Moorend Jock/Dora V) bred by Mr Atkinson of Kirkby Stephen, Cumbria, as she found him irresistible. She took him to the 1997 Dales Pony Performance show where he won the Dressage test and came fourth jumping coloured poles he had never met before. When Zana and her mother Angela set up the Yorkshire Dales Trekking Centre in Malham she used Dales ponies, 10 pure-bred, one unregistered and three part-breds. They are found to be ideal and much enjoyed by riders, both novice and experienced. For some years Mrs Anne Wall has also run a Trekking Centre from Raygill near Barnard Castle using some Raygill ponies.

In 1995 the Council of the Society was asked to clarify the height rule by the National Pony Society, as there was confusion about ponies over 14.2 being shown in affiliated classes when the breed standard stated a limit of 14.2 hands. Since the height for mares was lowered to fit NPS recommendations in 1964, ponies over 14.2 were supposed to be down-graded to Section B of the Grading-up Register. As the ponies matured so late this rule proved impractical to enforce. At the same time there was a greater concern that many ponies were significantly smaller than 14.2 hands. The ideal height for a Dales Pony is 14.2, a height which most buyers want. However the fear of breeding ponies over a strictly enforced limit had led to an overall drop in the height of the breed. The council has always believed that the influence of the over-height ponies was needed to rectify this and to provide a necessary

Mr D. Marsden's mares (left) Country Lane Gemma and (right) Country Lane Beauty, competing successfully against heavy horses in a ploughing match. This versatile pair win in-hand, under saddle and in harness.

wider gene pool for the breed. The problem had increased with the popularity of the ponies which were being exhibited in greater numbers at shows where height limits were strictly enforced. It was therefore decided that in future the height limit would be a 'preferred' one of 14.0 -14.2 hands, with no maximum or minimum limit stated. This allows a judge to appraise a pony according to conformation, action and performance, allowing over-height or under-height to be considered in the same way as a conformation fault. The only real change as a result of this clarification was that ponies were no longer measured at the Spring and Summer Breed Shows. However, height still forms an integral part of judging criteria in both show classes and assessment for Premiums.

In 1996, 162 ponies were registered, including two overseas foals. Geldings produced during the year numbered 37 with 16 entered and 21 re-entered. Twelve stallions were licensed and 91 ponies transferred to new owners. During the year the last 13 foals by the black 25-year-old, Stoneriggs Alick (Stainton John II/Spanham Bright Eyes) were registered. His fraternal grandsire was the Fell registered Master John by Black Jock II (2321 Dales) out of an unregistered mare by Seldom Seen (1628 Fell). He was Champion of the 1974 Spring Stallion show as a three-year-old and was a proflific sire with a propensity to damp out white markings in his progeny.

Entries were lower at 119 in 1997, which included 9 from Canada, 3 from France and 2 from Germany. Gelding numbers rose to 43 with 11 entered and 32 re-entered. Eleven stallions were licensed, one being Castle Hill Rob in the USA. One hundred and thirty-six ponies were transferred to new owners.

In 1998 all 134 registered foals were micro-chipped and issued with passports, including the 5 overseas entries. This was accomplished without too much difficulty and very few complaints. As a first attempt it was considered successful. Fourteen stallions were licensed including 3 in Canada. There was a good entry of 47 geldings, 20 registered and 27 re-entries and 134 ponies were transferred to new owners, including 9 overseas ponies. The council took satisfaction from the rise in the number of registrations which had showed no adverse effect from the micro-chipping. The gradual rise in numbers continues with promising youngstock coming forward to challenge the status of their seniors. It may be interesting to see how the colours fare in comparison to earlier days when dark bays and bays (browns) were dominant. In 1998 there were 96 blacks, 27 browns (bay & dark bay) and 11 greys. It seems the recent black dominance is persisting.

19
THE END OF THE 20TH CENTURY

THE 1990S HAVE BROUGHT many successes for the breed with Dales ponies taking a good share of Supreme Mixed Mountain & Moorland Championships. Many good ponies have qualified for the sponsored NPS Ridden M & M Championship Finals at Olympia: the Misses Well's and Daniel's Ashwood Delight (Stainton Prince/Village Lass) alias 'Lizzie Dripping' and her daughter, Danwell Alice by Copelaw Quickstep, both qualified twice and Rodger James's prizewinning bay mare Abdylane Nancy (Grey Rupert/ Heatherdowne Princess) bred by Mr Peter Cusworth, qualified five times. Of the five stallions which qualified over the years, it was Mr W. Ireland's Slaypits Black Magic (Raygill Jubilee/Rosie of Slaypits) bred by Douggie Hibbert and professionally ridden by Pamela Brown, who won the Supreme Ridden M & M Championship at the National Pony Show, Malvern, in 1996 and also became Reserve Champion at the Olympia Final in the same year. This was followed in 1997 by Glenys Cockburn's 10-year-old black mare, Highhouse Tilly (Waterside Prince/Kexwith Tilly) bred by the late S. Noble, who took a creditable 6th place in the Final. Tilly's son Carrock Billy Boy by Black Robbie, had won the Overall Championship of the DPS 1996 Summer Show.

Other successes in mixed native classes were gained by Mr Michael Gillett's stallion Stoneswood Easy-Go (Oakley Free & Easy/Stoneriggs Glory) who in 1990, ridden by Mrs Alicia Grant, gave a superb show to win an enormous qualifying round of 143 ponies at the National Pony Show. In 1995 Sue Peckham's six-year-old gelding Wharmton Brigadier (Raygill William/Lambton Rose), bred by J. W. Grant, won the first NPS Versatile Pony Championship. In 1996 Rodger James's grey Dartdale Peter Boy (Hett Shamrock/Castle Hill Heather) bred by Mr W. Eastwood in Kent, won the Shalbourne Cup for the Supreme M & M Stallion at the 1996 NPS show at Malvern. In 1998 Mr Billy Buck's bay mare Dartdale Nancy (Hett Shamrock/Stoke Heather) won the Dales championship and the Supreme In-hand Championship at the Royal Show. This mare also wins under saddle and is spectacular in harness. On their home ground judges are happy to find more ponies coming forward. Although mares remain generally of higher quality than the entires, there is now a greater selection of good stallions and promising colts coming on. It is said that the health of a breed can be told by the number of good geldings and it is pleasing to see a growing number of these. The standard of riding and schooling has improved dramatically over the last few years and performance classes are well worth watching. At the breed show the traditional ridden classes are maintained, trotting and walking only. Ponies which trot freely can also canter well and the Dales now often take the red ribbons in mixed Mountain & Moorland ridden, dressage and working hunter pony classes. Others compete successfully in one day events and hunter trials. It is therefore surprising that few are used in combined driving; those that competed in the past were considerably successful, particularly on the marathons and obstacle sections.

The history of the Dales pony is one of adapting to change and they have done it again. Doomed by some equestrian journalists of the 1950-1960s as small carthorses with little future, they have once more proved themselves as great-all rounders and are challenging the status of the popular Welsh cobs, which also had a narrow squeak following the last war. In an address given at the first Annual Dinner of the new Dales Pony Society in 1964, the President, Captain Miles Stavely said:

> 'In the Dales pony you have a pony full of substance, and breeders should keep it that way. You should turn more from training for harness, as 80% of the buyers now want them for riding but don't try to alter the type. A pony can be ridden and driven but will not get into the honours at the big shows unless trained to ride and trained properly, which you must try to do.'

The breeders have striven to keep the type and on the whole have been successful, but it has taken over thirty years for Captain Staveley's advice to come to fruition. The steady improvement in the standard of riding, turnout and general production over the last twenty years has helped greatly in achieving their full potential. As the century passes the society is moving into a world where very few have enjoyed a familiarity with working horses, either in war or peace. The old breeders may have gone but many have passed on the fruits of their long experience to this generation, who must now pass it on to the next. It is thanks to the Dalesmen and women now all gone, such as farmers Joe Hall who bred the Stainton ponies, Norman Harrison who bred Lowside ponies, Harry Barron of the Burdon ponies and Douggie Hibbert of the Slaypits stud, that so many ponies of good type are available for performance in mixed company; though sadly their

Champion performance pony bred, produced and ridden by Mrs Sue Hobday -
Sunglow Karalina.

prefixes have to now join other well-remembered ones in the long
history of the breed.

Other losses include that of farmer John Robert Longstaff of the
Lummas stud, born in 1916, who always stood a quality stallion; and
Joseph William Thompson of the Whitworth ponies, who was born in
1915 and who later worked as a horse keeper and showed pit ponies
for the National Coal Board throughout the country. Fortunately both
these studs have passed into the capable hands of sons.

The breed is lucky in having some good potential pony breeders
already appearing in the junior classes at the breed shows, where young
handlers and riders demonstrate their competence. These youngsters
seem to have absorbed a great deal of pony-sense and give immense
pleasure to their elders. It is comforting to realise that many long
established studs such as the Emerson's Wheatside stud which has
been in the family for well over 150 years; and later ones such as Mr
Robert Corner's Village, Mr Tommy Ramshaw's Wolsey, Mrs Betty Wall
and son, Robert's, Raygill, Mr Earnest Blockley's Hodgson Lane and

Mr Arnold Harrison's Tudor prefixes are still being carried by good foals. Most have younger members of the family taking a keen interest and eager to take the ponies forward. It is impossible to name all who have produced good ponies or stood sound stallions but they are all regarded with honour and appreciation by those who follow.

There is, however, some unease regarding whether or not new breeders and judges unfamiliar with the Dales breed understand the true type and realise that the amount of bone is no more important than the quality. New owners often talk about 'the old fashioned type' meaning ponies with tremendous bone and feather. It would be well to remember that at the turn of the last century when Dales ponies were at their very best and much admired as powerful, fast pony roadsters, 8" of bone was considered astonishing in a pony of that size, since it was comparable with that of a hunter. Great bone tends to be coarse and will not wear well. In those days a lot of feather was not appreciated on ponies working in towns or for the army and was always clipped. Though necessary for protection in winter the silky feather was mainly cast with the winter coat and there was little of it in the summer.

It is also important that the action of the Dales pony trot should be rhythmical and economical, with rounded high knee and hock action with tremendous drive from the hocks. This action always goes with a high head carriage and a very light forehand. Overbent ponies are never becoming and it is impossible for a real trot to be produced if the head is held down and in, the pony will then go on the forehand and trot into the ground.

It is hard to get to the bottom of a Dales pony which thrives on work and it is probable that any owner complaining of behavioural difficulties is usually not giving the pony anything like enough. London based stallions are driven daily and can be seen working the streets with 'totters' (scrap collectors) which keeps the ponies very fit. Most northern stallions and mares get driving exercise by the many skilled owner drivers.

Youngstock in County Durham and Yorkshire are usually yoked (broken to harness) as two- or three-year-olds. It is recommended that as Dales ponies mature late they should not be ridden before the age of four years; although a strong pony can be backed late in its third year and turned away for the winter. Dales ponies are very easy to get going in harness or under saddle. However, one discipline is very necessary: foals must learn that they cannot get away once haltered. These very strong ponies are prone to 'barge' if they have not learned this lesson early enough.

The council is keen to ensure that new owners and breeders fully understand the correct management and feeding of the ponies. Protein rich food, fertilised grass and added supplements can result in obesity and ensuing problems with skin, feet and behaviour. A Dales will thrive on natural meadow grass and hay with oats, carrots and low protein mixes if necessary for work or winter. These ponies are capable of high perfomances without competition mixes, and are extremely hardy, well able to winter out without recourse to rugs. Although they grow a dense double winter coat, they carry a very fine summer coat which gleams with quality. Many owners show their in-hand ponies straight off grass.

Those unable to understand the judging of a class by a Dales panel judge should attend a Dales Breed Show to study the true type. New owners often talk about pretty heads but the real emphasis is below the knee and hock. Dales ponies are judged from the feet up. If the limbs and feet are good and the action correct, the rest is worth looking at and good features will be a bonus. It should also be understood that the pony is being judged as a true all-rounder, able to haul up to a ton, smart in harness and comfortable and forward going under saddle. Any pony with smart action that goes up and down and nowhere is always penalised, as is a low moving 'daisy cutter'; Dales ponies should *really* move.

During the last twenty years the number of ponies has increased dramatically and there are a number of well-bred stallions around, thanks to the owners who stand them. There are also some grand mares to be seen. The class for brood mares with foal at foot is a sight not to be missed, at the Summer Breed Shows.

There are now established studs of Dales ponies in Canada, America, France and Germany with ponies in Holland and Switzerland. The ponies are in demand for competent teenagers and adults and more of them are finding their way to the top of the line in mixed Mountain & Moorland classes. The future for these rather old-fashioned ponies, which are still very like the old Roadster ponies in type and performance, looks reasonably assured as they continue to gather an increasing number of supporters throughout the world.

The policies of the Council of the Society seem to be sound. The Performance Show in Yorkshire and the Midlands and South Breed Show, which allow ponies based away from the hub in the north to be judged by Dales judges, seem to have been good moves. There are now enough good ponies for the council to have representatives at most equine events. The society is fortunate in having members who are willing to give time to such displays as that of the Royal Show, the

Miss R. Wells heading the Olympia qualifier class on Danwell Alice at the DPS Summer Show, 1993. Mrs D. Weedon stands second on Akehurst Daisy May.

Equine Event and the Pony Pilgrimage of 1998. In 1997 Mrs Sue Hobday took Sunglow Suzette (Raygill Jet/Sunglow Samantha) to the Essen Equitana in Germany, where the mare was much admired and greeted with cries of 'Ah! ein mini Friesian!'

The penultimate decade proved to have been a watershed as the Dales pony successfully climbed out of a vale of decline to the heights of regained popularity. Further progress has continued throughout the last decade of the twentieth century and there is every sign that this will continue. With the old virtues of hardiness, stamina and thrift, together with great intelligence, a very sensible temperament and high courage; the Dales galloways promise to trot into the twenty-first century with all the vigour of their renowned forefathers.

GLOSSARY

The Scotch Galloway was a recognised breed from which strong equines of 13 to 15 hands are known as galloways in the north of England and Australia.

A **hand**= 4″ or 10 cm approximately

A **hundredweight** (112lb)= 50 kilos approximately

A **stone** (14 lb)=6.10 kilos

H.H. or hh means 'hands high', e.g. 14.2 hh, which is also written as 14.2 hands or 14.2.

A **geld mare** is neither in foal or with foal at foot, a term used only in Fell and Dales breeds.

Tail male means the sire's male line. The **tail female line** through the dam's female line is usually known as **family**.

Registration numbers are placed before mares' names and after the names of stallions and also geldings, which have a G added , e.g. 164G. As Dales and Fell stock has been registered in both stud books the breed is given with the number where necessary.

Early stallions were described with the breeder's or owner's name following in brackets, some were retrospectively entered in Stud books then given numbers.

Early roadsters and trotters were entered in the Hackney Horse Stud book.

The Polo Pony Stud Book became the Polo and Riding Pony Stud Book and, eventually, the National Pony Stud Book.

The letters fs before a number denote an inspected mare entered as foundation stock in the Hackney Horse Stud Book.

ABBREVIATIONS

HPS   Highland Pony Stud Book
PPSB   Polo Pony Stud Book
NPS   National Pony Society
HHSB   Hackney Horse Stud Book
CHSB   Clydesdale Horse Stud Book

SELECT BIBLIOGRAPHY

F.T. Barton, *Ponies and all About Them* (John Long & Co., 1911)

Robin Birley, *Garrison Life on the Roman Frontier* (The Roman Army Museum Publications, 1991)

Robin Birley, *Hadrian's Wall* (The Roman Army Museum Publications, 1990)

George Borrow, *Lavengro* (John Murray, 1907)

Roy B.Charlton, *A Lifetime with Ponies* (The Abbey Press, 1944)

Barry Cockcroft, *The Dale that Died* (Dent, 1975)

Daniel Defoe, *A Tour Through The Whole Island of Great Britain*

A.A.Dent & D. Machin Goodall, *The Foals of Epona* (Galley Press, 1962)

The Druid, *Saddle and Sirloin* (F.Warne & Co. ,1870)

The Druid, *Silk and Scarlet* (F.Warne & Co., 1859)

G.M. Durant, *Britain, Rome's Most Northerly Province* (G.Bell & Sons Ltd., 1969)

Edward R. Fawcett, *Leadmining in Swaledale* (Faust,1985)

Sir Walter Gilbey, *Ponies Past and Present* (Vinton & Co.Ltd., 1900)

Sir Walter Gilbey, *Thoroughbreds and Other Ponies* (Vinton & Co.Ltd., 1903)

Daphne Machin Goodall, *British Native Ponies* (Country Life Ltd., 1963)

Frank Graham, *Dictionary of Roman Military Terms* (Butler & Butler, 1989)

Marie Hartley and Joan Ingleby, *Life and Tradition in the Yorkshire Dales* (Dalesman Books, 1981)

David Hey, *Packmen, Carriers and Packhorse Roads* (Leicester University Press,1980

William Howitt, *Rural Life of England* (1837)

Light Horses, Live Stock Handbooks, No. 11 (Vinton & Co.Ltd., 1907)

The Live Stock Journal, various dates.

Sylvia Loch, *The Royal Horse of Europe* (J.A. Allen,1986)

John M.Macdonald, *Highland Ponies* (Eneas MacKay, 1937)

G.MacDonald Fraser, *The Steel Bonnets* (Harper Collins, 1971)

H.Mattingly(Trans), *Tacitus on Britain and Germany* (1948)

T.A. Milburn, *Life and Times in Weardale, 1840-1910* (The Weardale Museum, 1987)

W.R.Mitchell, *Pennine Leadminer* (Dalesman, 1979)

Robert Myron, *Prehistoric Art* (Pitman Publishing, 1964)

Alfred E. Pease, *Horse-breeding for Farmers* (Macmillan, 1894)

Marjorie Quarton, *Breakfast the Night Before* (Andre Deutsch, 1989)

Arthur Raistrick, *The Pennine Dales* (Eyre & Spottiswoode, 1968)

Charles Richardson, *Cassell's New Book of the Horse* (1912)

Tom Ryder, *The High Stepper* (J.A.Allen, 1961 & 1979)

Vero Shaw, *British Horses Illustrated* (Published by Vinton and Co. Ltd., 1897)

The Sporting Magazine, various dates

The Standard Cyclopaedia of Modern Agriculture, 1912

Sir Humphrey De Trafford, *Horses of the British Empire* (Walter Southgate, 1912)

Transactions of the Highland and Agricultural Society of Scotland, 1905

ACKNOWLEDGMENTS

This book would not have been attempted without the help and encouragement given throughout the years of research by the Council and members of the Dales Pony Society, especially late President George H. Hodgson, the late Treasurer, Thomas Denham, and the past Honorary Secretary, Mr Peter Lawson, together with the late Council member, Douglas Hibbert, who used to accompany his grandfather on pre-War trips to the Dales to buy harness horses and ponies. I also gratefully acknowledge the enormous contribution given by the late Roy B.Charlton who kindly gave permission for the use of his father's collection of early Dales and Fell pony memorabilia. My sincere thanks to all who have helped in any way during the research, which include the Chairman Jeffrey Daley, Mrs E.E. Wall, Miss M.Emerson, Mr E. Blockley, Mr & Mrs F. James, Anni James, Mrs Jan Robertson, Thomas Ramshaw, Richard and Freda Longstaff, Clive Richardson, Dr David Hopkins, Mrs Sylvia Loch and Dr Wynne-Davies. I am deeply indebted to Mrs Eileen Drinkall for hours of initial proof-reading and Miss Valerie Russell for sound advice. Sadly many of the older generation who generously shared their knowledge are no longer here but are remembered with great appreciation, among them William Iceton, Roy Beadle, Joseph Thompson and Joseph Hall.

My thanks to the Beamish North of England Museum and the British Library which gave access to many old publications; also to the National Pony Society, the Fell Pony Society, the Hackney Horse Society, the Clydesdale Horse Society, the Highland Pony Society and the Welsh Pony & Cob Society for permission reproduce items from their studbooks.

Finally, thanks to my long-suffering but helpful family and to my publisher Annabel Whittet, for her patience in helping to bring the book to completion.

The author gratefully acknowledges permission to quote from the following:

J.A. Allen for *The High Stepper* by Tom Ryder on page 50 and for *The Royal Horse of Europe* by Sylvia Loch on page 23.
Marjorie Quarnton for *Breakfast the Night Before* by Marjorie Quarnton on page 57.
Dent for *The Dale That Died* by Barry Cockcroft on page 42.
Harper Collins for *The Steel Bonnets* by George Macdonald Fraser on page 34.

INDEX

Names in bold are names of ponies.

Colliery ponies 168, 186
Colour 12, 20, 23, 25, 27, 31, 92, 125, 132, 134, 148, 154, 159, 173, 190
Comet 55, 59, 61, 89
Comet II 38, 59, 61, 88, 89, 158
Comets 58, 59, 61, 104, 145
Copelaw Quickstep 163, 169, 178, 184, 191
Cross-bred equines 9, 10, 20, 26, 35, 57, 64, 69, 70, 100-105, 113, 115-120, 128, 137, 139, 150
Cumberland Fells 37

Daddy's Lad 59, 62, 79, 88, 93, 123, 131, 134
Dales cobs 78, 92, 93, 95, 97, 102, 103, 113, 123, 129, 131, 144, 168
Dalesman 78, 79, 90, 100, 101, 104, 106, 107, 109-111, 112, 123, 124, 126, 127, 128, 130, 131, 136, 138, 139
Dales Pony Enthusiasts Club 173
Dales Pony Improvement Society 7, 20, 78, 81-95, 101, 108, 109, 116, 121, 122, 125, 128, 133, 138, 147, 151, 152, 155, 168, 175
Dales Pony Society 7, 10, 20, 78, 81, 96, 97, 101, 107, 116, 118, 119, 121, 144, 147, 149, 150, 151, 152, 153, 155, 156, 167, 170, 171, 173, 175, 176, 180, 182, 188, 192
Dalton, J.W., 78, 79, 81, 95, 101, 102, 111, 112, 121, 124, 125, 127, 128, 131, 144, 151, 155, 159, 162, 168, 175
Darley Arabian 48, 73, 130
Dartdale Bobby 179
Daybreak 61, 78, 94, 104
Dun ponies 22, 23, 27, 31, 75, 87, 90, 92, 124, 125, 127, 128, 132, 134, 136

Emerson, T.V., 81, 84, 85, 92, 133, 136, 145, 154, 155

Fell pony sires 115, 116, 153, 154, 158, 159, 162, 163, 165, 166, 168, 178
Fell Pony Society 7, 96, 97, 105, 107, 110, 114, 116, 118, 119, 121, 122
Field, Norman, 94, 108, 114, 144, 147
Field, Mrs Olive, 147, 151
Fireaway, Jenkinson's, 50, 53, 54, 73, 89
FitzGeorge 75, 84, 87
Friesians 25, 26, 196

Galecian ponies (Asturian ponies) 23, 25, 26, 29, 35
Galloways 7, 26, 27, 32, 33, 34, 35, 36, 38-46, 47, 54, 55, 57, 58, 61, 64, 66, 77, 196
Galloways, Scotch, 33, 34, 35, 36, 134
Garrano ponies 23, 128
Glengarry 60, 73, 79, 97, 98, 101, 104, 106, 112, 115, 116, 117, 123, 124, 125, 127, 131, 136, 138
Grading-up Register 87, 130, 143, 145, 149, 156, 159, 160, 161, 165, 166, 168, 188
Grey Bobbie 146, 163, 167, 169
Guy Mannering 99, 106, 107, 112, 124, 127, 139

Hackneys 9, 11, 13, 18, 34, 49, 51, 53, 54, 55, 58, 64, 66, 67, 69, 73, 75, 76, 79, 87, 89, 94, 96, 97, 116, 126, 137, 177
Hadrian's Wall 24, 25, 34, 128
Haswell Outlook 168, 178, 184
Heather Boy 78, 79
Heather Boy II 157, 168, 169, 170, 178, 180
Heather's Model 77, 78, 89,113
Heather's Son 156, 165
Height 9, 11, 13, 14, 20, 25, 35, 36, 38, 65-67, 72, 77, 82, 97, 102, 116, 117, 118, 122, 159, 161, 168, 188, 189
Hett Real Fashion 154, 163, 179
Hett Shamrock 162, 163, 168, 179, 184, 191